T0375105

Knowing Pain

For Tony Morris

KNOWING PAIN

A History of Sensation,
Emotion, and Experience

Rob Boddice

polity

First published in 2023 by Polity Press

Polity Press
65 Bridge Street
Cambridge CB2 1UR, UK

Polity Press
111 River Street
Hoboken, NJ 07030, USA

ISBN-13: 978-1-5095-5054-8

A catalogue record for this book is available from the British Library.

Library of Congress Control Number: 2022946076

Typeset in 11.5 on 14 Adobe Garamond
by Fakenham Prepress Solutions, Fakenham, Norfolk NR21 8NL
Printed and bound in Great Britain by CPI Group (UK) Ltd, Croydon

For further information on Polity, visit our website:
politybooks.com

Contents

Figures

Acknowledgements

I began researching the history of pain in 2003. Despite the long gestation, the book came together quickly: an unexpected and positive turn after the conclusion of an unfortunate affair. For this I heap great praise on Pascal Porcheron at Polity and my stalwart agent Tony Morris for attaching rocket boosters to the idea for *Knowing Pain*. I am indebted to Joanna Bourke, Ian Miller, and Javier Moscoso for championing this book. It would not have been possible without the support of colleagues and family. Thanks to Pertti Haapala, Pirjo Markkola, Raisa Toivo, Ville Kivimäki, Bianca Frohne, David Turner, and Daniel Goldberg. Parts of the manuscript were shared at the colloque de l'Institut Éthique Histoire Humanités in the Faculté de Médecine, Université de Genève, thanks to Dolores Martín Moruno; at the 'Emotions, History and the Body' seminar at the University of York, thanks to Fay Bound Alberti; at the conference 'Establishing Empathy: Education, Emotions and Society in the Nineteenth and Twentieth Centuries' at Hamburg University, thanks to Esther Möller, Sylvia Kesper-Biermann, and Katharina Stornig; and at the cross-faculty seminar series 'Animal and Human Emotions' at the University of Newcastle, thanks to Lutz Sauerteig and Carmen Hubbard. Marie van Haaster materially helped with the placebo chapter. Sara Honarmand Ebrahimi was immeasurably helpful with Arabic and Farsi and, with Anneleen Arnout, in tracking down difficult-to-find texts. The book was written between Montreal and Tampere. It would not have been possible without Stephanie and Sébastien always close by. The context of disease, war, fear, and suffering would be paralysing without them.

Prologue

I am looking at my own brain stem. It is 1995.

Gazing at myself, sliced in sections, layer upon layer, I see myself but do not recognize these images as me. Stacked underneath the brain stem are the cervical vertebrae, each sandwiching a vertebral disc: sectional images, like postcards from the interior. Four or five into the sequence, the surgeon says, 'Ah-ha.' The disc between C4 and C5 is herniated, the split in its surface visible on the magnetic resonance image (MRI). *This is my pain.* The jellyish nucleus of the disc has been poking out of the annulus, touching off nerves that feel like hot needles, sending my neck and shoulders into paralysing spasms. By the point of discovery, this has already been going on for months. I have been in agony, doubled over like an old man, unable to turn my head left or right, sometimes feeling unable to move at all. It's taken some flexing to get a diagnosis. I am 17 years old.

My recovery, if I can call it that, is now in its 28th year.

I am recounting what I know about my own pain, what it is and what I remember of it, so that I can document its situatedness and its particularities, and so that I can dismiss it. It is pertinent not as an exemplar of chronic neck and shoulder pain, but as a particular experience of pain. I can show how and why this pain was meaningful, for the purpose of showing that it affords me no direct insight into the pain of others. If the evidence of my own experience is any kind of guide, then it is a guide only to the importance of context, structure, script, and culture in the meaning-making processes of subjective pain. A herniated disc and the genetic weakness that makes it happen again and again can be explained. Its associated effects and debilitations can be loosely predicted. But the quality and meaning of the pain depend upon all manner of ingredients that are not intrinsic to the spine. A pain in the neck is not simply *a pain in the neck*. Working out all these ingredients will involve a trip a bit higher up, to the brain, and a trip out, to the post-Thatcherite desolation of working-class South Derbyshire in the early 1990s, to the fine-grained distinctions of social class, and to the intransigence of an NHS general practitioner to the causes, consequences, treatment, and experience of chronic pain.[1] Should you herniate a disc, you would have to undertake a similar journey upwards and outwards.

Others had witnessed my decline. My posture slumped. Sitting at a desk became intolerable. Iron claws would grip my shoulders, above the collar-bone, and the thumbs of those claws would penetrate under the shoulder-blades. I was held in a vice with spikes.

It took courage to go to a doctor. Visiting came with guilt. Am I wasting his time? Am I imagining all of this? What if I don't feel it on the day? Will he think I'm a fraud? Shouldn't I be tougher than this? My self-examination was, in the event, in excess of the examination I received at the hands of the doctor. Quickly dismissed with a prescription for ibuprofen, without physical examination, I went on my way feeling that I had not been heard at all. I went back to the same doctor twice more. I was never examined, but simply prescribed stronger doses of ibuprofen. After the third visit, and many months, the dose was upped to 800 mg pink horse pills and there seemed to be no end in sight. The pills did nothing except cause alarm.

At this point, my parents intervened. They were self-employed, small-business owners. For a short period in our lives, we had private health insurance – BUPA – which was available as a means of avoiding the NHS queue for those willing to pay. None of us had ever used it. In a public health system, it was deeply divisive and hard to square with the principle of a National Health Service. I was not engaged in any of this. All I knew was that the doctor was not doing anything either to find the cause of my problem or to actively fix it.

A new appointment was made, with a different doctor at the same practice. The story, which by this point was a story of being in agony and being ignored, was recounted. My dad mentioned that we were in BUPA. At a stroke, the game changed. We were asked whom we would like to see. My dad mentioned the name of a surgeon he knew – not personally, but because he was the go-to guy for Derby County Football Club – and in no time at all I became his private patient, in his rooms in part of his own house. An MRI scan was quickly scheduled in a private hospital (it had carpets and did not smell of disinfectant; it felt more like a hotel) with a diagnosis following on directly. A course of physiotherapy followed, without further waiting. In school, since I'd had time off, my form teacher asked me about it in front of the whole class, and I explained in the context of my dad's own long struggles with cervical spondylosis how, as the surgeon had put it to me, 'the emergence of dad's problem' in me had occurred remarkably early. Her response was a snort of derision: 'You don't have a cervix!' She apologized the following day, in private, having consulted a dictionary. It did not undo the humiliation. All the time the same questions, before a variety of authorities, ran in my mind: 'Am I allowed to have this pain, this condition? Does it help to say I've got *this* – a specific condition with some impenetrable jargon? Why isn't the fact of being in pain enough to be believed, to be taken seriously?'

To know about the injury behind my pain was something of a relief. The prospect of recovery was an analgesic. But the process of finding it out had been an eye-opener. I could see how, without the magic wand of private healthcare, and without a parent advocate who at least knew enough to properly game the system, I might have been stuck in an infinite loop of medicated despair. I could see a route out and I could see that it was unjust.

The physiotherapist was not a listener either. She did things that hurt. In my mind, she did things designed to hurt. At one point, as she jammed her thumbs into my neck and as I yelled, it felt like a torture session. 'Is that *your* pain?' she asked, repeatedly. She had found it and was pressing it, making me own it. Of course it was my fucking pain. Who else could it have belonged to? But the cause of the pain was shifting, from a deficiency in my own body, to this person and her boring thumbs; to this room of strange equipment that put my jaw in traction; to the ultrasonic devices waved in front of me like (utterly ineffective) magic wands, and to the other people in that room, all in agonies of their own. The atmosphere that defined the room was one of pain, not of hope or recovery. Maybe, over weeks, the therapy helped. Constant attention to my posture and giving up snooker probably helped more.

The pain never went away. Or, rather, the shadow of pain never left. I know, now, that I can herniate that disc at any moment, by any innocuous activity. A long writing session at the wrong desk will do it. Standing for too long will do it. Even putting on a coat can do it. I stave it off by running (something my erstwhile physiotherapist told me never to do). About once a year, I'm out of action for a couple of weeks. I know right away when it's happened, and I know what to expect. Every time, my mind casts back to the first time. I remember it, curse it, and try to mark the differences. It's not the same pain now as then. Why? Because I know about it. I know its causes and its limits. I know what to do and what not to do. I know that in a pinch I can seek help from a doctor, without guilt or fear, and with the knowledge that I can request the examination and the assistance I did not receive when I first approached a doctor at the age of 17. My pain is mine. It is entangled in its own narrative that is constantly being re-written. It has been made worse or better to the extent that I am the author of that narrative. At 17, I was in control of very little and knew very little. That is no longer the case.

Introduction
Disrupting a Definition

Everyone knows their own pain. How? This book explores the answer to this question historically, demonstrating the relationship between the pains people have known and the changing frameworks of philosophical, medical, religious, and scientific expertise that have claimed to know what pain *is*. It is, therefore, a contribution to current knowledge about the experience of pain, produced in a transdisciplinary space comprising perspectives from history, philosophy, anthropology, psychology, psychiatry, neuroscience, politics, art, and literary studies. *Knowing Pain* illuminates a history of painful experiences, a messy assemblage of many worlds of suffering, which disrupts commonplace appeals to the universality of pain. Here you will find: pain as specific, particular, mediated, and contingent; body-minds whose agonies are connected to the cultures they inhabit; brains that *produce* pain that makes sense only in and through the context of its experience; authorities that make and disseminate the situated concepts of pain, through which suffering is made meaningful; historical politics of the medical and moral valuation of pain; pains that count, and pains that are *invalid*. You will find claims that patients do not know their own pain at all and the provocation that your pain belongs to someone else's discrimination.

This book cuts against the grain of 'common sense' about the pain that people think they know. It documents well-known but under-appreciated phenomena, such as the history of extraordinary and devastating injuries that, nonetheless, did not hurt; the history of overwhelming suffering unconnected to any injury at all; the unreliability of the senses as either a signal for pain or a method of measuring pain; how these mutable senses, in combination with equally contingent emotional concepts, can change the experience of pain. It shows pain as a virtue and as a pleasure, and how much of the history of human pain has fallen beyond the ken or the interest of medicine. The world of medicine nevertheless plays a big part in the story, both in terms of the production of knowledge of

1

what pain is and how to alleviate it, and concerning its role in creating limited definitions of pain that seemingly either overlooked or failed to treat a great tide of suffering. I delve into the lived experience of pain in all its physical, emotional, social, and cultural entanglements to reveal the kinds of apparently invisible pain that millions, nonetheless, have known and shared.

Aside from collating these phenomena, this book puts forward an original pain agenda. Ranging from antiquity to the present, and taking in pain knowledge and pain experiences from around the world, I draw upon the methodology of the history of the senses, the history of emotions, and the new history of experience to weave a narrative about the mutable patient, or the situated sufferer, often alone, sometimes in a collective.[1] It is predicated on critical engagement with a strain of social neuroscientific and neurohistorical research that explains how the concepts by which humans express their experiences play a central role in the production of experiences. A history of pain concepts and pain practices becomes a history of the contextualized plastic, biocultural brain-body system. Pain, an embodied, embrained, but above all *meaningful* experience, is in and *of* the world. It may be something that almost every human has known, but there is nothing in the evidence of our own experience that affords us automatic insight into the pains of others, or into the pains of the past. To that end, this book is a sustained denial of universality, and a denial of easy recognition of the other in pain. I lay bare the difficulties and the politics of knowing pain – your own, someone or something else's – and the way that the experience of pain is mutable, historical, and unpredictable. I aim to show the connections between the construction, use, and *experience* of pain, understanding as a first principle that knowledge claims about pain *occupy* what pain is like.[2]

Definitions: A Contemporary Overview

Since one major purpose of this book is to historicize the experience of pain, to show that it can and does change over time, a necessary first step is to disrupt any operative definition that delimits what pain *is*. The formal definition of pain has focused the worlds of medicine and medical science on the kinds of pain research that are pursued and the kinds of pain that receive priority for treatment. Disrupting such definitions is essential if the varieties of pain experience, in the past and in the present, are to be recognized. In chapter 1, I will explore the historical formulations of pain, but I begin with the present and the possibilities current formal definitions afford.

The International Association for the Study of Pain (IASP) formulated a formal definition in 1979: 'Pain is an unpleasant sensory and emotional experience associated with actual or potential tissue damage or described in terms of such damage.'[3] Critics across the disciplines found this definition inadequate, and it was finally augmented and complicated (and improved) in July 2020. A series of qualifications and clarifications have been added. They make the formal definition less pithy and supply new possibilities for the study of pain, especially in historical terms:

- Pain is always a personal experience that is influenced to varying degrees by biological, psychological, and social factors.
- Pain and nociception are different phenomena. Pain cannot be inferred solely from activity in sensory neurons.
- Through their life experiences, individuals learn the concept of pain.
- A person's report of an experience as pain should be respected.
- Although pain usually serves an adaptive role, it may have adverse effects on function and social and psychological well-being.
- Verbal description is only one of several behaviors to express pain; inability to communicate does not negate the possibility that a human or a nonhuman animal experiences pain.[4]

The most welcome parts of this revision are as follows. First, the notion of pain as an objective phenomenon – something that can be mechanically measured or rated – is rejected in the first clause. Pain, it confirms, is *subjective*. Later, I'll explore the boundaries of this claim, showing that sometimes pain is not 'personal', but 'social', analysing the relational dynamics that colour the experience of both pain and relief. For now, it is helpful to think of pain in these terms, as different from person to person, and from time to time.

Second, the formal definition of pain has finally introduced a conceptual wedge between 'pain' and 'nociception'. The confusion, which is long-standing, and which has obfuscated scientific communication about how pain works, lies in the conceptual linkage of sensory perception with pain perception. Nociception, deriving from the Latin *nocēre*, suggests that the nerve endings in the body that detect external stimuli – the cutting, burning, or compression of the skin, for example – are *pain* detectors. Those nerves then send 'pain signals' to the brain, which responds. This is based on an understanding of *nocēre* as 'to hurt', when it might more usefully be translated as 'to damage'. Those nerves detect damage, and they send damage signals, but damage does not imply pain. Only when damage signals reach the brain does the brain produce pain, if the circumstances are right for such a production. By no means do all damage signals result in the experience of pain. The formal separation of pain and nociception is useful because it puts an end to the notion that pain is formally correlated with injury. I will return to this at much greater length.

The third qualification here is also useful but requires further revision. It is important to acknowledge that people learn what pain is: that it is not a simple human universal to which everyone has the same access; it is a complex human variable that is accessed in all manner of ways, according to place, time, and other intersectional criteria. The further implication attached to this conceptual learning process is that there is not one thing called 'pain', but many different *pains*, each according to the way in which life experiences unfold. I seek to understand what is precisely meant by the phrase 'life experiences', how they are formed, and how they might change over time.

Fourth, regarding subjective reporting of pain, this is an important step forward in wresting formal control of the definition, diagnosis, and treatment of pain from the hands of doctors and placing it instead in the hands of patients. The modern history of an objective science or measurement of pain is the history of either ignoring or amplifying subjective reporting of people in pain, and is revealing of the unseemly history of racism, misogyny, classism, and ageism within the medical and allied professions. It should be enough for the medical establishment to endorse subjective reports of pain as truthful accounts of the experience of pain. As this book will illustrate, this has not typically been the case.

The word 'usually' in the fifth qualification could be struck because it is counterproductive. It is widely acknowledged that one of the biggest challenges facing medicine is the prevalence of chronic pain syndromes, which fall precisely into that category of bringing 'adverse effects' to the people who suffer from them. The need to cling to the idea of pain as adaptive is related to other medico-historical impetuses to try to know pain objectively and positively; to explain pain in ways that accord with the scientific need for natural laws. This is not to say that there is not an adaptive role for pain in evolutionary terms, but that the acknowledgement of the social and subjective construction of pain tends to make allusions to such rigid categories of analysis as 'natural selection' moot. In practice, both the experience of pain as suffering and the encounter of the medical community with people in pain fall into the category of dealing with 'adverse effects'.

The sixth and final definitional caveat is a good one, disrupting the assumption that pain experience can only be gauged through pain utterances. Many scholars have pointed out that such utterances are, paradoxically, both extraordinarily rich and yet somehow inadequate in putting pain experience into the world. Several questions arise from this: if language is not the be all and end all of pain signs, what are the other signs and how does anyone know how to read them? If pain is social, personal, subjective, based on conceptual learning and life experience, how can the pains of others be accessed? It seems a difficult task when considering another human being, presenting in the clinic. What if the person is an historical figure, reachable only through the vagaries of a partial archive? What if the pained subject is not a person at all? How do we assess or come to know the pain of an animal, without resorting once again to the scientific temptation to objectify or to project?

Sense and Emotion

As a form of experience, pain is affectively produced.[5] It has no direct or predictable relation to sensation, but where sensation is involved it is only through the construction of meaning that the sensations can be experienced as pain. This admixture of sensation and meaning-making involves an emotional repertoire: emotions, too, are meaningful ways of making sense of what is happening. Without meaning there is no pain. In effect, this means that without the meaningful interpretation of the senses and without emotion there is no pain. This observation is not new. It has been argued by physicians based on first-hand experience with patients;[6] it has been argued by pain scientists researching the physiology and neurology of painful phenomena;[7] it has been argued by neuroscientists looking for the similarities in the brain between pain associated with physical injury and suffering arising from social injury (hurt feelings, if you will) and by cultural psychologists trying to break out of the laboratory silo;[8] it has been proven, by oblique means, by looking at the phenomenon of pain asymbolia or congenital analgesia, in which people experience injury consciously but attach no meaning to it and therefore do not experience it as pain.[9] Psychologists, philosophers, anthropologists, and historians join the ranks of pain experts who acknowledge this fundamental affective dimension of pain. Not all of them follow its logical implications, but as a rule, the loose agglomeration of disciplines that makes up 'pain studies' agrees that pain is only pain if it is meaningfully and affectively produced. For all intents and purposes, the expression of a painful experience – whether the plaintive scream; the shedding of tears; the sharp intake of breath; stopping suddenly in your tracks; screwing up your face in a certain way; writhing (there is no limit or universality to such signs) – is an emotional experience, connected to the context in which it occurs, according to the expressive repertoire of the person in pain, according in turn to their own accretion of experience. It is bewildering to admit that despite a general multidisciplinary consensus, across vast schools of thought, about how to begin to think of pain, and how to come to know it, there remains an intractable urge among certain medical authorities to think of pain only in terms of a mechanical and automatic *sensory* function. There is also a huge communication gap about what pain is with the lay public at large. The equation of pain with the affective productions of the brain in relation to the world might be understood as tantamount to saying that the pain is 'all in your head'. However much one might try to explain the profound complexity of the relationship between the brain, the nervous system, and the world from which meaning is derived, that it is not – or not necessarily – a dismissal but a means of unlocking the variety and mutability of pains, this is a difficult thing to sell. Most people, especially in moments of pain, or in their long-endured sufferings, want to hear about what can be done for their *finger*, or for their *back*, because, somehow in a common-sense way, it *must* be a structural or a functional problem; it must be an *injury*; it must have a *place*. It must be something's fault. To say that pain is in the world, or between the world and you, seems like an intellectual abstraction. But pain does lie in between in this way.

If you cut your finger, you feel the pain *there*, and you staunch the bleeding *there*, and you cleanse and bandage *there*, and these acts, on the spot, help ease the pain. The bandage, just like the rubbing of a banged shin, or the kissing-better of tumbled toddler, is itself a salve. Its effect seems to take place at the point where it hurts. In the chapter on placebo, I'll explain the complex relationship between belief and expectation and the internal pain-killing system that makes this magic work. But people do know, on an everyday practical level, that this kind of inter-relational social and material behaviour does in fact help, and from this can be gleaned the essence of the reality of pain. Mere *damage* is not pain. Damage is painful only when attached to meaning. Meaning, produced by the brain, is derived from the world. For the same reasons, feeling better is meaningfully derived from this dynamic relation of brain and world. It is about *feeling* beyond the narrow sensory definition, at the entanglement of sensory information with emotional experience, knowledge, and an appraisal of the contextual situation. These are integrated systems but they are unstable, largely unpredictable, and can be understood only by a multipronged approach that understands that the brain-body in pain is never isolated from the world in which pain has meaning.

This is still only a part of the pain-is-emotion story. I mentioned 'hurt feelings' already, and I want to underscore this point. While modern medicine, in its pain research, has overwhelmingly focused on the wound, on sensitivity, on damage in the body or dysfunction in the nervous system, much can be gained by an understanding of emotional pain – grief, exclusion, depression, despair, anxiety, *Angst*, sometimes fear and anger – as pain. The late-modern understanding of the affective quality of pain suggests that researchers look in this direction, but there remains a kind of divide between pain that is the purview of medicine and 'pain' that is social, the purview of culture, family, community, or self-reflection. The division is unhealthy and unhelpful, which is not to say that all these emotional conditions and an endless array of others in situated historical contexts should become the purview of medicine. Rather, the boundaries of the medical and the medical-scientific should be open, porous, alive not only to the physical body and the functions of the brain and the nervous system, but also to the possibilities of learning something from coming to know pain in its infinite cultural varieties. This knowledge, of pain as emotion, must disrupt pain knowledge per se.

My intention, as already stated, is to historicize pain. My approach to this topic has been formed by many years working in the field of the history of emotions. The premise of this field of study is that emotions have a history: they change over time; they have origin points and some disappear altogether; they are culturally and temporally specific; they are *always* present, even when – in the realm of political debate, law, science – it has been politically expedient to argue that they are not. Emotions are not merely the affective consequence of the unfolding of events, but causal, effectual parts of chronicity. I refer the reader to the relevant literature instead of expounding on this at length.[10] Suffice to say that if emotions are historical and pain is an emotion, then pain is historical too. Its history can be accessed via the same methods as other works in the history of emotions: through an understanding of the plasticity of the brain and body and their dynamic relationship with the specific, situated world in which they are caught. This is a study of pain contexts, pain conceptual repertoires, situated pain experience – how it felt – and situated pain meanings. It is about language, material culture, belief systems, and knowledge just as much as it is about the brain and the body.

The book is written as a history, but pain studies is both intellectually and practically a multidisciplinary affair. What we know about pain is always situated, and I am constantly running contemporary epistemologies of pain against their forebears and asking questions of the ways in which knowledge is produced and changes over time. Critically, however, contemporary pain studies increasingly includes the testimony, experiences, expressions, and opinions of people in pain.[11] It has enlivened a field of study by connecting formal frameworks of knowledge to often creative forms of putting pain into the world, which in turn has helped change and develop those formal frameworks of knowledge and suggested new forms of care and relief. In many ways, this openness, which starts with the opening of academic studies of pain to vastly different disciplinary approaches – biological, psychological, sociological, anthropological, historical – and flourishes with the inclusion of patient-led practices of management and protest, has been a perfect demonstration of the ways in which what is known about pain and how pain can be experienced can change in real time. It emphasizes the dynamic relation of knowledge and experience: what is known frames what is experienced, but access to experience can frame new knowledge. A new practice or expression might lead to a new feeling, which, if properly harnessed, might produce a new theory that can lead to the formalization of new therapies. It was, I will argue, ever thus, but that relationship is much easier to see now than it was in many historical contexts. All that is available to the historian, often, is the record of knowledge formalized in canonical works of medical authority. The experiential must be inferred. No one discipline can be master of this kind of holistic analysis. No one discipline can call the shots, whether it concerns what pain is, how it works, how to treat or prevent it, how to read or measure it, or how it feels.

I want to stress the necessary disruption of any implicit notion of a disciplinary hierarchy here. Pain studies is, or *should be*, a truly interdisciplinary affair. There are not pain sciences and then 'softer' pain humanities. There is no pain science without the crucial work of the humanities and social sciences that helps complete the picture of pain's experiential contingency. I make no attempt to hide or otherwise obfuscate my own disciplinary background and training, but I make a concerted attempt to draw together diverse threads. In so doing, it sometimes becomes apparent where the interdisciplinary production of knowledge about pain is dysfunctional. Knowledge does get produced on parallel and even on divergent tracks, such that what we know about pain becomes paradoxical. As different disciplines claim incompatible truths, it is essential that probable errors all around are addressed. The primary error, in almost all cases, is the assumption, often unrealized, that a particular disciplinary approach is all that is required to unlock the secrets or solve the problems of pain.

Given the interdisciplinary scope, I have eschewed a typical historical narrative. I favour neither a chronological sequence nor a place-based focus, and the book is not limited to one period or to a regular notion of periodization. The coverage is global, from antiquity to the present, encompassing many different languages and cultures. Sometimes there is theoretical or thematic overlap; sometimes there are sharp distinctions and departures. The broad scope is reined in by thematic staging and by specific episodes of either source-based analysis, context-based analysis, or focused histories of sub-themes. Within each chapter, therefore, the reader can expect to find great leaps over time and across space. The point isn't to be comparative or to show consistency across history. Rather, it is to exploit a certain historical method to show that it is possible, however partially, to uncover the relationship between pain knowledge and pain experience, and to exemplify elements of this method as the circumstances demand. My sources, therefore, are especially diverse: paintings, pottery, sculpture, photographs, diagrams, diaries and other ego narratives, letters, epic poetry, medical and scientific texts and treatises, a corporal-punishment device, novels, film, and a basilica. I have heard the charge that historians of emotions, senses, and experience are, despite their best intentions, essentially no different from cultural historians. To whatever extent they claim to be historicizing feelings and sensations, they are primarily researching in the realm of text, the word, what people said about what they felt. I hope to show by this approach that there is rather more to it than this. The word, the linguistic concept, is *vital* to the argument of this book – it deals in pain concepts in, I think, sixteen languages, to the meanings of which I have tried to be contextually faithful – but it is not the only important element. Through this wide array of sources, I aim to recover the body in pain, the lived experience of pain, and the richness of the history of communicating pain – putting it in the world – beyond the word.

ONE

Scripting
The Politics of Knowledge

What is beyond and what is behind the process of defining pain? How has knowledge about pain been produced, developed, and disseminated? Knowledge is never produced neutrally. It always serves someone. Something is always at stake. There are always inclusions and exclusions, whether wilful or not. Knowledge is political and pain exemplifies this. This chapter examines the politics of knowledge from the point of view of medical authorities, probing at the formation of experiential frames of reference from antiquity to modernity. It is about the politicization of pain knowledge on several fronts. First, it documents the formation of one strand of historical pain scripts, which have roots in Greek antiquity and a distinctive historical development in early medieval Persia, and from there to medieval Spain and then throughout Europe. To complement the Greek and Arabic schools, I examine the canon of traditional Chinese medical knowledge on pain. In all cases, I am mindful of the ways that formative scripts – the most significant medical canons of pain knowledge – have later been erased by the cultural authority of modern medicine. The logics of ancient and medieval medicine have been overridden in the name of either connecting the knowledge claims of historical medical authorities with or disconnecting them from the knowledge claims of contemporary medicine. Throughout, I connect the formalization of pain knowledge to the way that the experience of pain was scripted. It does not matter so much who was right and who was wrong – this would even be a misdirection – for the experience of pain takes place within the epistemological framework that exists.

From Greek Pain to Arabic Pain

Bleeding as pain therapy was remarkably long-lived, stemming from time immemorial until the nineteenth century as a central pillar of medical practice, and lasting until today for specific cases. In its classical form, as iterated by Hippocrates and Galen, it was a central therapeutic strategy in alignment with humoral and meteorological understandings of human anatomy, function, and disease. The human temperament (the word literally refers to the specific mixture of the humours) was dependent on the balance of humoral substances: melancholy or black bile (cold and dry), yellow bile or choler (warm and dry), blood (warm and moist), and phlegm (cold and moist). The predominance of one humoral substance in the body over the others was indicated in the corresponding four types of temperament: melancholic, choleric, sanguine, phlegmatic. A pathological imbalance of the humours was caused by climatic conditions or food or activities that were out of accord with a person's temperament. It is possible that the idea behind these four humours came from what happened to blood when it was separated out – something that can now be done by putting a vial of blood in a centrifuge. Melancholy, for example, would appear as a darker substance at the bottom of the tube – in fact, clotted blood. When the four humours were in balance in the body, which is to say, in proportions correct to each other, then the person was healthy and well disposed. If the humours were out of balance, this was the cause of disease. In the case of general excess of all the humours (plethora), balance could be restored by bleeding. One sign of excess was pain. If the humour-containing vessels were distended by a plethora of substance, leading 'to a feeling of tension, soreness or pain', then relief was to be achieved by bleeding, among other therapies according to the patient's age, strength, and even the time of year.[1]

Galen was born in Pergamon, situated in what is now the west of Turkey, near the Aegean Sea, in 129 CE, and died in about 216. The shadow of his medical influence falls across a millennium and a half and cannot be overstated. Galen's innovation concerning pain was to connect sensory perception to the brain, that is, to the cognitive processing of sensory information, such that the subject becomes aware of it. Under that generality, there were numerous causes of pain, all of them related to the specific balance or imbalance of the humours and their specific qualities. To this extent, Galenic pain is sensory, physical, nervous, cognitive, and affective, but all of these terms risk anachronism, for pain according to Galen pertains to the qualities of humours and to the location of the soul in the brain, and to the physical relation of the former and the latter. Inflammation was one cause of pain; physical injury (discontinuity) was another; and there was room for something like psychosomatic pain, where pain in a certain part of the body is unrelated to imbalance, inflammation, or injury of that part. There is, in Galen's apprehension of the process of pain, a notion of a kind of nervous pathway, between an affected part and the brain, but it is only in the brain's reception of sensory information that pain is perceived.[2] In any case, ancient Greek concepts of pain, suffering, and toil – ἄλγος (*álgos*), λύπη (*lúpē*), ὀδύνη (*odúnē*), πάθος (*páthos*), and πόνος (*pónos*) – could all indicate both the physical and mental aspects of pain, situated in a general understanding of the passions that did not (could not) attempt to disentangle affective phenomena from bodily phenomena. While Greek culture had complex notions of the division of the soul and the body's relation to it, the mind–body dualism that has been the hallmark of modernity would have been alien to Galen and to the hundreds of years of Greek civilization that preceded him.[3]

How could a medical man access the experience of someone in pain, whether for diagnostic or therapeutic purposes? How could pain be known and shared? To some extent, Galen understood that people experienced pain in common with other people. Courtney Roby calls it an 'experiential consensus'.[4] Yet at the same time, he mistrusted a patient's capacity to make sense in verbal terms of a pain sensation, or to correctly describe what was happening in their own body. Galen set about delimiting the descriptive categories of pain to avoid slippages that obfuscated the experience, its bodily location, and its medical implications. While Roselyne Rey highlighted four broad categories of pain that were operative for Galen – throbbing (or pulsating), weighty or heavy, stretching and lancinating – there were many other types of pain that he abided by on the basis that they were 'so widely known' they required no 'special explanation': pricking pain (*νυγματώδη*), tearing (stretching) pain (*διατείνοντα*), violent or vehement pain (*σφοδρὸν*), severe or powerful pain (*ἰσχυρὸν*), violent or forcible pain (*βίαιον*), constant or continuous pain (*συνεχῆ*), and intermittent pain (*διαλείποντα*). That this list contains numerous 'or' words is testimony to the vagaries of translation, but in terms of physical description, Galen's typology of experienced pains sound familiar enough.[5] Yet all these types of experience must be situated within both the patient's and the medical authority's understanding of cause (humours) and therapy (bleeding, often), such that the experience is likely some distance from the closeness that translation tends to imply. Besides this, there is a whole culture of painful experience outside of the medical purview that nonetheless inflects the medicalized 'experiential consensus'. I refer back to this culture at various points throughout the book.

The Galenic tradition was preserved, yet altered, in the medieval Persian world of Ibn Sina (Avicenna to the Europeans), whose medical *Canon* juggled Galen and a host of other medical expertise, from India and China, and from his own immediate culture. Hellenistic influence in Persia is well documented, and all the available Greek works of medicine were in Arabic translation by the early eleventh century CE.[6] While this involved the creation of formal Arabic terminology, by the time of Ibn Sina this was well established. The *Canon* was written over at least a decade, in the cities of Ray (now a part of Greater Tehran) and Hamadan (mid-western Iran), and published in 1025. Until the Greek revival of the sixteenth century in Europe and, for many, long afterwards, Ibn Sina remained the principal medical authority, with the *Canon* the main medical text. While agreeing in broad principles with Galen about the ways in which pain was carried to the brain (not the heart), Ibn Sina nonetheless has been understood in recent scholarship to have expanded the causes of pain from injury to temperamental changes (any sudden change, for example in temperature, could cause pain, as could sudden change in the mixture of the humours in a particular organ) and to have expanded the number of types of pain from Galen's four to fifteen. It should be noted that Galen himself drastically reduced the number of medically viable pain descriptors that he had found in Archigenes, on the basis that they were unintelligible and confusing, but, as already noted, it is incorrect that Galen reduced the typology of pain to four types.[7] In some instances (numbness, for example), Ibn Sina restored a category of 'pain' that Galen had explicitly rejected. Scholars have gone to great lengths to try to map Ibn Sina's pain categories onto contemporary descriptions of pain (others have done the same for Galen), such that they might even foreshadow the classificatory system of the McGill Pain Questionnaire (explored at length in chapter 4 on chronic pain).[8] This is to be indulgent in translation, perhaps, and to play fast and loose with situated meanings, for all of the types of Ibn Sina's 'pain', and Galen's too, were based upon a humoral understanding of human physiology. The implication, according to the antihistorical tradition of joining straight lines between Ibn Sina's knowledge and contemporary medical knowledge, is that a pain description served a particular experience of pain that, the under-lying context of the description notwithstanding, does not change. The analysis cannot work. The category of 'pain' that appears in both Galen and Ibn Sina is a broad category that includes feelings and symptoms that most contemporary medical authorities would not class as pain at all.

I have tried – through a reading of Ibn Sina's 'pain' categories in Arabic that has no a priori agenda to connect them to anything like present-day pain categories – to arrive at the situated meanings of these terms, resisting the temptation to label each one as 'pain'.⁹ In the list and description of these categories in Ibn Sina, each one is marked as a type of *Waja'*, which could be translated as 'pain', hurt, ache, or disease, or, per Ibn Sina's own definition, 'a feeling of incongruity'.¹⁰ Most scholars acknowledge this breadth of meaning, yet obscure it by insisting on listing types of 'pain'. Instead, I list a range of them here as categories of *dis-ease* – a term that perhaps more neatly captures this notion of a feeling of incongruity, and which preserves the latitude of medieval 'pain' as encompassing troublesome and discomforting experiences that go beyond physical hurt. In each case, I give the Arabic transliteration with original script in parentheses, followed by the Farsi transliteration and original script, followed by its meaning in English.

The first named dis-ease, telling enough for the point I wish to make, is *Waj'-i-hakkāk* (الوجع الحكّاك), *Dard-e Khāreshī* (درد خارشى), meaning 'itchy'. The Arabic might indicate something like scraping or chafing sense of harm, a sensation of friction, but it makes sense simply to settle on the feeling of itchiness. Most scholars prefer 'itching pain', but I do not think this should apply. It is caused here by acrid or sharp humours and treated accordingly. Once we remove the need to translate *Waj'* into a narrow definition of 'pain', the meaning of an itchy discomfort emerges. It appears in a general list that includes things recognizable as physical pain because it shares in an aetiological explanation: the humours.¹¹

The second dis-ease is *Waj'-i-khashin* (الوجع الخشن), *Dard-e Zebrī* (درد زبرى), which is often translated as 'irritating pain'. The circularity of the textual description does not help much, since it advises that this kind of pain is caused by this kind of humour, so it is important to know what *khashin* means: rough or raw or rude. Something unrefined in the humoral condition equates to something similar in the character of the experience. Is it 'irritating'? Maybe. But that doesn't seem to get to the heart of the intended meaning. The Farsi indicates something rough or spikey. So, this is a feeling of roughness or rawness.

Waj'-i-nākhis (الوجع الناخس), *Dard-e Khalande-h* (درد خلنده), is often translated as 'stretching pain' or sometimes 'tension pain' (I suspect to fit with later Latin translations, and to fit with Galen, but see more on this below), but it seems to refer to a sting or prick. Again, there is circularity in the description of the cause, since this dis-ease refers to the action of a humour that has this quality of effecting the muscles and nerves. *Waj'-i-momaddid* (الوجع الممدّد), *Dard-e Feshārī* (درد فشارى), is pressure or compression, and could be a physical pain, but it could also be the experience of feeling compressed: of a weight bearing on a part.

One begins to see the point that these descriptions are both diminished and rendered confusing if it is insisted that they be made narrowly to conform to a modern western notion of pain. Rather, to understand them, it is necessary to relinquish this narrow understanding and to embrace a category of pain that is far broader, nearer to a sense of dis-ease. Two final examples clinch the argument. Ibn Sina's *Waj'-i-rikhw* (الوجع الرخو), *Dard-i Sost* (درد سست), has been translated as 'relaxing pain' – most confusing – and could be something like a 'soft' or 'loose' ache, but it is the feeling of flaccidity that makes most sense. The Farsi is suggestive of looseness, but also *numbness*: a category that Galen had explicitly rejected as a type of pain, for reasons that are rather obvious. Something that is loose, relaxed, flaccid, or numb does not make sense as a pain, but it does make sense as a dis-ease. Ibn Sina's text gives a precise circumstance for this loose feeling, in which a muscle is stretched but not the ligaments and tendons. One might be troubled by such a condition without experiencing pain. In a final example, *Waj'-i-I'iyāi* (الوجع الإعيائى), *Dard-i Khastigī* (درد خستگی), often translated as 'tired pain' or 'fatigue pain', is simply a feeling of fatigue. While there is a temptation to connect this to the pains experienced in chronic fatigue syndrome, again this does not seem to be implied here. The cause is given as overwork, so why not simply understand this as it was intended: an uncomfortable feeling of tiredness?

How could it be that such a well-studied text has become so mangled in modern translation? There is, without question, a desire to connect Ibn Sina to modernity, to emphasize the profundity of his medical vision, but this is rather undermined (a) by the argument that his 'pain' categories map comfortably onto something like the McGill Pain Questionnaire and (b) by the fact that they contain such confusing examples as 'relaxing pain', 'itching pain', and 'tired pain'. I suspect that the intention is compounded by a reading of Ibn Sina through its Latin translation.

One only needs examine the Latin translations of Ibn Sina to see that his fifteen types of dis-ease were given a different feel by translators looking to make sense of pain categories in medieval Europe. I am here relying on the translation of Gerard of Cremona in manuscript form, from the late thirteenth-century copy, a printed version of Gerard of Sabbioneta's thirteenth-century translation, produced in 1489/90 (both housed at Yale), and a later Latin translation of 1658.[12] Consistently, from the first translation, Ibn Sina's category of *Waja᾿* is rendered as *dolor*. *Dolor* in medieval use could indicate physical pain, grief, anguish, and resentment. It was, like the Arabic concept, broadly indicative of *suffering* and therefore appealed to the physical and the emotional alike, but it missed the sense of *disease*. As *dolor* made its way into vernacular European languages – French *douleur*, Spanish *dolor*, Italian *dolore* – there was no strict tightening of definition. It could still indicate suffering – emotional anguish such as grief, say, and not just physical pain – but it could not be readily used to talk of disease. *Dolor* does not, in my understanding, capture that feeling of incongruity, of illness, of dis-ease, that the Arabic seems to emphasize. The Latin translations are clear enough, for the most part. One finds a list of conditions connected to humoral causes that includes qualities like itchiness and tiredness. The feeling of looseness, for example, is rendered in Latin, first of all, as *laxativ*, and later as *laxus*, but it is consistent with the Arabic to translate this same way, as a feeling of looseness, not a 'relaxing pain', caused by a flaccid muscle. If this passage is thought of as being about the causes and types of 'suffering', then the interpretation of it, even if missing the sense of 'disease', will not be too far from Ibn Sina's intention. But in modern medical parlance, especially from the twentieth century onwards, all these varieties of *dolor*, as well as its English correlate 'pain', have come to stand for physical bodily pain in a narrow sense. The power and influence of this narrow conceptualization of pain in modern medical history have made it extremely difficult to read the Latin text of Ibn Sina with sensitivity to its conceptual contextuality.

In short, what has been routinely taken to be Ibn Sina's pain knowledge is in fact a knowledge of certain presentations of *discomfort*, disease, and sometimes what a contemporary reader would understand as bodily pain, each with discrete causes based upon a humoral understanding of the human body. To think through these categories of dis-ease as pain requires the re-scripting of 'pain' to conform with historically contextualized, situated meanings, to be able to include in it the various kinds of discomfort and illness and their wide variety of causes. While the various translations of Ibn Sina's *Canon* into Latin, beginning in the twelfth century, preserved some of the breadth of the original, over time it has had the effect of concretizing the flexible category of *Waja* into *dolor*, and from there it has come to be understood that Ibn Sina was talking narrowly of pain, instead of broadly about disease.[13] Despite the efforts to join up the dots between his categories and modern ones, the effect of this reduction is to render him incomprehensible and to miss that which is historically distinct. A modern pain script has colonized a medieval pain script and ventriloquized it. Thus, Ibn Sina's pain categories are mapped onto those of the McGill Pain Questionnaire, developed in the 1970s, and make a claim either for the constancy of types of pain experience over a millennium or else for the genius of Ibn Sina in discovering all these different types of pain, or both.[14]

My inclination to sever this eminent genealogy is not born of a desire to relegate the importance of the work, or its influence. Rather it is to try to capture the ways in which knowledge has been interpreted and re-interpreted to both make and reflect experience. It cannot be expected that high medical knowledge had no colloquial or vernacular iteration among the lay public who had to approach medical men for treatment for their ailments. Then, as ever, patients sought out doctors with preconceived ideas of what was wrong with them, based on appropriated and internalized ideas about how the body worked and what made it go wrong. Medical encounters were distinctly unequal negotiations of subjective experience and expertise, situated within a broader context of belief systems and sensory and moral evaluations. Diagnoses, treatment, and experience lie in the balance of such negotiations. To have an itch, or a stretching pain, or a boring pain, in Avicenna's terminology, was to understand the humoral conditions that caused such a pain, and the kinds of external causes – food, climate, injury, etc. – that had brought about the change in temperament. It was to see cause in a specific range of possibilities and to seek cure in a specific range of therapies. The attitude to the experience of pain cannot be disconnected from this kind of knowledge, however loosely or vaguely it was known.

Ibn Sina was no less a reflector, of Galen, of other medical traditions, than he was an innovator. This knowledge is borne of scholarship and 'clinical' experience, where presentations of disease are understood through diagnostic epistemology and are formative of that epistemology. The world of humoral medicine, of *Waja* ' meaning pain, suffering, and numerous types of disease – is experientially distinct from worlds of medicine predicated on different understandings of human physiology, different categories of pain and disease, and different cultural frameworks for expressing and making sense of one's body and mind when they feel out of sorts. The Latin translators of Ibn Sina, and the European upholders and disputers of Arabic medicine throughout the medieval period, were performing their own elisions and slippages, to make a knowledge framework function (or fail to function, for the critics) in their own situated context. This kind of adaptation, which looks like continuity but is actually veiled change, makes it difficult accurately to periodize changes in either medical epistemology or diagnosis and, more importantly, changes in the way pain has been experienced.

From Arabic Pain to Renaissance Pain

One potential avenue of elucidation is in the history of therapeutic measures to alleviate pain, suffering, and dis-ease. I return, therefore, to the primary method of correcting humoral imbalances from Galen through the eighteenth century: bleeding. According to the Galenic script, at the onset of disease the humours divert to the problem area, leading to inflammation. Early intervention, therefore, depended upon the idea of getting the humours to flow in the opposite direction, to evacuate the excess, by bleeding, at a far-away point ('revulsion'). If, on the other hand, intervention occurred only after the accumulation of the humours at a specific point in the body, then they had to be evacuated from that point ('derivation'). Subtle changes in the way that scripts were read emerge, as do more dramatic changes that lay behind shifts in reading cues. The question of how to bleed, where and when to bleed, and the reasons why, all say something about the nature of the experienced pain, for each method contains within it the rationale of cure. I focus here on a flashpoint of controversy – early sixteenth-century pleurisy, which was literally a pain in the side – that connects Ibn Sina, the European followers of the Arab school of medicine, their Galenic opponents, and a new methodological rationale, which in turn heralded the undoing of the practice of bleeding in general.

The precise meanings and methods involved in discriminating between bleeding options and their therapeutic pros and cons were obscured over the passage of centuries, but came to a head in the sixteenth century, in part because of a revival of the study of Greek (and therefore renewed attention to Galenic texts, and explicitly in opposition to Arab influences and supposed corruptions of the original Greek) and in part because of empirical observation. The efficacies, risks, and types of bloodletting came into focus during an epidemic of 'pleurisy' in Paris in 1514, and in Evora, Portugal, in 1518, with the therapeutic practices of Pierre Brissot (1478–1522). Brissot attempted to shift typical revulsion practices, which were painted as Arab errors, insisting on the letting of blood from the arm of the affected side, as opposed to a distant point on the foot of the opposite leg. Couched in Galenic logics of therapy and staunch opposition to Arab influence (Avicenna's advice was *ineptissime*, or foolish), Brissot claimed the proof of observed therapeutic benefits.[15]

Drawn into the controversy with a mind to settling it, Vesalius wrote the bloodletting letter, the *Epistola docens venam dextri cubiti in dolore laterali secandam*, in 1539. It is a staging post on his way to his magnum opus, *De humani corporis Fabrica* (1543): a clear point of departure from the Galenic tradition and knowledge base, towards the production of new knowledge based upon empirical observation. It is an important example of the ways in which systems of knowledge about pain and about the human body in pain have been overturned. For Vesalius, the prevailing knowledge on human anatomy was mired in ignorance and misunderstanding. His aim was in part to correct prevailing misinterpretations of Hippocrates and Galen, and in part to correct medical knowledge by direct observation. The operative point was to locate the correct place from which to draw blood in the case of *dolor lateralis*. While this term was understood to relate to pleurisy, Vesalius makes an extensive case that Hippocrates referred to general pain in the area, with certain precise delimitations. It was a subject, he said, upon which 'even the most erudite dispute fiercely among themselves, with unbridled enthusiasm and by contentious subtlety in open and wordy contradictions', and yet Vesalius presents himself as the corrector before a community of wrongdoers, 'eager to defend an obvious heresy'. These men were, in Vesalius' view, digging in the wrong place. The vein, he thought, 'should be opened in line with the affected side'.[16]

What is clear is that certain kinds of pain in the side were relieved by the action of letting blood. If relief was not attained, it was simply because the blood had been let from the wrong place. Hence the debate. Vesalius serves a useful point about the tenacity of pain knowledge. While his empirical observations set about correcting heresies, he nevertheless continued to operate within a framework of knowledge in which the nature of disease and its symptoms, in this case pain in the side, were rooted in humoralism.[17] Patients labouring under such a pain would expect to be bled, and may have formed an opinion, according to their exposure to medical debates or the authority of the physician treating them, about from where blood should be drawn. Without entering too much upon the question of efficacy, it should suffice to say that therapeutics stemmed logically from knowledge of a pain's cause, and that this framework of knowledge, even under substantial pressure of observation and experiment, changed but slowly.

Nonetheless, Vesalius' approach set in motion a culture shift in medicine that put the onus of argumentation on the results of experimentation. As John Saunders and Charles O'Malley argued back in the late 1940s,

> Up to the year 1539 every participant had marshalled his arguments from the pronouncements of authorities or from empirical observations on the outcome of illness, but thereafter, if he was to attack the Vesalian thesis effectively, he must adopt the new objective method of dissection. ... The physician, therefore, if he was to remain in the mainstream of what was to him logical and rational medicine ... must take up the scalpel and stain his hands in the cadaver.[18]

At stake was the core of how knowledge was formed and upon what authority. While the debate is about the why and where of venesection, the context is the whole of human health and illness, the causes of pain, and the means of pain relief. Pain knowledge was couched in Galenic tradition, seemingly obscured by Arabic influence, subsequently duly scorned by Galenic revivalists, and then, in the context of Galenism, altered irrevocably (if slowly) by innovations in method. What is known, and how it is known, directly relates to the vicissitudes of medical practice. Practice is justified by knowledge claims. The experience of pain, trust in medical authority, and the relief of pain are all tied to these knowledge claims. Changes in the status of knowledge, therefore, have direct consequences for the experience of pain, for they disrupt the basis of trust in medical authority, disrupt the practices and procedures of therapy, and disrupt the patient's own (colloquial) understanding of what they are suffering and why. While Vesalius settled a point about the place from which to draw blood for a certain type of pain, his method opened the way to research practices that would ultimately change the understanding of human physiology, its pains and diseases. The disruption was not simply epistemological, but at the heart of seismic cultural shifts in understandings of what human beings are, how and why they suffer, what that suffering means, and what to do about it.

Eastern Schools

The trip from the Roman empire to the Renaissance takes in various parts of Asia, Persia, and Europe, but that still leaves vast swathes of the global history of pain knowledge untouched. The humoral understanding of the human dominates western medical history and its interaction with Arabic knowledge, but the boundary further to the east was porous, with other knowledge frameworks for the understanding of pain steeped in medical and religious beliefs and practices. If Arabic *Waja*ʿ allowed for the possibility of disease as well as pain and western *dolor* did not, other cultures had correlates. Sitting alongside the Arabic production of formal knowledge about pain was the situated Persian culture, the language of which was Farsi. In Farsi, the word *dard* did all of the work that *Waja*ʿ did, and indeed still does. *Dard* encompasses everything from uneasiness to extreme physical pain, from mental anguish to grief, and is at the core of Hindi and Urdu conceptualizations of pain in South Asia.[19] In broad terms, Hinduism is accepting of suffering as 'part of the unfolding of karma'. It has a kind of cosmic sanction, being the 'natural consequence of the moral laws of the universe in response to past negative behavior'.[20] In medical terms, the Islamic adoption of Greek principles of medicine, known as *Unani Tibb*, was exported eastwards in Arabic translation, where they 'thrived under the patronage of the Mughal Emperors and various regional rulers', translated into Urdu and other languages.[21] This medical culture remains enormously popular. As Judy Pugh has documented, the way Indian metaphors of pain traverse the physical and the affective 'reflects the integrated mind-body system of Indian culture', which 'effects the simultaneous manifestation of physical and psychological suffering'.[22] Pain's causes, as per Galenic Greek, lie in the diet, in the climate, in the 'emotions', or an 'emotional balance' (but which is rooted in humoralism), and in physical exertion and lesion. At a colloquial level, this kind of integration is present in western cultures (broken heart, anyone?), but it has not been endorsed through most of modernity by the gatekeepers of medical authority. What *counts* as pain in the clinical setting, in the medical encounter, therefore differs greatly, with the consequence that the way in which pain is experienced also differs. Within Indian medical culture, the script for pain behaviour is further mediated by social codes relating to caste and gender. The coding of pain behaviour, as well as an understanding of the causes of pain, equates to the ways in which pain is treated, such that the entire experience of pain, from onset to diagnosis to therapy to cure (or lack thereof), is contained within the cultural framework. This perforce goes beyond the world of medicine in a narrow sense to the broader cultural framework in which medicine is itself situated, where acceptance of pain/suffering is virtuous or positively meaningful, where religious belief is inseparable from the experience of daily sufferings, grief, accidents, and diseases.

Some will readily recognize the similarity in South Asian culture (Hinduism, Islam, and Buddhism) to religious cultures of pain and suffering in medieval and early modern Christianity, with its double emphases on the virtue of suffering (literally *patience*, from the Latin *patior*, I suffer) and on the virtue of quiet endurance that, for Christians, was encapsulated in the *imitatio Christi*, the imitation of Christ's passion (I return to this in chapter 3). It is a meaningfulness largely lost in western pain scripts, but it is essential to recognize the ways in which cultural inflections directly alter the ways in which pain is experienced. In the clinic, as Pugh discovered, this makes for an encounter in which formal medical knowledge, rooted in classic Arab texts, is negotiated through the patient vernacular, each validating the other. While there may be an asymmetry between doctor and patient in terms of what they know, the exchange is based upon a common understanding.[23] I cannot improve upon Pugh's conclusion, which holds good for contemporary experiences of pain according to the pain scripts of modern-day India as much as it does for encounters in antiquity or medieval Persia: 'Sensation, expression, and etiology and cure form interconnected facets of pain experience. The meanings which weave them together and ground them in the sufferer's life show the work of culture on the process of suffering. Culture molds pain in both everyday life and medical systems and constitutes their relationship.'[24] The only thing I would add is the element of power or authority: the politics of the pain script.

This is exemplified by the Chinese example.[25] The *Huang Di nei jing* can be literally translated as the *Inner Canon of the Yellow Emperor*. Like other classical medical texts in Greek and Arabic, it exerts an enormous influence over the cultures that produced it, over a period of about a thousand years, though nobody can say for sure when the text originated. Perhaps it is as old as 475 BCE; perhaps it was begun in the Han dynasty (206 BCE–220 CE). Whatever may be the case, the texts were in continuous use and were continually adapted and altered up to 1053, having been formally compiled and rearranged in the mid-eighth century. The edition that remains in use is from the eleventh century, produced by the Imperial Editing Office. It has remained of central importance in Chinese traditional medicine over the ensuing thousand years.

The text is presented as a dialogue between the Yellow Emperor and six ministers. These dialogues are themselves works of literature, for all the interlocutors are mythical. The Yellow Emperor's reign is dated to 2698/7–2598/7 BCE, some two and a half millennia before the *Inner Canon* was begun. He is considered a deity. The *Inner Canon*'s production is connected to the cult of the Yellow Emperor that bloomed in the Han dynasty.

Reading the text for the formalization of pain concepts is beset with difficulties. Not only does it represent a millennium of editing and alteration, but its literary form and the shifting context of its reception in Chinese culture also make it difficult to offer a situated analysis. One could read for the reception of the *Inner Canon* in many different contexts across Chinese history, and doubtless different interpretations of its language and the knowledge it conveys would emerge. I have relied heavily on the monumental translation of Paul Unschuld and Hermann Tessenow. Their own subtextual annotations are strongly suggestive of a text about which there are many debates, corrections, and suspicions of error. Following the textual trail across the different editions and making clear translation choices are, in a work as grand as the *Inner Canon*, a philologist's dream (or nightmare). These kinds of textual uncertainties are plain in the sections concerning pain, what it is, and what to do about it.

At the core of the *Inner Canon* is *qi*, which might be translated as 'air' or 'breath', but which denotes the energy or the vital force of a living being. It is central to traditional Chinese understandings of health and illness. If the flow of *qi* is checked or otherwise disturbed, illness and pain follow: 'Harmed qi causes pain.'[26] The operative concept here is 痛 (*tóng*), which translates to pain and ache as well as sorrow and sadness, showing a conflation of somatic and affective experiences. *Qi* flows through conduits or vessels that are networked through the body and is affected by diet, season, weather, and so on. Blockages or imbalances of different kinds of *qi* (yin and yang) could be treated by piercing the skin, sometimes drawing blood, sometimes not, to release the 'evil' energy. All this falls within a metaphor of the body as a kind of regime, with 'palaces' (*fu*) and 'depots' (*zang*) that served as storage and handling spaces and organs that ruled over subordinate organs and functions via networks of *qi*. As Unschuld puts it, the *fu* 'are enclosures housing and sheltering something important. In its original sociocultural context, this may have been literature in a collector's library, or a prince, a king, or an emperor in a palace; it is the blood, the essence brilliance, and so on, in the human body.'[27] The body becomes the image of empire writ small, as if imperial governance were composed of the same kind of structures and energy flows, subject to the same kinds of blockages and pains. A close examination of either could reveal the other:

> The ruling organs in the human body sit in 'palaces' just as the governors
> in the various regions of the empire. As the latter are responsible for

administrative functions and rule over people, the organs in the body fulfill important administrative duties such as 'the supply of qi' and rule over subjects identified as 'vessels,' 'skin,' and so on.[28]

Thus all bodily conditions, including pain, were understood through both political and philosophical frames of reference.

Pain could be caused by wind (itself a complex multitude of phenomena), as well as by injury, but special significance is given to *qi* pain. *Qi* flows continuously in the 'conduit vessels', but this flow could be interrupted by cold, diminishing the blood if occurring outside the vessels, and blocking *qi* if inside the vessels. The result of both would be 'sudden pain'. The Yellow Emperor asks about all kinds of pain, experienced in different ways and with different adjoining symptoms. The narrative explanation of all the types of pain is an imaginary account of internal swelling and movement. Cold makes the vessels shrink, causing curving and tension, which causes them in turn to 'pull on the small network' vessels 'outside'. Heat stops the pain, unless there have been 'multiple strikes by cold', in which case 'pain will persist for long'. If 'cold qi' resides in the conduit vessels and 'strikes against the heat qi', then 'the vessels become full', causing an ache that hurts to touch. If the 'cold qi stagnates and the heat qi follows' it upwards, 'then the vessels are full and big and both the blood and the qi are in disorder', causing 'extreme' pain. These vessels should not be pressed. Other pains could be dispersed by pressing, such as that caused by cold *qi* in the intestines and the stomach, because the act of pressing allowed for the blood again to flow. But sometimes the cold *qi* was too deep, and no matter how deeply one pressed, one could not reach the blockage. All over the body, vessels of varying dimensions are seen to flow or be blocked, and to pull upon surrounding organs, muscles, and bones, though physical ties. The exterior of the penis, for example, is described as 'the ceasing yin vessel', which 'encloses' the sex organ, and this was in turn 'tied to the liver' and spread to the diaphragm and the flanks. Cold *qi* here, therefore, caused the 'ribs in the flanks and the lower abdomen [to] pull each other', resulting in pain. Abdominal pain with '[constant] outflow from one's behind' was caused by cold *qi* settling in the small intestine.[29]

All these types of pain had their external signs, especially in the five colours of the face. Each of the five depots and six palaces of the bodily interior had corresponding sections in the face, and the colours of the face (red, yellow, white, green-blue, and black) each had diagnostic associations. This could be augmented by palpation: the physical state of the vessels was discernible to the touch.[30] Every kind of emotion, sensation, and temperature had an effect on *qi* and could therefore be pathological, with distinct signs of disease.[31] In every case, the physical appearance or feel of the body, or else its obvious external symptoms (sweating, vomiting, etc.), was evidence of what was wrong with the flow of *qi*, but *qi* itself could not be seen. The sites and vessels of *qi*, the overall good or ill functioning of the bodily regime, could be seen and measured and understood through the balance of yin and yang and the flow of *qi*.

There is no point in debating whether *qi* is real, for it is central to a major belief system, and such central concepts have functional and experiential consequences that are empirically researchable and verifiable, just as the belief in a Christian God has real-world effects at the level of experience, especially for those in pain. To debate about the *fact* of *qi* is to misunderstand the central importance of *qi* as a core linguistic and conceptual element of the medical explanatory and political and philosophical framing of the body. It is analogous, in my estimation, to the notion of wiring, signalling, and networking in modern western medicine's theorizing of pain pathways and pain mechanisms. These pathways were more self-consciously employed as figurative language, perhaps, but structurally they serve the same purpose. The evidence of *qi* in the body stands for the evidence of *qi* itself, just as, in western medicine, the evidence of pain has stood in for the evidence of injury, however invisible, or for the evidence of a pathway, or for the evidence of once unseen Greek-sounding 'components' (*neurons, axons, synapses, ganglions*), or as proof of sin and of God's love.

When the Americans sent a delegation of pain specialists to China in the 1970s, led by John Bonica (1917–94) (who was himself formative of the study of pain in the post-war United States), condescension and suspicion were baked in. They attempted to look behind the metaphors, to decode them, to see what was *really* going on, and to understand the functioning of practices like acupuncture according to western physiological standards. To their bewilderment, acupuncture seemed to work, whether as analgesic or as anaesthetic.[32] But their attempt to fit acupuncture into a contemporary American model of pain and pain relief in the pseudo-electrical-engineering metaphor of the 'Gate Control' (see the next section of this chapter) failed to understand that the experience of pain and its remedy were entirely situated within the conceptual framework of *qi*. To export the practice of acupuncture without exporting the whole web of meaning in which acupuncture took place would make little sense. Hence it was dismissed as akin to hypnotism.

Modern Pain Pathways

If flows of humours and *qi* were a part of the pain imaginary, the turn in early modernity to material and embodied notions of pain did not make the phenomenon of pain any more visible. The break with the past is usually identified with René Descartes, who visualized the relationship between sensory damage at a part of the body and the brain's awareness of and reaction to that damage. While the language is of animal spirits, there is nonetheless an embodied sense of a signalling flow, or, perhaps more prosaically, a bellpull. Just as a distant bell rings when the rope to which it is attached is pulled, so the brain bell rings when activated by input at the periphery. This is famously illustrated in the *Traité de l'homme* (1664) as a man with his foot in the fire, his realization of burning, and the mechanics of withdrawal. Insofar as the human *soul* suffered, this was a matter of reflection on the damage, but the mechanics of pain were automatized, witnessable in the animal machine as well the human. The fact that animals had no immortal soul put them beyond moral concern.[33] The kind of specificity theory afforded by Descartes puts pain reception in the body's periphery, in bodily material that detects the 'pain' and then sends messages, by some internal means, to the brain, where the pain is processed by a specific part adapted for this purpose. Modern pain scholars, from the late nineteenth century onwards, came to understand this peripheral bodily material as nociceptive nerve endings – that is, as pain detectors – as if the pain happened at the point of injury. The greater the damage (or input), the larger the pain, the message being encoded at the site of injury and sent to the brain.

Thus begins a series of modern pain theories that look for the pathway, the circuitry, the wiring, or the matrix of pain in the stuff of the body. One could match many accounts of this kind of model of pain to that of Descartes, and while the specific idiom may change over time, the basic explanation of pain remains the same. I would argue that, for many people, this remains the 'common-sense' understanding of pain. From the 1930s, based on the ideas of J.P. Nafe (1886–1970), the picture began to complicate. Nafe surmised that different afferent nerve fibres 'fired' in different ways, and in different combinations, according to differences in sensory stimulation. Bodily sensation was 'coded' according to this 'composite of activity'. This was known as 'pattern theory'.[34] Thereafter, different types of nerve fibre, specifically myelinated Aδ fibres and unmyelinated afferent C-fibres, were shown to be activated by different magnitudes of sensory stimulation, and to signal 'damage' in different ways and at different rates. It was not until 1965 that Ronald Melzack (1929–2019) and Patrick Wall (1925–2001) produced a theory that would change the simple directionality of these mechanical models, in an attempt to match their clinical experience with the varieties of pain after injury.[35] The unpredictability of pain experience was well known, but the sheer scale of injury afforded by two world wars had acutely focused attention on the strange phenomenon of the absence of pain accompanying serious injury. The leading anaesthesiologist Henry Beecher (1904–76) suggested that more than two-thirds of seriously injured soldiers felt no pain in the immediate event and aftermath of their wounding in the context of combat.[36] The mass breakage of bodies and their mysterious absence of pain in injury provided copious empirical proof that there was no specific relation between injury and pain.

Melzack and Wall's 'Gate Control Theory' stayed within the idiom of electrical engineering and automaticity, but in placing a 'gate' between the peripheral damage signal and the brain, they could theorize the variable relationship between pain and injury. A variety of different types of electrical and chemical signal enter the 'gate' and their specific combination determines the message that gets further transmitted up to the brain and what noise is filtered out. The same 'gate' receives regulatory signals from the brain, which determines the colour of pain, its magnitude, and so on. It eliminated the search for a specific pain nerve, instead understanding the experience of pain as a more complex relationship between damage, afferent signalling, and efferent signalling. The size and type of nervous signal, in combination with the cognitive and affective evaluation of the situation, modulate and modify what pain feels like.

All of this could still be reduced to the imagery of a circuit diagram, the contextual and emotional component notwithstanding. The human being was reducible, still, to its wiring, its processes, its systematized automatic functioning. Over time, the metaphor of electrical engineering gave way to the metaphor of the computer. To a large degree, pain research languishes in this metaphor in which the human as situated, active, relational, evaluative being remains impoverished. As Howard Fields noted, the 'neurobiology of the evaluative component is still an open question'.[37] That 'component' is not wholly in the body, but in the relation between body and context. So long as neurobiologists continue to seek answers in neurobiological terms, the question will remain 'open'.

While the Gate Control Theory took pain research on a step, it could not explain chronic pain states. Why did pain sometimes endure, even after the injury was healed? I will return to this question later. For now it is important to state that the line from Descartes to Melzack and Wall had painted medical science into a corner in which the focus on the relation of damage and pain would frustrate viable theories of pain without damage and of pain that endured. There were clear indications, from Beecher onwards, and especially in the work of Melzack, that neurobiological models would never entirely suffice to explain either pain mechanisms or pain experience. Another product of two world wars – the survival of large numbers of men who had lost limbs – would crystallize the problem of chronic pain and the deficiency of existing models of explanation.

There is robust scholarship on the pain syndromes of amputees, particularly the phenomenon of phantom limb pain, which is the experience of pain in the limb that is missing.[38] The phenomenon has been known since at least 1552, documented by the French surgeon Ambroise Paré (c.1510–90).[39] Descartes mentioned it in 1641.[40] Opportunities to study it came about with advances in both modern warfare and modern medicine, which meant that seriously wounded soldiers were more likely to survive their injuries. Silas Weir Mitchell (1829–1914) studied phantom pains in American Civil War survivors. The twentieth century would see an enormous swelling of cases.[41] The existence of pain either in the stump or in the space beyond it where there was no longer any body confounded both medical science and the social mechanisms employed to support veterans. Character, psychology, and moral fibre were all questioned as potential explanations for a pain state that made no sense. The experienced physical pain was often exacerbated by being officially displaced by diagnoses of nervous illness, shell shock, hysteria, and so on. It removed the pain patient to the psychiatric gaze.

In a series of papers between 1989 and 2006, Melzack returned to the problem of phantom pain and the potential, through understanding it, of cracking the problem of chronic pain and the deficiency of the pathway model.[42] The metaphor was computational. The specific insight was the 'neuromatrix'. In this theory, the connection of the experience of pain to the location of the injury is finally severed, focusing on the production of experience in the brain irrespective of where the harm might initially have been. Melzack theorized an individual construction of a 'neurosignature' in the brain which amounted to the brain's internal image of the bodily self, comprising the whole array of incoming information. He conceived of this neuromatrix as plastic, being a composite of genetic, sensory, and affective information, including the proportionality of the body and the relationality of all its parts and the meanings attached to the body through cultural situation. Melzack understood the brain to arrange this wide array of information and transform it into a 'symphonic' output that amounts to what is perceived as the body-self. An injury somewhere becomes part of the array of information coming in, and the output of the brain locates the injury in the appropriate part and identifies it as belonging to *this* body.

Since all experience comes *from* the brain, rather than to it, the removal of a limb may not necessarily alter the image of the body-self in the neuromatrix. Thus it is possible to sense experience in the missing part. The experience becomes pathological when the expected signal from the part in question does not arrive. The brain responds through additional nervous activation, as if asking the question of the missing limb, amplifying the descending signal in the continued absence of an answer. This process of sensitization can itself cause burning pain *as if* in the missing limb. Similarly, central commands to move are amplified because of a lack of response, and this can lead to the experience of cramp in the missing limb.

These are not settled questions, and their metaphorical framing keeps them locked, to some extent, in an understanding of the human as automated machine.[43] Melzack, perhaps more than any other twentieth-century medical-scientific pain specialist, wanted to break out of that idiom. While pain researchers now know the Cartesian model to be incorrect (nociception is not pain; the extent of sensory input does not determine the magnitude of pain; the production of pain is more like an output of the brain, not a collection of incoming data), it is remarkable just how tenacious this idea is. Researchers still think in terms of 'peripheral pain sensors', and still frame their understanding of what pain is as the 'sense' of harm and the automated response of withdrawal. They still think of a distinction between physical, nociceptive, and neuropathic pain, and all of the emotional effects of those essentially mechanical problems, even shoehorning those emotional effects into the mechanical explanatory. One can readily find explanations that emphasize signals, electrical connections, mechanisms, systems: automatic, autonomic, biological reductions; the human as model railway.[44] This kind of research has a narrow understanding of what pain is and, in describing how sensory messaging to and from the brain works and the bare physiology of homeostasis, perhaps misses pain altogether. It explicitly limits its horizons to the exclusion of cultural context in its formulation of pain in the present and the future of pain knowledge. When looking for an explanation of 'varying levels of pain experience by people', it looks to genetics, not to the vicissitudes of experience. This is not to say that genetic research might not contribute useful knowledge to the picture of pain, but insofar as a better future can be envisaged in terms of what is known about pain and how it can be treated, it lies in the abandonment of narrowly mechanical, essentially seventeenth-century views in modern medicine, opening up the neuroscience of nociception to the worldedness of bodies and brains, senses, and emotions. In many respects, this might be effected by a critical look at the richness of much older historical constructions of pain.

The increasing sense of doubt about the specificity of pain to an injured part led to parallel theories of pain, outside of neurobiology, that re-focused the 'where' of pain to a compound aggregation of biological, psychological, and social factors. Without having looked back, this nonetheless captured some of the conceptual holism of earlier pain knowledge. Crucially, the theorization of this compound comes without spaces in between the parts: the *biopsychosocial* model of pain. In practice, the divisions remain open. The model was suggested in 1977 by American psychiatrist George Engel (1913–99) as a potential replacement for a flawed biomedical model of illness and disease, encompassing the 'social, psychological and behavioral dimensions of illness'. It would allow, for example, medical authorities to understand when grief was a disease, and why it presented with physical symptoms.[45] It has been influential across a range of specialisms, including pain, but it has frequently butted up against neurobiological intractability and the fantasy of the pain machine. It has, at least, afforded new approaches to the question of chronic pain that include the 'social' not merely in terms of pain's effects, but as part of pain's experience.[46]

Ask the operative question, 'Where does it hurt?', and the biopsychosocial answer is complex. Imagine, for example, that you have just trapped your finger in a door. Is the pain in your finger? Is the pain somehow intrinsic to the door? Is the pain in your head? Is it, in fact, coursing through your body, between the door, finger, body, and brain? The answer, with many qualifications, is that pain is in all these things. It is at once everywhere and reducible to no single element. It does not reside in the specific injury, but the specific injury – not only in terms of its physical damage, but also in terms of how and what caused it, when, under what circumstances – is a constitutive part of how pain will come to be experienced, in the moment, in the short term, and in the process of recovery (or, perhaps, in the failure to recover). It might seem strange to say that the pain is, to some extent, in the door, but this is a shorthand way of understanding the trapped finger in relation to the world, just as it is related to the brain. To say, similarly, and with equal weighting, that the pain is in your head is not to dismiss the experience of pain as a phantom or a psychosomatic delusion. All pain is in the head, insofar as all pain requires a brain. The trapped finger triggers a set of signals, electrical and chemical, that the brain ends up processing. It may be painful and it may not. The circumstances, the individual experience of the finger owner, the cultural repertoire in which the finger owner is situated, will play a large role in the way the brain manages the signals, working out whether this is painful or not. When you trap your finger in the door, your finger might hurt. It would be right, in a purely practical sense, to tell a doctor or nurse that your finger hurts. It would be wrong, both analytically and technically, to say that the pain was located in the finger. It is located in the process of the finger being damaged in a specific context. Many recent studies of pain attempt to capture this through imaging, as if the lit-up sectors of the brain, courtesy of functional Magnetic Resonance Imaging (fMRI) techniques, reveal that pain was in your head all along.[47] Unfortunately, a great deal of doubt hangs over the technological reliability of these instruments to say that pain is *there*.[48]

Take another example, more complex. You, like millions of others, like me, suffer from chronic low-back pain. There is, for all intents and purposes, nothing wrong with you: no physical injury, no obvious lesion external or internal, no structural deformity. But your lifestyle, sitting for hours each day in ergonomically non-ideal circumstances, with poor posture and little recourse to correct it, leaves you in agony. Where is the pain? In your back? In the cheap office furniture? Is it in your head, in the pejorative sense? Have you – have I – succumbed to the indolent complaints of decadence? Or is it in the structure and logic of the capitalist society that puts you in the cheap office chair, day after day, pursuing someone else's enrichment? Unlike the finger in the door, which in most circumstances will sort itself out in a short time, the chronic low-back pain of the seated worker seems to be tied precisely to the conditions of survival. For many it has become the price of survival. Thus inescapable, the pain manifests in the flow of complaints that come in the wake of the intractable problem: depression, anxiety, withdrawal, loneliness. If acute pain is everywhere, chronic pain syndromes are all-consuming. They are everywhere in a cultural and social and economic sense. They afflict people in their millions and, at the same time, contribute to the making invisible of those people who lack the means – as most of us do – to change their circumstances.

Pain is programmed in the system.

Pain scripts come from somewhere – from a place of education, literacy, scholarship, experience – and their success is borne upon the authority that inheres in these things. When one argues that culture *does* something, one risks removing the agents of that doing. Who are the imposers, the gatekeepers? Who or what is it that translates formal, esoteric, exclusive knowledge into everyday practices that open, in however a rudimentary a fashion, this high knowledge to the person in pain? If the vicissitudes of the experience of pain are to be understood, then the writers and adapters of the terms of pain must be given their due. Formal pain knowledge, which I have shown here in cursory ways to be contingent, heavily mediated by language and belief and cultural inertia, is lived out as situated pain experience. This relationship, between the production of, or claim to, knowledge about pain and the lived experience of pain, is central to this history. It fundamentally disrupts an all-too-common notion that how one feels, especially when one feels pain, is *natural* and universal. Rather, the feeling of pain is *produced*, even if one feels it *as if* naturally. It follows a script and exists within a situated frame. The key, both to understanding the history of pain, and to the contemporary politics of pain in present-day pain-knowledge production, is to make visible these easily hidden or obscured processes of making pain. It matters whether the person in pain understands what is happening to them in terms of energy flows or humours or wiring or computational processes: how it feels is directly related to common understandings of how it works.

TWO

Experiencing
Objectivity versus Subjectivity

To say that how it feels is directly related to the common understanding of how it works does not mean that how it feels always (or ever, perhaps) *accords* with the given conceptual framing. The available pain rubric may be a poor fit for the feeling of pain. This in turn might occasion more suffering, unnameable and inexpressible. The notion of a 'script' raises the question of what happens if you cannot 'read' it, or if there is room for improvisation.[1] This chapter explores the relation of pain knowledge to the medical practices for measuring and assessing pain. I focus on the effect of modern understandings of pain sensitivity, pain thresholds, and pain as an automatic and autonomic function of biology with its own logics of reflex, reaction, and display. They are at the root of scientific attempts to make pain into an objective phenomenon that can be studied and measured without reference to the experienced feelings of the person in pain. Aside from the obvious erasure of patient testimony, the claim of objectivity was always inherently political. Discourses of differential biological sensitivities to pain are underwritten by racism, misogyny, class chauvinism, ageism, and speciesism. Objectivity is the story of the categorization of the unfeeling, the over-sensitive, the unimportant, and the validated according to mechanical or visual proof. The mechanical measurement of pain has been used as a way of scripting both what pain looks like – whether on a body, a face, or a mechanically drawn graph – and how it feels. The history of this measurement must therefore explore how the tools of measurement have been used to operationalize the scripts formed by medical authorities about who and what can suffer and to what degree.

Insofar as these processes have erased subjectivity, there are parallel scripts of pain, both medical and extra-medical, that depend entirely on subjective expressions and practices of pain and their cultural codes. This pertains to what is now understood as emotional pain, or social pain, or psychological *trauma* (or post-traumatic stress), and this has its own political history and its own way of categorizing pains that count and pains that do not. What has been the effect of constructing pain on these parallel tracks – the physical and the emotional – and what has been the effect of attempts to make them converge? What is the experiential relation of physical and emotional pain? Here the focus shifts to the implications of biopsychosocial understandings of pain – attempts to put the body and the mind in the world to get at the phenomenon of suffering – and to the metaphorical language of 'trauma'. What does one have to know – what script must one read, or perform – to have emotional pain acknowledged, especially where this no injury? And how do people come to know such scripts? How do they access and employ the concepts that pain authorities have constructed? To populate an approach to these questions, I turn, first, back to the humoral world of medicine, and the script for melancholia in early modern England, and from there back to Greece, specifically to the figure of a grieving Achilles. One of the consequences of the medical focus on pain's function in the body has been the parcelling off of painful experiences into emotional categories that lie beyond the sphere of medical intervention – grief, loneliness, depression – opening up an apparently separate field of emotional pain signs and practices. I want to highlight a long history of cultural validity for this kind of pain experience, in the context of the politics of securing medical validity in modernity.

Pain by Numbers

How can one measure pain? If I am to know your pain, do I not need some method by which to rate it? If scientists are to understand pain, do they not need a scale by which to categorize it? These kinds of questions seem rational and logical but they come from a certain political orientation that assumes that to know is to provide or produce an objective gauge of an experience, as if the simple fact of you telling me about or showing me your pain could never be sufficient. Perhaps the telling and the showing never can be sufficient, but they will at least get me some of the way there, some of the time. To objectify your pain, however – to try to put it on a scale that applies to anybody, anywhere, based upon the fact of your humanness, your nervous system, or some essential quality of the brain – is to risk ignoring or rhetorically outranking your own testimony. It comes bundled with many other dangers.

The allure of measurement is easy to understand. As with many other great physiological and psychological ambitions, the promise of cracking the code of humanity, to be able to say simply and elegantly what 'we' are and how 'we' work, with accuracy and predictability, is attractive. If a pain-measuring device could be contrived that would accurately describe the experience and intensity of pain, for anybody and at any time, based on a reading that does not depend upon the vicissitudes of metaphor or the ambiguity of gesture, then we would be diagnostically and therapeutically advantaged. Much as this is a consummation devoutly to be wished, the historicity, mutability, and contextuality of pain make it impossible. This has not stopped attempts being made, and they have had an effect, even if the effect has not always been helpful and has, to the contrary, sometimes been harmful. To chart the history of pain-measurement techniques and devices is to mark the history of the intention to know pain and the hubris of those who claimed to have come to know, definitively, what the experience of pain was and how to measure it.

From the late nineteenth century, devices began to be conceived that bracketed the subjective experience of pain and its associated reporting as irrelevant and misleading. The scientist was searching for a way out of the confusing and ambiguous mire wrought by patient testimony.[2] The character or morality or emotionality of a patient in pain, and the ways in which these qualities could be understood as features of sex, race, and age, were all thought to skew the real presence of pain towards over-reporting or under-reporting. Real pain, according to this logic, was embodied, mechanical, and universal. The quest for a measuring device, for human pain at any rate, was predicated on the relative valuelessness of what the person in pain could relate. This reduced the quest for objectivity to the search for a sensitivity index.[3] At what point does a human come to sense a peripheral stimulus, and at what intensity does that stimulus change from a bearable sensation to an unbearable one, from a mere awareness of touch, or heat, or cold, or constriction, to a feeling of pain? Some understood, prior to the experiments to find ways to measure pain, that there would not necessarily be a single scale of pain sensitivity. Rather, the point at which pain became detectable and the point at which pain became unbearable would be indicative of degrees of civilization, criminality, and race in a *true* way, beyond unreliable verbal reporting. Nonetheless, as pain-measuring devices and techniques proliferated, it became necessary to try to conceive of an experimental setting that was devoid of emotion: a place in which the controls ensured that none of the noise of gendered or racialized affective complaint could taint the 'pure' pain data. Such a context proved elusive but the intent is itself telling. The devices fabricated to measure pain thresholds were pre-destined to confirm the *a priori* assumptions of the researchers who built them.

They entangled, in a lasting and increasingly damaging way, the experience of pain and the presence of injury. What was being measured, in most cases, was sensitivity of the skin. The operative assumption was that pain was *always* related to a physical cause, experienced by the peripheral sensorium. If there was no such physical cause – if the experience of pain could not be matched to the technology designed to measure it – then perhaps the pain was not real or should be ascribed to a mental deficiency. Thus the impetus to measure had, from the outset, the consequence of ignoring (at best) and invalidating (at worst) those pains that were beyond the technological capacities of the researchers. This 'functional correspondence' between injury and sensory intensity would come to be definitive of the approach to pain in western medicine throughout the twentieth century.[4] In practical terms, the observation that 'algometers' or 'dolorimeters', 'despite their name, do not measure pain' became moot, because the thing they *do* measure – the intensity of a stimulus, the sensitivity of a subject to variable stimuli – came to stand in for a subject's relative experience of pain.[5]

One such 'algometer' was deployed by the criminal psychologist Cesare Lombroso (1835–1909), who assumed that there was such a thing as the 'criminal type' of person and set about proving it through the political and methodological logics of his time.[6] Using a device designed by the German physiologist Emil du Bois-Reymond (1818–96) that was to record the sensitivity and pain thresholds via electrical stimulus, Lombroso was able to confirm that pain in the criminal type was 'much less acute and sometimes non-existent'. One pole of the electrical device was placed on the back of the subject's hand and moved towards the index finger. The current was raised until the subject felt it, to establish 'general sensibility', and then raised again until the subject felt a sharp pain. To make such an appraisal depended on the uncertainties surrounding heritability in the second half of the nineteenth century, a problem exacerbated by leading evolutionary scientists' vacillation on just this point. Lombroso *knew* that criminality was heritable and he *knew* that the signs of it were physical; his research therefore proved what he presumed to know. On opening up the body of a notorious criminal, he experienced a 'revelation' on finding a 'distinct depression' on the skull that reminded him of the skulls of 'inferior animals'. It was a sign, if not an explanation, of criminality. The criminal was 'an atavistic being who reproduces in his person the ferocious instincts of primitive humanity', which included 'insensibility to pain' among a host of undesirable qualities such as the 'craving for evil' and the desire to kill and 'mutilate the corpse, tear its flesh, and drink its blood'. The algometric testing demonstrated to his satisfaction that 'the criminal shows greater insensibility to pain as well as to touch', and that in some criminals this reached the extent of 'complete analgesia or total absence of feeling', which Lombroso averred was 'never encountered in normal persons'. The degree of insensibility could be plotted against specific types of crime, such that murderers were less sensible than burglars, for example.[7]

The pain measurement not only equated physical sensibility to specific types of criminality, but also mapped out in broad terms the consequences on a social level. To be cruel depended 'on moral and physical insensibility'. If a person is 'incapable of feeling pain', then he is more likely to be 'indifferent to the sufferings of others'.[8] Lombroso's research suggested that the capacity for emotional extension to the suffering of others – sympathy – could be estimated from the sensitivity of the skin.

Lombroso's assumptions were baseless and his research was worthless, but this is nothing to the purpose. He and others like him acted upon what they believed to be true, and their actions had real-world experiential effects. The assumed ability to detect essentially moral qualities in the skull, the features of the head or body, or the skin was undergirded by a typological study of photographs of criminals and a widely heralded method that understood genealogy through inheritance of acquired habits and characteristics. Men like Lombroso took pain out of the mind, opposing trends in psychological research, and put it in the skin and the body, where it was positively measurable.

Not everyone agreed with Lombroso. Multiple possibilities about what could be known about pain were active at the same time. One of Lombroso's contemporaries, Paolo Mantegazza (1831–1910), knew that pain was a 'subjective experience, a fact of consciousness', and therefore contingent, situated, variable.[9] According to Dolores Martín Moruno's reading of Mantegazza, attempts to reduce pain to 'physical and chemical changes in a nerve or in nerve cells' were mistaken, for pain was formed 'in relation to the codes, norms, and institutions that prevailed' at the time.[10] Mantegazza was ahead of the curve. Such a view predicts current knowledge on pain, but it did not prevent him from rooting these observations in essentialist physiology, measuring physical changes not as the effect of pain but as the evidence of pain. Nor did it prevent him from a conscious pursuit of pain in the laboratory, studying and measuring it through the controlled infliction of a whole variety of wounds on a menagerie of experimental animals.

Elsewhere, the history of the algometer reflects debates about the way pain works, framed by historically specific forms of chauvinism, bigotry, and arrogance. Noémi Tousignant has shown that competing algometric devices in the late nineteenth century were devised in the hope of settling the question of pain function: along a specific pain 'pathway', or as a 'pattern' of sensations that added up to pain. There were Swedish attempts in the 1880s to 'map' the 'distribution of sensory spots using needles, faradic current from a single electrode, narrow jets of hot and cold water, cork points and small drops of ether' and German attempts to measure precisely where the perception of sensory stimulation on the skin began.[11] Meanwhile, with results that Lombroso would doubtless have lauded, algometric readings taken by anthropologists in the Torres Strait in 1898 claimed proof that 'Murray Islanders were only half as sensitive to pain as English men and boys.'[12] This fed upon a literary and political trope of the unfeeling inferior other that lay at the heart of colonial logics of expansion and displacement. As Xine Yao documents, Thomas Jefferson had marked the 'inherent insensibility' of black people in 1785: 'Their griefs are transient. Those numberless afflictions, which render it doubtful whether Heaven has given life to us in mercy or in wrath, are less felt, and sooner forgotten with them.'[13] The generalization encompassed indigenous peoples, in whom the white gaze detected only vacancy and numbness, with Stanley Stanhope Smith remarking, in

1787, on the 'uncommon power of supporting pain' among American 'aboriginal tribes'.[14] Such views were mild for the times. Smith is seen as a minority counterweight to the thrust of the racist foundations of academic anthropology, which maintained the racialization of pain sensitivity throughout the nineteenth century.

As algometric research proliferated, in conjunction with psychophysiological experimentation on emotions on a grand scale, so the emphasis shifted. One strand of research understood emotions as physiological phenomena – visceral responses to stimuli – collapsing 'the borderline between physical and emotional pain'.[15] Subjective testimony, however it was expressed, could still be ignored according to this logic, because emotions could be plotted on graphs according to changes in blood pressure, heart rate, sweat, and traceable alterations in the functioning of different organs, just as pain sensitivity could be mechanically recorded. If there was variability, the body would let the researcher know. The patient's, or the experimental subject's, own testimony was *noise* to be filtered out. Another research strand in the United States from the 1930s seemed to reinstate that 'borderline' between the physical and emotional, arguing, according to Tousignant, that '[d]ifferences in sensitivity to pain … were an artefact of the contamination of the sensory pain threshold by elements of subjects' *reaction* to pain, influenced by mood, attention, disposition, etc.' If these reactions could be controlled, filtered out of the experimental setting, then sensation could be completely isolated. The Hardy–Wolff–Goodell dolorimeter, which projected heat onto the blackened forehead of the experimental subject, claimed to have achieved such an isolation, proclaiming 'constancy of physiological sensitivity in all neurologically normal individuals, independent of gender, personality, fatigue or emotional state'.[16] Nevertheless, it remained clear that, sensory uniformity notwithstanding (and sensory uniformity was not reliably reproducible anyway), the experience of pain was not uniform.

That lack of uniformity threw the focus back onto racial, gender, and class categories of affectivity to explain the varied response of different kinds of subject to the same stimulus. The physiological fact of pain was, it was routinely assumed, embodied and measurable. If the experience of that embodied pain was variable, this must then have to do with personality, which in turn could be rooted in broader categories of difference (the norm being the educated white male). If personality was psychological and this psychology was connected to the state of the brain, then it was clear that emotionality was not simply visceral. Psychology and physiology would have again to diverge, or, rather, it was no longer sufficient to say that bodily changes were themselves the presence of emotions, but rather that such changes were the bodily *responses* to emotions that could account for different reactions to standardized painful stimuli. Dolorimeters were increasingly employed as a control in psychosomatic research, in combination with personality testing and invasive surgical techniques such as lobotomy. With great rapidity, American researchers began to understand that the response to a painful stimulus was the result of complex mind–body interactions, though they did not relinquish the notion that a physical stimulus – the simulation of an injury or lesion – *should* be painful. The extent to which it was tolerated was a matter of personality, rooted in the brain, such that it was possible to conclude, by the 1960s, that 'pain tolerance was linked to perceptual style – a way of experiencing the world'.[17] This was in alignment with new theories of how pain 'worked', especially the Gate Control Theory.

Pain measurement, from the first, connected variations in sensibility to *a priori* assumptions about racial hierarchies, sex and gender differences, age, morality, and so on. Historical prejudices gained new power through the *proof* of mechanical objectivity. Theoretical and methodological flaws were rendered invisible by the prevailing ideology. The history of objectivity in pain measurement is therefore defined and characterized by its political utility, serving white, male, colonialist and classist interests. Moreover, most attempts to measure pain have depended upon the narrowest reduction of the pain experience to sensory intensity. In the early 1970s, Ronald Melzack and Warren Torgerson (1924–99), who were, alongside Patrick Wall, forging new frontiers in the scientific understanding of pain, highlighted this problem. 'The tools currently used to measure pain', they wrote, 'treat it as though it were a single, unique quality that varied in intensity only.' It was akin to describing the 'visual world in terms of light flux only, without regard to pattern, color, texture, and the many other dimensions of visual experience'. This was despite the recognition among clinical researchers of the many varieties of pain. Qualitative descriptions of different types of pain were often crucial to effective diagnosis, but there was no formal means of assessing them. Melzack and Torgerson found 'no studies of their use and meaning'.[18] They set out to remedy this lack, with a focus on the language of chronic pain. It put the subject of pain measurement on a new footing, but insofar as it embraced metaphor and subjectivity, it also attempted to supply the language of pain. I discuss this in chapter 4 on chronic pain.

These observations notwithstanding, the era of the algometer did not end. Late twentieth-century American medical pain politics continued to grapple with racial and gendered notions of differential pain sensitivity, reinforcing white, male, privileged stereotypes. Kenneth Woodrow and others showed in the early 1970s that it was easy to find statements such as 'men tolerate pain more than women' and 'Whites tolerate pain more than Orientals, while Blacks occupy an intermediate position', but each example of such rhetorical appeals to racial and gender hierarchies of suffering was countered by another study or statement that refuted it.[19] There are even recent attempts to inscribe ethnic and cultural variations in pain expression and display onto a genetic explanatory, with a view to pioneering specific pain management strategies targeted at different ethnic groups, such that an observed cultural difference is institutionalized as a biomedical standard.[20] For every instance of attempts to uncover racial hierarchies of pain sensitivity, there are analogous attempts to show either that women are more or less sensitive to pain than men or, at any rate, that they complain much more about it.[21] It is not uncommon to find that perception and expression are conflated in the 'measurement', or else they cannot be disambiguated through the measurement tools. For example, one study from 2006 speculated that 'women generally report higher levels of pain than men' because of 'early childhood socialization', but noted that it 'is also possible that women … reported more pain because they felt more pain', noting the importance of 'the interaction of gonadal hormones with pain mechanisms'.[22] The research only begs more research, in an endless procession of fundamentally uninformed and unsophisticated understandings of what gender and ethnicity are. In much of this, the conflation of a sensitivity measurement and a pain experience has been paramount, despite multidisciplinary pressures to disambiguate nociception from pain.[23] There is, doubtless, diagnostic utility in being able to detect insensibility or reduced sensibility, especially if a problem has a pathological or physiological cause. But there should be resistance to the temptation to extend the implications of degrees of sensitivity to the magnitude of pain, or to the experience of pain across individuals who may share a physical complaint or illness.

The Figural Face

Running prior to and then in parallel with attempts to create machines that would provide objective measurements of pain were anatomical arguments that attempted to measure pain, across all people and all species, according to an idea of the universal face.[24] As recently as 2000, Esther Cohen conceded to 'anthropologists and neurologists' that 'certain uninhibited expressions of pain and grief are both universal and virtually indistinguishable. Weeping and its facial gestures, the turned-down mouth, the drawn brows, the cry, are common to all humans.'[25] A couple of decades later, all those conceded universals are up for grabs.

Shortly after his death, Charles Le Brun's (1619–90) treatise on the drawing of the passions – *Méthode pour apprendre à dessiner les passions* – was published. In terms of its motivation, it was Cartesian in its operative thesis though paradoxically scholastic in its notion of the passions. Passion, according to Le Brun, is a movement of the *sensitive* soul.[26] The body approaches what the soul thinks is good and recoils from what is bad. Whatever causes passions in the soul causes the body to act. From this it was a mere step to inquire what those bodily actions, precisely, were. To know them would be to know the soul itself. Chiming with Descartes, Le Brun put the soul in the brain and not the heart, insisting that whatever might be felt in the heart was a mere effect of the impression received in the brain. From these beginnings, Le Brun described expressions of the passions, both textually and pictorially, including different types of pain.[27]

A bodily pain is marked by eyebrows lowered in the middle, with a mouth lowered at the sides, for example. If sadness is caused by bodily pain and the pain is acute, all the movements of the face are said to appear sharp, with the eyebrows rising and converging, hiding the eyes, and the nostrils flaring, making a fold in the cheeks, with open mouth, roughly square (Figs 1–4). All the parts of the face would be more or less marked according to the severity of the pain.[28] There is a variety,

45

from extreme bodily pain to acute pain (or sharp pain – the ambiguity in *douleur egüe* is problematic), and then, following on from the face of the sharp pain of body and mind, the movement of pain. The notion of capturing 'movement' was a problem for Le Brun, and it has dogged the science of facial expression ever since.[29] How could a static picture capture the essence of something that was experienced in motion? Le Brun's movement of pain captures what? An intermediate stage? Photographers would later run into the problem of the face in movement in a much more profound way. The face in motion didn't look like anything. It was not a recognizable indication of any experience. The beginnings of a universal pain face therefore contained an untested assumption about the point at which an expression reached its appropriate appearance. Many of the plates in the early printings of Le Brun's treatise are simplistically rendered – uncomplicated line drawings – but more elaborate portraits of the passions were produced. As the fame of Le Brun's treatise grew, with engravings made by Martin Engelbrecht in Germany, so some of the descriptions began to obfuscate.[30] Le Brun's 'sharp pain' became 'simple bodily pain' for Engelbrecht in 1732, preserved in a later English engraving around 1760. Thus, despite the best intentions of Le Brun, the appearance on the face of the movement of the soul acquired more than one description. The universal pain face had more than one name.

Nonetheless, Le Brun's faces of the passions became the reference point for artists. These expressions achieved the status of orthodoxy. The confusing descriptions and the sheer unlikeliness of many of the expressions depicted did not prevent them from becoming widely accepted as the truth of the human face and the movements of the soul. As individual captures of isolated emotions, they may strike the present-day viewer as far-fetched. It is important, therefore, to appreciate the fact that most viewers throughout the eighteenth century did not form such an impression. Le Brun's faces of pain were *the* faces of pain.

Charles Bell (1774–1842), the Scottish surgeon, anatomist, and artist (among other things), demurred. Not only was Le Brun's philosophy faulty, but his anatomical prowess was wanting. The whole history of art as it concerned the depiction of the face was in error, in Bell's estimation, because the history of portraiture was the history of impossible muscular contortions. The face could only do so much and in certain ways. The purpose of the pain face was to communicate pain, and

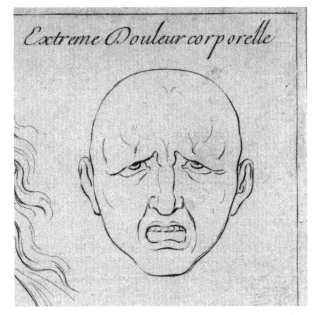

Figure 1. Charles Le Brun, *Extrême Douleur corporelle* (1702). (Metropolitan Museum of Art.)

Figure 2. Charles Le Brun, *Douleur Egüe* (1702). (Rijksmuseum.)

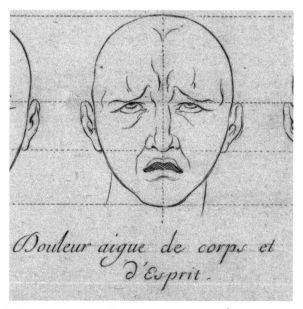

Figure 3. Charles Le Brun, *Douleur aigue de corps et d'Ésprit* (1702). (Metropolitan Museum of Art.)

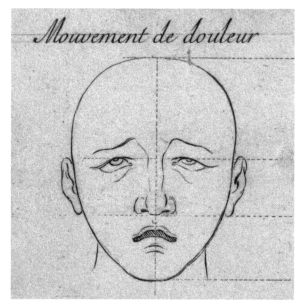

Figure 4. Charles Le Brun, *Mouvement de douleur* (1702). (Metropolitan Museum of Art.)

the reason for it was divine. For Bell, his anatomical investigations were a deep dive into the realm of intelligent design, of the human being as given – *fixed* – by God. The muscles of the human face were especially and uniquely designed (for Bell had no truck with animal souls, and therefore discounted any purposeful communication of emotion on the animal face) as the 'organs' of a 'natural language', universal in its scope, which 'produces something like the effect of innate sympathy and seems to be independent of experience or arbitrary custom'.[31] Implicit here was an exclusive and exclusionary politics of human being and a blueprint, developed from Le Brun and Descartes, for a science of expression that would prove enormously influential.

Although Le Brun was not explicitly mentioned by name, his pain faces were rejected. Bell's descriptions of pain faces, according to his own philosophy, clinical practice, and anatomical research, could not have been further removed from Le Brun's. 'In bodily pain and anguish the general cast of the features is like that of grief; but instead of the torpid state of the muscles … there is in the muscles much tension and action' (Figs 5 and 6). He first depicts the pain of a man 'sick, and in some degree subdued by continual suffering'. He notes 'the confined nostril', for Bell marked that except in extreme agony the 'nostrils are narrow and depressed', though 'an occasional pang will dilate the nostril, cause the teeth to grind, draw wide the lips, raise the eyebrow, make the eye sparkle as in extreme rage, and inflate all the features'.[32] Either way, there are clear distinctions in the shape of mouth, nostril, and brow. Bell's continual suffering of the sick looks akin to Le Brun's *extrême douleur corporelle*, but Bell's own rendering of 'the utmost extremity of pain' revealed other differences: 'convulsive motions in the cheeks and lips, and in the throat … a violent tension is upon the whole face'. Bell describes an encounter with the victim of a gunshot wound in the arm, with a face 'turgid with blood; the veins on the forehead and temples distinct; the teeth strongly fixed, and the lips drawn so as to expose the teeth and gums; the brows strongly knit, and the nostril distended to the utmost, and at the same time drawn up'. He rendered the face in a composition depicting a 'man who has received a mortal blow, but who is infuriated like a beast', commingling despair and rage and pain, with muscles exerted to the utmost. 'The muscles which shut the jaw are stronger than those which open it; the jaw is therefore strongly

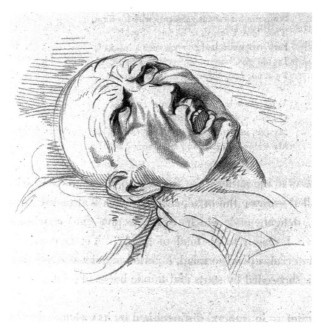

Figure 5. Charles Bell, *Pain of the sick, and in some degree subdued by continual suffering* (1806). (Wellcome Collection.)

Figure 6. Charles Bell, *Utmost extremity of pain* (1806). (Wellcome Collection.)

clinched.'[33] If anything, this resembles Le Brun's *extrême désespoir*, but it is difficult to find a close parallel.

In later editions of Bell's work, he included a sketch of 'true Opisthotonos' (tetanus), which would come to be characteristic of the hysteric under the gaze of Jean-Martin Charcot (1825–93) in Paris (Fig. 7; see also chapter 3 and Fig. 16). Here, we see the exertion of muscles and the rigidity of the pain face extended over the whole body. The purpose was again critical and productive. Bell criticized the ways in which those possessed by the devil were represented by Renaissance masters, showing through the arch of tetanus exactly what postures were bodily possible. Indirectly, it is critical not only of the artists who depicted pain in the way they did, but also of past cultures for having *seen* it there and therefore to have given it credence.[34] The anatomical argument is unswerving in its positivism. Once one knows the extent of the human body and its capacity for movement, one cannot then take seriously any representation of pain that does not conform to this universal structure. Still, Bell fell afoul of the same problem as Le Brun in these terms, for what notion of movement could be captured in painting? He was explicit that a face not in agreement with itself is 'farcical and ridiculous' and that the countenance had to be 'systematized' to be properly read, but that left a question mark over the status of the face in motion. While Bell couched his argument in terms of divine design, it has, in only slightly varied form, survived in the modern physiological and psychological imagination. God, to be sure, was cast out along the way. The explanatory framework for why there are only these muscles that work only in set ways has changed beyond recognition. But the conclusion, that only certain expressions are possible and that they betray readily identifiable emotional and sensory experiences, still tends to hold sway.

Enter the photographer and a new set of problems. A science of emotions began to take shape around the middle of the nineteenth century, driven in part by the formulation of an academic study of psychology dovetailing, not always comfortably, with the development of evolutionary theories.[35] Photography was an enabler, providing an air of mechanical objectivity to images that had, previously, depended on the skill of the hand. This neutrality was a phantom. At the root of the modern pain face was a complete absence of pain. The favoured photographic subjects of Guillaume-Benjamin-Amand Duchenne de

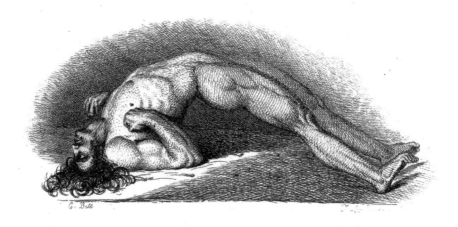

Figure 7. Charles Bell, *True Opisthotonos* (1824). (Wellcome Collection.)

Boulogne (1806–75) were a man who had no sense of feeling in his face and an actor. The features of the former could be manipulated with galvanic apparatus – electrical current – into the archetypal expressions of emotions that Duchenne *desired* to see (Fig. 8), and the features of the latter were willed into the 'correct' aspect by the skilled performer. Having identified a muscle behind the eyebrow as the 'pain muscle', it was a matter of technique only, not experience on the part of the subject, to produce a variety of degrees of pain face at Duchenne's command.[36] Hence, the actor could produce '*douleur extrême*' to the point of exhaustion, where the subject seemed to succumb to suffering (*souffrance*). To this a note was added: '*tête de Christ*'. Yet there was no such suffering on the part of the actor. Similarly, on the benumbed face of the other subject, Duchenne could produce '*douleur et désespoir*' (pain and despair), later qualified as pain and *l'abattement* (dejection, perhaps).[37] Duchenne was conjuring with the whole palette of physical and emotional experiences and the ways that they materialized on and through the face, while at the same time having the complete absence of all such physical and emotional experiences as the bedrock of his methodology. The viewer always reckons with the photographic evidence of the pain face through the suggestive framing of the accompanying narrative.

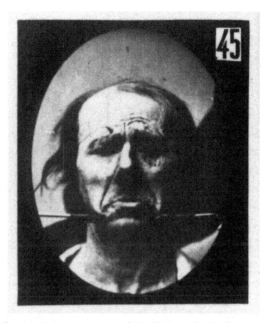

Figure 8. Guillaume-Benjamin-Amand Duchenne de Boulogne, *Pain and Despair* (1854–6). (Wellcome Collection.)

The technology was alluring, such that its fundamental aim to fabricate the face was lost in the overwhelming appeal of objectivity. Charles Darwin (1809–82) employed Duchenne's photographs, some of which were rendered as woodcuts to remove any evidence of the manipulative galvanic apparatus and present the archetype of various emotional faces. Darwin was at once ready to dismiss Le Brun and revise Bell, aiming for the evolutionary explanatory that underlay expression, not as communication of pain, but as an effort to achieve relief. There had to be, in Darwin's working over of pain, an evolutionary point to pain expressions, even if that point had long since been lost, the expressions being a vestige of inherited habit. On that score, he could not help at one moment calling pain expressions 'purposeless'.[38] But this was revised by the assertion that 'the writhing of the whole body, the grinding of the teeth, and the uttering of piercing shrieks, all give relief under an agony of pain'.[39] He was careful when describing pain, noting that 'it is well known that pain is increased by attending to it', and he was fully alive to the ways in which cultural prescription and proscription for physical signs of pain altered the ways it was experienced, subjectively and intersubjectively.[40] But the common takeaway from Darwin and his reliance on Duchenne has been the forceful argument of universality of expression.[41] In other words, while foregoing proponents of the universality of the pain face were right in principle but wrong in their depiction of it, Darwin et al. are considered right in principle and objective in their production of such an expression on a real face. The fact that Darwin was more nuanced than this has not seemed to matter much in the formation of an intellectual genealogy.

Suggestive narrative framing, in the idiom of mechanical objectivity, is supposed to be invisible. The legacy of the universal pain face constructed through photography can be found in the basic emotions theory of Paul Ekman, who directly connects his own work to that of Darwin, and who in many ways repeats the methodological errors of the pioneering scientific photographers.[42] Ekman remains committed to the view that the face is an accurate, predictable, and universal indicator of emotions that transcend culture and time. While he does not directly treat of pain, his acolytes do. Ekman's Facial Action Coding System (FACS), which depends upon a range of simulated expressions captured by photography, was profoundly influential among those behavioural psychologists who wished to prove the universality of pain. If the relation of expression to experience was 1:1, then finally nailing the 'true' face of pain would be a major epistemological leap forward, with profound clinical implications. Hence the desire to find and fix the universal pain face. In parallel moves that seem strange in the light of more recent foci on pain language and pain concepts, researchers turned to two entities that could not speak, though it was assumed that they could suffer: the humble laboratory mouse and the neonate. Ekman's FACS was adapted for the newborn human, introducing the 'grimace scale' as a way of divining suffering in those who cannot otherwise intelligibly relay their pain to an observer. The circularity of the reasoning is breath-taking, for there is no way to assess actual experience of pain among neonates, even if it is necessary to state that human infants experience pain. Rather, the experience is divined from the expression, on the basis that the expression is itself directly revealing of what lies behind it. The meaning of expressions must therefore be defined *before* they are researched.[43]

The neonatal grimace was extended to animals, especially mice, with the result that animal grimace scales were put forward as evidence of the universality of pain.[44] The argument is based on analogy, or evolutionary proximity, but the methodological problem is the same. How does anyone know how the mouse feels? While some call for the installation of automated surveillance systems that can constantly monitor the well-being of laboratory mice by using AI facial recognition of mice grimaces, others have begun to ask if mice can hide their pain faces.[45] And if they can, what might humans be capable of? I ask this rhetorically, because I suspect most people reading this will implicitly understand the notion of putting a 'brave face' on a hurtful situation. The advocates for AI might claim to be able to see through such brave faces. This is a science in disarray.

These grimace scales have ultimately been extended to human adults and used, through the logic of Ekman's FACS tool, to argue for the presence of a universal pain face, based upon small sample sizes and a narrow injury intensity = pain intensity logic (which is known to be deeply flawed).[46] In addition, a bid to find the essentials of the human pain face led to the cancelling out of facial 'noise': that is, the parts of an expression that were not commonly witnessed across the range of experimental conditions. By so doing, a small number of facial movements could be said to be the fundamental indicators of pain, the rest being secondary. To cap a great tradition, such studies include pictures of pain faces (see Fig. 9). The distance between Le Brun and the recent past is collapsed in an instant.

It is important to recognize what these grimace scales and claims for the universal face are. While at some level they represent an epistemological claim, about universality, they are of a piece with the algometers of a century and more ago. The grimace scale is a way of measuring pain, objectively, according to its intensity. Because it assumes, as the algometer designers did, that the intensity of a sensory stimulus will correlate with the intensity of the pain experienced, and because it assumes that the face is a reliable indicator of experience, the method is flawed. When the premises are so flawed, any possible conclusions drawn from research based upon them must be equally flawed. What are the ethical risks?

If one concludes, as Kenneth Prkachin did in 1992, that 'a relatively small subset of actions convey the bulk of information about pain

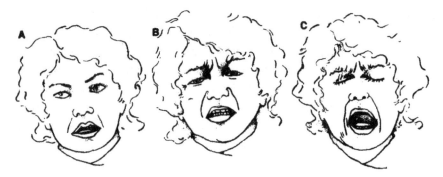

Figure 9. A sequence of facial changes showing the emergence of the four principal facial actions. (Kenneth M. Prkachin, 'The consistency of facial expressions of pain: a comparison across modalities', *Pain*, 51 [1992]: 297–306, at 304. Reproduced with permission.)

that is available in facial expression' and that 'pain expressions may be universal',[47] then the absence of this relatively small subset on any given face under any given conditions may be treated as the absence of pain. Conversely, the presence of these few facial indicators of pain will be treated as the presence of pain, even if there is no experience of pain. Under-treatment and over-treatment are both implied. The testimony of patients – their words, their other gestures – become under-weighted in the clinical environment in favour of what can be read on the face. To give Prkachin his due, he and his colleagues have pointed to the clinical necessity of combining methods of pain communication, and even of the dangers of the medical misreading of the pain face because of habituation.[48] While the study I am using as an example did include the caveat that 'cross-cultural consistency' would have to be researched to back up the claim of universality, the weight of the argument was strongly in favour of the conclusion of universality even though such research had not been carried out.[49] The politics of pain is always present, even and perhaps especially in those attempts to make the study of pain neutral and objective.

If Prkachin knew, in 1992, that a universal claim could only be made through cross-cultural testing, such testing was not forthcoming. In a 2001 article, Prkachin, along with Kenneth Craig and Ruth Grunau, summarized the pain face research but noted, still citing a raft of publications by Ekman, that 'no studies systematically examining cross-cultural variations in nonverbal displays of pain have been undertaken, despite their potential importance'.[50] Rather, Ekman's claims about the 'cross-cultural consistency in facial expressions of emotion' were treated as a reliable basis upon which to infer the same thing about pain faces. Now that Ekman's research has been thoroughly critiqued to the point of total rejection across the disciplines, should not the pain face inference go with it? Ten years later, in a review of the literature on facial pain expression, Prkachin again noted that 'consistency across cultures' had *still* not been 'addressed systematically'. At that point, 'all studies reported used participants from developed, western cultures'. This was a 'significant shortcoming because of the widespread belief in profound cultural differences in pain expression'.[51] Still, he theorized that the form of the pain face would be the same, even if the circumstances that made it arise differed. Let us not mince words. Over twenty years, a pressing research need was known and not addressed. The basis for the need – that Ekman's FACS tool had revealed the likely universality of the pain face – now stands in serious question. Yet the need to research and study the pain expressions of people beyond 'developed, western cultures' remains.

Then there is the problem of the smile. In the late 1980s, the Wong–Baker Faces Pain Rating Scale was found to be preferred among children as a means of communicating the degree of pain they felt as a result of a variety of medical procedures. Six circular representations of faces – they would now be called emojis – are lined up horizontally, each with a different facial expression (Fig. 10). The instructions for the use of the scale are to

> Explain to the child that each face is for a person who feels happy because he has no pain (hurt) or sad because he has some or a lot of pain. Face o is very happy because he doesn't hurt at all. ... Face 5 hurts as much as you can imagine, although you don't have to be crying to feel this bad. Ask child to choose the face that best describes how he/she is feeling.[52]

It implicitly asks, therefore, for pain to be translated into an emotional category. Or, perhaps better, it understands on a fundamental level that pain exists only through a meaningful emotional evaluation. Naturally

Figure 10. Wong–Baker Pain Faces Scale. (Donna Lee Wong and Connie Morain Baker, 'Pain in children: comparison of assessment scales', *Pediatric Nursing*, 14 [1988]: 9–17, at 11. Reproduced with permission.)

enough, one might think, no pain is equated with happiness, and therefore with smiles, and lots of pain is equated with sadness, and therefore with downturned mouths and possibly (but not necessarily) tears. While children demonstrated a preference for this way of reporting their pain, the researchers concluded that it was not superior in 'validity or reliability' to other tests. In a discussion of the research's limitations, they acknowledged that there was no objective means of knowing that the way in which children ranked painful events was 'a valid estimate of their perception of pain'. The authors expressed the remarkable (and true) opinion that 'there is no way of proving that pain exists other than believing the person in pain'.[53] So, as with the McGill Pain Questionnaire, analysed in chapter 4, there is an onus on trying to tap the patient's experience of their own pain, while at the same time *supplying* the language of that pain for them. The prevalent use of such scales, which define and apportion emotional categories to pain intensity, must be understood to be developmentally formative. They have an active role in the ways in which painful experience is constructed. They are part of the conceptual fabric that makes up how experience will feel (and when it will feel out of place). This has not prevented pain researchers from actively trying to disentangle pain experience from emotional experience, and indeed the widespread use of the Wong–Baker Scale does not seem to have built much awareness of the fundamentally affective quality of painful experience.

In 2001, the IASP launched a revised version of the Faces Pain Scale, specifically to 'score the sensation of pain' and with the 'advantageous' removal of 'smiles and tears'. A number of studies had raised concerns about the 'affect-laden anchors' of the Wong–Baker Scale, leading to these changes.[54] Explicitly, the instructions for using the scale say not to 'use words like "happy" and "sad"', because the 'scale is intended to measure how children feel inside, not how their face looks'.[55] Nonetheless, children are still being asked to infer an inner experience from a sensory experience *through* a facial expression. While the more extreme pain faces now resemble something like the pain faces from the time of Le Brun, it is hard to escape the smile of level 0 or the downturned mouth of level 6. People report their pain according to the conceptual framework and received representational forms of their time and place. Smiles and frowns, happiness and sadness, have, since at least the 1980s, been equated with pain severity when people are asked to report their pain. But there is a snag.

In a 2013 paper, Miriam Kunz and Stefan Lautenbacher, along with Prkachin, explored what they considered a 'surprising phenomenon', an expression 'incongruent' with the 'core set of pain-indicative facial actions': the smile. Yes, people in pain often smile. This observation entailed the pulling apart of the orthodox association of the smile with happiness or with positive emotion, which first required the enumeration of types of smile and then a careful consideration of why people smile. A narrow view of pain remained, discounting the circumstances in which pain is enjoyed: 'By definition, pain is an unpleasant experience and thus, it seems unlikely that smiles occurring during pain are *enjoyment smiles*.' Nonetheless, the focus in this paper was on the 'social motives' for smiling, with the conclusion that 'the properties of the relationship' between the person in pain and others in the room 'had a considerable impact, with smiling being reduced in the presence of a formal other, whereas the presence of the partner significantly increased the smiling behavior'. Thus, 'the smile of pain might be less of a sign of the underlying affect than a reflection of social motives'.[56]

The problem with all pain-face claims, from Le Brun to the present, is thus summed up. Sometimes, the pained person wears an expression that is, to the observer, strange. The observer must decide how to feel or what to do about this odd look of pain. The oddness, the strangeness, the incongruence, is, in the end, not a measure of inscrutability on the part of the person in pain, but a measure of the untested assumptions – the *a priori* expectations – of the witness. If it seems odd to you that a person smiles when in pain, then that is your problem, not theirs. In every instance that a pain face has been described, drawn, photographed, or videotaped, the idea of the pain face in the mind of the artist or observer has preceded the evidence of the face. Thus, facial noise must be removed, explained away, assigned to other causes. The smile presents a challenge in this respect because there is such a strong psychological orthodoxy undergirding the assumption that it should not be there. That Kunz and her colleagues concede multifunctionality to the face is telling but ultimately destructive of the whole notion of divining experience from facial expression. How is anyone to know that certain 'core' facial actions are signs of the 'underlying affect', but that other facial actions are not? The idea of a social 'motive' suggests some degree of agentic control, but there is by now broad agreement that all emotional expressions are *always* social. Even if one can find a physical space to which to remove a human to see a test subject outside of all social influence, the sociocultural repertoire – the emotional regime – lives inside a person's head. It's part of who and what they are. Pain faces are no less practices than any other expressions.

In 2020, Prkachin was still describing Ekman's FACS as the 'gold-standard for dissecting facial movements' (it should be remembered that this 'dissection' is meant to reveal the underlying emotion, based on an essentially inflexible relation between the inside and the outside of the emotional human), and the quest for the pain face continues. Yet the purpose has shifted, subtly. Whereas it is taken for granted, dubiously, that some of what is on the face is indicative of what is behind the face, the assertion that these faces 'evolved largely, if not primarily, as a means of transmitting something about the sufferer's experience to others' shifts the inquiry elsewhere. We are far from Darwin, who argued the opposite. This assertion requires researchers to test the claim that the universal pain face is 'indeed socially meaningful'. While this would seem to disrupt the distinction being striven for in Kunz et al.'s smile paper between those expressions connected to the underlying affect and those that are 'socially motivated', the social impetus of the research has not led, or at least not in this case, to actual social research. Rather, a concern about the confounding of judgement by things like 'the timing of the actions or the co-occurrence of other movements'[57] – that is, the existence of the contextualized whole body and facial response to pain in the real world in real humans – has turned the research away from humans altogether.

All this extra noise could be cancelled out in the production of the avatar in pain.

This over-striving for control ultimately undermines any results for, as with every iteration of the pain face and every attempt to achieve objective measurements, the social and the cultural are always there. Neutrality is never neutral. While it might be possible, with a computer-generated person, 'to manipulate other features of the face, such as its apparent gender, age, skin colour, etc.',[58] the 'social perception' of this avatar in pain is never going to be divorced from the fact of its artificiality. Moreover, the programming of its pain face, to measure its social impact, again fails, as did Duchenne and Ekman, to understand the suggestive quality that this imposes upon the research. It is precisely in the context, the thing here that is subject to an attempt at erasure, that meaning is made. Looking at the pain faces of an avatar (Fig. 11) is not a lack of context, but its own context, with its own associated meaningfulness. If a person recognizes pain in the face of an avatar, are they detecting *pain*? Surely they *know* that avatars do not experience pain, or anything else. Does not this implicit knowledge affect the relationality, the readability, that is precisely the thing at the heart of the study? Are these pain faces, irrespective of the results of the study, any more definitive of what pain faces *actually* look like than any of the other pain faces going back as far as the seventeenth century? In whatever ways control is wrested from the social, it is lost in untold and immeasurable ways.

Nonetheless, with this most recent research strand on the pain face, there are reasons to be cheerful. The authors of the avatar study note that 'it is misleading to still present only one prototypical facial expression of pain when asking individuals in decoding studies to observe pain in others'. The study in question tried five different pain faces, including a 'stoic' face with 'no visible facial expression'.[59] One wonders what the truly inexpressive face looks like. The plurality is at least encouraging, even if the attempt at control confounds the results. Combining the views of Lisa Feldman Barrett, that we have to see the whole expression of the whole body in its context, and the views of Daniel M. Gross and Stephanie Preston, that such controlled conditions are detrimental to our understanding of the human in the 'real world', it only remains to urge this kind of research into

Clusters based on Kunz & Lautenbacher 2014	Clusters created by FACSGen
Cluster I: 'narrowed eyes with furrowed brows and wrinkled nose': Scoring highest on AU6_7 with a slighter co-activation of AU4 and AU9_10.	**Cluster I:** AU6 and AU7 (intensity of 0.8), AU4 (intensity of 0.5), and AU9 and AU10 (intensity of 0.4).
Cluster II: 'opened mouth with narrowed eyes': Scoring highest on AU25_26_27 with a slighter co-activation of AU6_7.	**Cluster II:** AU25 & AU26 (intensity of 0.8), AU27 (intensity of 0.3), and AU6 & AU7 (intensity of 0.6).
Cluster III: 'raised eyebrows': Scoring highest on AU1_2.	**Cluster III:** AU1 (intensity of 0.9), AU2 (intensity of 0.6).
Cluster IV: 'furrowed brows with narrowed eyes': Scoring highest on AU 4 with a co-activation of AU 6_7.	**Custer IV:** AU4 (intensity of 0.9), and AU6 & AU7 (intensity of 0.7).
Cluste V: 'stoic:' No visible facial movements.	**Cluster V:** AU43 (intensity of 1). We chose a blinking face instead of a totally static one, so all faces are animated.

Figure 11. Pain avatar. (Eleonora Meister et al., 'Decoding of facial expressions of pain in avatars: does sex matter?', *Scandinavian Journal of Pain*, 21 [2021]: 174–82, at 178.)

greater collaboration with historians and anthropologists, and with the insights from the medical humanities in general.[60] The quest for the pain face has endured for more than three centuries. We are no nearer its end, precisely because those invested in finding it continue to start from the wrong place.

Feeling the Flow

Algometric devices and pain rating scales have failed in their attempts to objectify pain. In large part, despite the best of scientific intentions to the contrary, this is because pain is a *subjective, intersubjective,* and *biocultural* experience, irreducible to equations or sensory predictions. This is the under-researched foil to the medical-scientific quest for the universal and the objective. It is effectively demonstrated by an example of the experience of pain caused by the humours, carried forward across the centuries and still at the heart of medical understandings of pain in the seventeenth century. The meaning of being out of balance might have shifted, but the experience of pain was inextricable from its supposed cause. Thus, for Robert Burton (1577–1640), humoral imbalance could be understood as the effect of disease, or heresy, or sin. Moreover, the humours and their relative proportions denoted the character, or temperament, of a person. Galen had noted nine humoral 'mixes', the ideal being perfect balance, with four slight variations, and four patho-logical cocktails. These latter four – the sanguine, phlegmatic, choleric, and melancholic temperaments – essentially marked out the principal medical diagnoses *and* character problems for hundreds of years of history, and they would survive Burton. Each faulty temperament corresponded to the specific qualities of the humour in question. The melancholic temperament – introverted, moody, thoughtful – was cold and dry, like the earth.

Burton set about collecting everything then known about melancholy, the substance and the disease, allowing him to present it as both a cause and a symptom. He was an Oxford scholar, somewhat obscure, lost in the library, as it were. His life appears through loose anecdotal and often contradictory gestures, a pattern that extended to his death. He is rumoured to have hanged himself, but there is only morbid speculation to be had here. To say that he was 'depressive' would be to employ an anachronism, since 'depression' as it is now known did not exist. It seems more fitting to speculate according to the conceptual framework of his times that Burton suffered from a melancholic temperament. His master work, *The Anatomy of Melancholy*, seemed to combine scholarly erudition with a deep personal understanding of the subject. Some wonder whether his book was not a form of self-medication or, as he said himself, 'being busy to avoid melancholy'.[61] A melancholic disorder could be caused by God; the devil; witchcraft; astrology; a quirk of bodily composition; fear; imprisonment; poverty; grief; other diseases; fevers (agues) or distemper of the heart, brain, spleen, liver, and so on; exposure to the sun; a bump on the head; constipation; piles; or eating too many onions. What was the experience of suffering with melancholy like? Head melancholy – that is, a preponderance of black bile in the head – manifested itself in physical disorders (headaches, insomnia, a dry body, etc.) and mental or emotional disorders (fear, sorrow, suspicion, etc.). Hypochondriacal melancholy had a different kind of effect, causing basically a dyspeptic disposition in the body or a fearful, anxious, lascivious mental outlook.

Hypochondriac must be taken literally, as referring to under (*hypo*) the upper abdomen, below the ribcage (*chondros*). It was a physical complaint that, at the time, was synonymous with melancholia. Burton cites the collaborator of Martin Luther, Philip Melancthon (1497–1560), in this regard, under the heading of melancholy caused by 'sorrow':

> the gathering of much melancholy blood about the heart, which collection extinguisheth the good spirits, or at least dulleth them, sorrow strikes the heart, makes it tremble and pine away, with great pain; and the black blood drawn from the spleen, and diffused under the ribs, on the left side, makes those perilous hypochondriacal convulsions, which happen to them that are troubled with sorrow.[62]

As for 'sorrow', Burton called it *insanus dolor* – crazy pain – and, with Hippocrates, proclaimed it the 'mother and daughter of melancholy', its 'cause and symptom'.[63]

Finally, melancholy was marked by a universal blackness of body and blood, and a fearful, sad, and solitary mind. Every passion, in fact, was a potential source of pain for Burton. Fear, for example, makes men's 'hearts ache, sad and heavy … in continual pain'.[64] Shame caused 'bitter pangs', and was 'as forcible a batterer as any of the rest'.[65] Likewise, envy 'crucifies' the soul. An envious man can know 'no greater pain' than 'to hear of another man's well-doing'.[66] Worse still were the connected affections of emulation, hatred, faction, and desire of revenge, which Burton described through Cyprian (d. 258) as 'a moth of the soul, a consumption, to make another man's happiness his misery, to torture, crucify, and execute himself, to eat his own heart'.[67] All forms of discontent and misery were causes and symptoms of melancholy, for the 'most part accompanied with anguish and pain'.[68] It is important to remember that in all instances these were not 'emotions' – productions of the brain, as they are now known by western science – but passions and affections with bodily causes and bodily consequences. If one was in an irascible humour, there was something physically, humorally wrong. To scoff at or scold a person prone to melancholy was to wound deeply, worse than any mere 'bodily pain', for the ill humour was so aggravated by it that it could make it a 'perpetual corrosive'.[69]

It is not apt to say that melancholy, as a noxious substance, a physical presence in the body, does not exist – just as in the case of *qi* – or to attempt to re-diagnose such conditions as Burton described through contemporary diagnostic categories. Even if I could say that all the maladies Burton describes account for something else, and even if I could rationally explain contagion and disease, depression and anxiety, grief and fear, indigestion and heat stroke, I would be doing Burton, and his ilk, a disservice. For to enter into the world of someone like Burton, it is necessary to acknowledge the reality of melancholy and ask what it was like to be melancholic. These conceptual categories, which have been bequeathed as metaphors, were *real* to him. They were productive of his experience.

To be diagnosed or self-identify as melancholic came with a set of cultural expectations. A melancholic person could be identified, and a person behaving in a certain way or manifesting certain symptoms would be diagnosed and treated as melancholic. But a melancholic person in this culture would know what was expected of a melancholic person – would unconsciously struggle to match how he felt inside with what the people around him would recognize as melancholic. Certain bodily practices, expressions, movements, utterances, would follow from the melancholic individual. The way in which a feeling is described is drawn from the available repertoire of emotional and sensory expressions. In this effort to make feelings *fit*, the feelings themselves are acted upon, translated, altered. Some call this 'performance', though they do not mean *acting* in the theatrical sense.[70] The feelings of a melancholic like Burton were *authentic* feelings, where authenticity is understood not as some timeless, essential, or objective biological process, but as befitting the conceptual and contextual world of a particular body and mind, diseased as they were according to the notion of disease at that time.

65

There is a lasting memory of the lexicography of humoral theory. One might still lose one's *temper* or be in an ill *humour*. People might still be described as *sanguine, melancholic, choleric, phlegmatic*. All such things are, now, metaphors for real substances with real qualities – historical bodily material – that no longer exist. This hangover of language attests to the cultural pervasiveness of understandings of the body and the emotions that modern science has rejected. The qualitative meanings of these words are still useful, even if they do not refer to anything substantial. Keeping the knowledge of these categories alive is especially important for the historian, for past experiences cannot be explained according to knowledge frameworks that come after them. Experience is a product of what is known or claimed to be known (there is not much difference) at the time. Robert Burton was not depressed. He suffered from melancholy. That is the only possible framework for speculating on his variety of pain.

Trauma

In an extraordinary 2021 interview, Lady Gaga (Stefani Germanotta) spoke of the lasting effects of trauma after having been raped in 2014. She gave the interview as part of a series on 'mental health [*sic*]'. In 2019, she experienced 'full-on pain' before becoming numb. She said she could not 'feel [her] own body'. This pain came as if from nowhere and had no apparent physiological cause: 'I've had so many MRIs and scans where they don't find nothing.' The pain, numbness, and associated sickness were connected to the rape. '[Y]our body remembers,' she said. 'The way that I feel when I feel pain was how I felt after I was raped.' She 'realised that it was the same pain that I felt when the person who raped me dropped me off pregnant on a corner, at my parents' house, because I was vomiting and sick. Because I had been being abused, and I was locked away in a studio for months.' This 'total psychotic break' lasted 'a couple years', where 'getting triggered' would bring back these physical, visceral pains.[71]

Trauma is the Greek word for wound. Contemporary speakers of English use it almost entirely unaltered. Trauma is a wound, an injury. It is used metaphorically to talk about pain because of the ease of associ-ation between a wound and a pain, like the 'break' above, even though there is no direct correlation between the two. But modern trauma has an added new sense of figural meaning, transferring trauma from body to mind, loading the conflation of damage and pain into mental phenomena in which the wound is not visible at all.[72] The notion of psychic or psychological trauma is not old but it has by logical extension been applied to historical contexts in which this kind of trauma did not yet exist. Situated expressions or diagnoses of hysteria, neurasthenia, and shell shock all crowd the widening definition of trauma.[73] Moreover, the late modern diagnostic category of post-traumatic stress disorder (PTSD) can conceive of the initiating trauma as either a wound or psychological damage or both. As such, there has been a scholarly interest in projecting back the notion of trauma (as well as grief and depression) to ancient times, finding PTSD in the Homeric battlefields around Troy and everywhere else since then.[74] In typical constructions of this condition, the stress disorder that follows *post* trauma is itself trauma, as if the constant experience and re-experience of the original 'wound' is the living presence of that wound. It is why Lady Gaga's pain fits the PTSD framing, for while she was dealing with a traumatic event that had already happened, the trauma was evidently ongoing, real, in the present. If its explanation is rooted in a past traumatic event (or series of events), that does not make the manifestation and experience of pain part of the category of *post* trauma, locatable in the separate category of 'stress disorder'. Self-evidently, the experience of 'total pain' was of the present. It was not related to any physical injury, though it stemmed from a violent violation of the body.

What do people hear when they hear about this kind of 'total pain'? It should be possible to take Lady Gaga at her word, to take her literally, that this trauma that required psychiatric treatment was *physical* pain. That is my understanding of what people mean when they say their bodies are in pain. Yet the way it is reported, in a filmed interview, the subject comfortably seated, and breaking down in tears, comes with the weight of figuration. When an uninjured person sheds tears and speaks of pain, it is still all too easy to read 'pain' as a metaphor for emotional suffering, even shame, and thereby relegate it.[75] It is an example of the ways that western cultures still labour under the artificial division and stratification of emotional and physical suffering. The argument that 'pain is grief' must still be forcefully put.[76]

How should trauma be handled historically? Some say that the enduring effects of traumatic shock might be a sign of universality in human affectivity.[77] Others demur, pointing to the situated variability – the context dependence – of even the most basic physiological functions, such as homeostasis and its disintegration.[78] I have said elsewhere that caution is necessary because 'diagnostic categories delimit experience. They formalise what counts and what does not count. A new category compels the sufferer to think with and express through its terms, and there is always therefore the potential for a bad fit, or for a repetition of the process of being not believed.'[79] Even if the sufferer is not aware of any formal diagnostic categories, which is a distinct possibility, one can imagine that this ends as soon as they encounter any kind of medical authority, and this in turn will frame their experience. There is a significant value, from the point of view of analytical convenience, in opening up the history of 'mental trauma', on the understanding that (a) it is the pursuit of a wound metaphor that stands in for the experience of real pain and (b) the situated concepts and context of the historical experience must be used for any deeper analysis. This will keep the historian alive to the politics of 'trauma' in the recent past, as well as critically aware of the kinds of 'trauma' that do not usually trouble historians of medicine at all, such as grief, shame, ostracism, and bullying.

Regarding the politics of trauma, PTSD was only incorporated into the *Diagnostic and Statistical Manual of Mental Disorders* in 1980, after Vietnam War military veterans had lobbied for its inclusion. The aim was to achieve formal recognition for a type of pain and suffering that could otherwise be dismissed as a character flaw, psychological weakness, figment of the imagination, or malingering. Formal recognition of a new *condition* not only opened up medical attention, medical treatment, and new kinds of therapy, but also impacted the political credibility of veterans who sought compensation, honour, or a pension. To be diagnosed is to be validated, and this comes with social, economic, political, and personal benefits, even if it does not in itself set the sufferer on the road to cure. It nonetheless changes the experience.[80] The insight is useful for historical inquiries into emotional pain, or pain without lesion, because the premise can be translocated even if the specifics cannot be: the metaphors of wounding that are particular to a time and a place can be researched and analysed according to situated meanings and framings to gain access to the ways in which trauma *avant la lettre* was conceptualized and experienced.[81]

Regarding the pain of typically non-medical purview – social pain, emotional pain – there is a wealth of research yet to be done. The word 'pain' in these usages is itself usually understood to be a metaphor for something else, something *lesser*, a kind of suffering that does not rise to the bar of bodily pain. Nonetheless, neuroscientists are showing social and emotional pains to be categorically indistinguishable from pains caused by physical injury.[82] Naomi Eisenberger's cyberball experiment tracked the real-time effects of social exclusion from a game and found that the brain's affective responses mapped onto brain responses to painful physical injury.[83] The same insight has been reached through the study of congenital anaesthesia or pain asymbolia: a rare condition in which a person is fully aware of the sensation of bodily damage but applies no meaning to it. It is the lack of affective response – fear, hesitation, anxiety, withdrawal, caution – that accounts for the impossibility of experiencing bodily pain.[84] Nikola Grahek concluded that there could be no pain without meaning, and that meaning was derived through affective processing: a product of the situated brain. This has been re-confirmed by experiments using acetaminophen (paracetamol) to regulate emotional pain and social distress.[85] Since we know emotions themselves to be situated and contextually mutable, these 'products of the brain' cannot be reduced to the brain and must be understood as part of the dynamic, ecological relationship between the plastic brain-body and the world in which it is situated. There is a world of pain across the historical record that has been recorded in contextually specific affective terms that has yet to be substantially explored.

Whether one calls this the history of emotional pain or the history of trauma, one is perforce exploring the history of human attempts to give voice to pain through affective utterance, gesture, embodiment, and bodily practice. The history of grief, for example, has not been on the radar of pain scholars despite the conceptual conflation, in so many languages, of grief and physical pain. One could make a similar point about the history of nostalgia (literally 'home pain').[86] Just as medical-scientific languages are situated, and the knowledge about pain they produce is implicated in the experiential delimitation of pain, so the pain concepts people use outside of a medical idiom are knowledge claims and delimit experience. When historical actors claim that their bereavements, broken hearts, exiles, and social snubs *hurt*, I take them literally.

Achilles: Grief Personified

Though the ancient Greeks had the word *trauma*, they preserved it for physical wounds. The word does not appear at all in the Homeric epics, though they were not short of wounds. But I turn to the *Iliad* to try to understand one aspect of the suffering it contains in situated terms. Elsewhere I have argued that while the *Iliad* is usually thought to be about 'rage' or 'wrath', these are poor translations for the *menis* that is the principal theme of the poem.[87] For the *menis* of Achilles makes him withdraw, become sullen and obstinate, and fundamentally inactive. Achilles does not act in anger at all in the *Iliad* until after he has relinquished his *menis*. In other words, all the acts of violence (including the desecration of Hector's corpse) that are usually associated with Achilles' rage only take place after *menis* is put aside. This is the only way to begin to understand the shift in the poem from Achilles' inactivity to activity, and it affords us a framework for understanding why *menis* is considered virtuous and praiseworthy.

The disappearance of *menis* is, by itself, insufficient explanation for why Achilles rejoins the fray with such vigour and indomitable violence. In the final books of the *Iliad*, Achilles kills in anger but his anger is activated by something else: grief. The *Iliad* pivots on Achilles' grief, which is the most excruciating pain in the poem. It is, more so than *menis*, the definition of Achilles, who bears this pain in his name.[88] Patroclus, his friend, comrade, lover(?), persuades him that he can fight in his stead, and, as a sign of his relenting *menis*, Achilles agrees, lending him his armour for the purpose. Once Patroclus is slain by Hector, the remainder of the epic is concerned with the experience and practices of grief, whether in violence, the spirit of revenge, rituals of lamentation, funerary rites, the cutting of hair, or Achilles' refusal to release Hector's slain body. When hearing of Patroclus' demise for the first time, Achilles is engulfed in a black cloud of ἄχεος (*ákheos*), which is usually translated as grief. The word appears frequently in the Homeric canon, and often refers to the distress of the heart and to grief, but it is also a standard word for pain (as is the word used interchangeably for grief in the *Iliad*, πένθος [*penthos*]). Achilles throws himself in the dirt, tearing his hair out, while his attendants wail in grief. Hearing his cries, Thetis, his mother, announces that he will have this grief, this pain, for the rest of his life and that there is nothing she, or he, can do about it. When Patroclus' body is finally recovered from the battlefield, Achilles leads the lamentation, replete with tears, wails, and groans. He is, famously, like a lion whose cubs had been killed by a hunter, whose pain was taken over by anger (χόλος [*cholos*]) and the desire for revenge. Achilles vows not to have the funerary rites for Patroclus until he has slain Hector and brought back twelve Trojans to slay before his funerary pyre (a promise that he carries out).[89]

At the beginning of book 19 of the *Iliad*, Thetis, who has come to present Achilles with his new divinely made armour, finds him clinging to the body of Patroclus, and with weeping all around. I want to focus on this moment, but at a stage of remove from the text itself. Other historians of emotion have eschewed the *Iliad* and Achilles because this purely literary character is part god, too distant from anything recognizably human. Yet the *Iliad* served as the central cultural text for hundreds of years of Greek history, framing ideas about virtue, history, religion, warfare, ritual, and so on, and modelling the way in which passions were to be tempered. It was, arguably, the most important pedagogical ingredient in Greek self-fashioning throughout the classical period. Not for nothing was it the central intertextual ingredient of Plato's *Republic*. As such, the practices of things like grief can be found in the traces of Greek material culture, making direct reference to the *Iliad*, but depicting it in ways that the poem itself does not reveal. Through these tangible traces of Greek culture, therefore, what grief-pain looked like and how it was practised can be recovered. When we see Achilles in grief in Greek pottery of the fifth century BCE, perhaps some three hundred years after the *Iliad* was first set down in writing, we are being given a glimpse of Greek grief at that moment, as it was then practised. It not only helps us to understand how the emotional trauma of the epic poem was received, but it also allows us to see how such emotional trauma was lived in contemporary Greek life.[90]

My source is an Attic red-figure volute-krater – a vessel for the dilution of wine with water – from about 460 BCE (Fig. 12). It is the kind of pottery typical of museum pieces the world over: the archetypical emblem of ancient Greece. This piece captures the moment when Thetis arrives with Achilles' armour. While the poem indicates that Achilles is the only one of those assembled who can look at this divine armour, here he is depicted alone apart from his mother, and his eyes are covered. His entire body is veiled in a loose shroud, save for the top of his head, and the symbolic presence of the heel of one foot. There are further differences: in the text, Achilles and his comrades are openly weeping and wailing aloud. There is no mention of any attempt to cloak this lamentation.

Douglas Cairns understands veiling as a prominent display rule in ancient Greek culture to conceal tears. The shedding of tears, he says, is 'governed by display rules that are context-specific. It is not that

Figure 12. Thetis presenting Achilles with his new armour, c.460 BCE, Attic red-figure volute-krater, Louvre, Paris. (Photograph by Marie-Lan Nguyen.)

Homeric characters are fundamentally uninhibited and spontaneous in their display of emotion [*sic*], except in a few well-defined situations.'[91] Achilles' loud wailing and crying are atypical. The re-rendering of the scene on the krater makes it conform to more generally accepted practices of the hiding of signs of grief, which, Cairns speculates, is a symbolically feminine act but not in such a way as to diminish the masculinity of the grieving party.[92] To shed tears openly may contravene a social norm, for the outpouring of grief bespeaks a 'vulnerability' that is shielded by the veil, to protect the self from a diminution of status and to protect others from the painful and discomfiting sight.[93] The veil is the symbol and practice of Greek grief *par excellence*, a sign of pain that is the concealer of pain. Here we find Achilles so depicted, even though there is no such veil in the Homeric account of his grief. The visible hair is a further important symbolic aspect of grief, since, as the carrier of the soul, it was torn and cut in lamentation practices.[94]

Achilles in this depiction is not recognizable as Achilles, but only as the sign of grief. The fact that this sign conceals almost the entire body suggests both the depth of this pain and the social necessity of removing it from view. The finessing of this scene into an orthodox conformity of the practice of grief is indicative of a greater fidelity towards fifth-century social convention than to the depiction of epic poetry. It spares the viewer, holder, or user of this krater the spectacle of Achilles wailing over a corpse, while nonetheless silently and knowingly indicating that the wailing is taking place behind the veil. It is a showing/not showing: a paradox of expressing pain by concealing it. If nothing else, it shows us that *trauma*, if we take a more distant analytical view, could be understood in affective terms. Its experience and its practice were themselves subject to shifting scripts, conventions, and framing.[95] Already by the time of Plato, Achilles' grief was difficult to handle socially. Homer spoke/wrote literally of Achilles' pain, his tears, his groans and wails. In depictions such as this krater, and in depictions of grief more generally in ancient Greek culture, the veil is the expressive way of saying 'I am in pain', and it should be read as such.

There is no way to talk about pain without metaphor; no means of objectifying it neutrally or of subjectifying it without recourse to something outside or beyond the self. To whatever extent the scientific or medical understanding of pain, with its own situated metaphors of pathways and process, makes its way into the cultural consciousness of the population at large, people understand their own experiences of pain, and their attempts to find relief, through them. Pain experiences are formed through what people know of pain colloquially, personally, communally, and collectively. The experience of pain draws upon metaphors that exist in parallel with, sympathy with, or opposition to the metaphors of medical science, depending on time and place and circumstance, but these metaphors exist in tension with cultural-historical shifts about how to be in pain and how to show it. When a sufferer is confronted with an orthodoxy of experience in the form of formal pain knowledge, their experience may well not fit. Sometimes pain has to be veiled and sometimes pain *is* the veil. There is a wrinkle of uncertainty about how to express, manage, and live one's pain. It is to the vicissitudes of expression and management that I now turn.

THREE

Worlding

Expressing and Managing

I turn here to the myriad ways pain is put into the world. 'Worlding' refers to an understanding of expression that dynamically connects experience to context. Expression, as indicated by the veil of Achilles, goes beyond language. I focus on gesture, facial expression, and other forms of representation, including material culture, art, and place, to demonstrate the enormous range of pain signs and to chart change over time in giving voice or presence to the experience of pain. It is increasingly recognized that finding creative or innovative ways to express pain is not only diagnostically useful but also of material advantage in managing pain. Painting, photography, music, and poetry do not objectively capture pain, but subjectively express it and can, in so doing, act as therapeutic devices. People have always found creative outlets for their pain, sometimes as a means of formulating a scream, and sometimes as a means of making sense of, and a salve for, the pain they know. These creations foreground the emotional experience of pain, centring the meaning of its experience in unstable and changing affective categories.

In a path-breaking book from the mid-1980s, Elaine Scarry (b. 1946) made great strides in developing the study of pain as a multidisciplinary effort. It concerns the horrors of torture and war, and the 'unmaking' of the world of the sufferer in exquisite pain. The focus is on the collapse of language to describe the experience of pain, and with it, the inability to put a successful pain expression into the world. Pain, at its extremes, is unshareable, according to Scarry.[1] As such, it destroys the person. Much is still to be gained from careful reading of Scarry's book, but the core argument has, in recent years, been rejected or revised. Many scholars have pointed out that there are rich languages of pain: an endless repertoire of simile and metaphor that precisely locate specific incidences of suffering in the world in which they occur, even if they do so inadequately. There has been an explicit attempt, by those specializing in pain therapeutics in medicine, to *supply* a vocabulary of pain for sufferers, such that physicians might be able better to access the experience of the person in pain. These linguistic and conceptual registers of pain have much to do with its situated experience. They express it and are formative of it. But beyond language there are other ways and means of putting pain into the world, which is to say, ways of giving meaning to experience by making it available to others. The body itself, and the face, speak a language of pain that is particular and contextually specific.

Our Lady of the Tumours

The Basilica of Santa Maria Maggiore in Ravenna is the bit the tourists skip. In a complex with the much more celebrated Byzantine wonders of the Basilica of San Vitale and the marvellous mosaics of the Mausoleum of Galla Placidia, this stylistically confused place of worship holds few treasures for the passive gawker. Dating to the sixth century, it was heavily modified in the 1670s. From before that time, one underwhelming fragment of a fresco, re-housed in the chapel and surrounded by baroque stucco work by Martinetti, was an object of particular devotion. Nothing about it seems to speak of pain or suffering, disease or illness. The infant Christ looks playful enough. Mary regards Christ's hand on her wrist. Some have tried to suggest she looks unhealthy or diseased: she is also known as the *Madonna delle enfiagioni* in reference to her swollen face, making some connection with the signs of incurable disease.[2] But her rosy cheek may as well be a sign of robust health as any kind of malignancy. Nevertheless, this is *Sancta Maria a tumoribus*, St Mary of the Tumours, an icon of hope, commiseration, and meaning-making in pain for cancer sufferers. Breast cancer sufferers have made their way for centuries to pray at the fresco. The logic of the pilgrimage is made plain in a printed prayer, made available in the Basilica. Mary offered her suffering (*sofferenza*) beneath the cross to unite the world in pain (*dolore*) with her for Christ. Christ healed the world from sin (a conflation of a consuming *male*, meaning disease, with the more thoroughgoing *male* of sin). Since Christ came to cure the otherwise incurable sin, hope is offered up that he might offer salvation to the sick (*malati*) from the incurability of cancer.[3] For centuries, people have found solace in this chapel: a place to express the sufferings of a painful disease; a place that gives order and meaning to earthly suffering in a much grander cosmological vision. There is misery here, to be sure, but there is also a hope that transcends earthly considerations.

When I visited the Basilica in 2014, I was unmoved by the fresco and perplexed by the postcards of the image for sale. This reminds me that there is nothing obvious about the ways in which objects, expressions, spaces, and places contain or convey meaning. One needs to be inside a culture – inside its logics of suffering and salvation – to get it, and that presents a major barrier for the historian. One can reach an academic appreciation of the relationship of image, suffering, and hope through the context of Catholic understanding and management of sin over the centuries. There is divine meaning – a potentially virtuous import – in disease as an analogy for sin, for the sufferings of such maladies are embodied reminders of the way Christ suffered for the sins of the world. To forbear, to re-express faith, to commiserate with the suffering of Christ and with the sufferings of Mary in her grief – to conflate *piety* and *Pietà*, as is so readily done in Italian – gives a function, a colour, and a positive meaning to the unlooked-for mortification of the flesh.[4] It might be expected that cancer pain feels differently after a prayer is offered up at this altar.

If 'Our Lady of the Tumours' gives no obvious visual clue of cancer suffering, swelling notwithstanding, there is a stark reminder of this just a few steps away in the form of another painting. It seems to provide the atmosphere of the Basilica, though it is seldom mentioned in descriptions of the place and virtually nothing has been written about it. Painted in the Mannerist style by Luca Longhi (1507–80), a lifelong resident of Ravenna, it depicts St Agatha being visited by St Peter when imprisoned. It is unusual in its theme and arresting in its depiction of the results of torture. To understand why it is unusual, and why the painting matters in the context of Our Lady of the Tumours, a brief detour to the life and martyrdom of Agatha is necessary.

Agatha of Sicily was martyred in about 251 CE. Her story comes from written sources, the earliest of which dates to the tenth century, but they in turn reflect centuries of veneration. Her life story is centred on a vow of virginity made before God, and her adherence to this vow despite the repeated offers of marriage of a Roman prefect, Quintianus. Quintianus had her tortured, but she reaffirmed her faith. Agatha's story and ordeal are redolent of other martyrdoms – St Agnes's in particular – suffering the rack, burning, and flaying. The most significant act, which became the mark of Agatha, was to have her breasts removed with pincers. She did not relent. Agatha was imprisoned, where she received a visit from St Peter, who came miraculously to heal her wounds before she was tortured, once more, subsequently dying peacefully in incarceration.

Most depictions of Agatha either show her in the moments of her torturous mastectomy or else represent her breasts on a platter. Longhi had himself painted her holding her breasts aloft on a plate for the Church of Sant'Agata Maggiore, also in Ravenna. Her removed breasts are symbolized by cherry-topped iced buns on her feast day in early February, especially in Sicily. Unsurprisingly, therefore, Agatha has become the patron saint of breast cancer sufferers. In the context of a theological understanding of pain and disease, of virtuous suffering and faithful devotion in adversity, Agatha's wounds and her fidelity made an obvious connection with women who suffered from cancer. Longhi must have been already familiar with the veneration of St Mary of the Tumours when he painted Agatha for this church, in singular fashion, at the moment her body is about to be miraculously restored (Fig. 13). Her breasts are not in the picture at all. Two circular open wounds appear on her chest, as St Peter is about to apply an earthly-looking medicinal salve (another singular feature of this composition), dipped in a bowl held by an angel bearing a candle: the light of Christ. Agatha herself points her right hand to the heavens, her arm following exactly the line of the angel's candle, as if to invoke divine intervention, but despite the severity of the wounds there is no obvious sign of suffering. In her other arm she holds the palm of martyrdom – a recognized symbol of the victory of spirit over flesh, and a sign of defiance to Quintianus. Agatha has an activated stance, a robust frame (the model for Agatha's body may well have been male), and a face apparently unmoved, relaxed, unlined. There is a triangulated focus in the exact centre of the picture, incorporating the keys to heaven, the miraculous power of medical attention, and the light of Christ, which encapsulate both the virtuous end of suffering and the potential of medical intervention. This provides the essential dialogue with the St Mary fresco, in whose direction the figure of Agatha looks from her position in the aisle to the right of the nave, signifying the hope of miraculous cure while graphically capturing the symbolism of suffering a rent body.[5] To pray at the chapel altar of St Mary of the

Figure 13. Luca Longhi, *St Agatha* (sixteenth century), Basilica de Santa Maria Maggiore, Ravenna. (Photograph by the author.)

Tumours has, for many centuries, framed cancer pain, given it meaning, even intention, and structured the hope for salvation from disease and from sin, if not in this life, then in the next. This is the clue to unravelling what may at first blush seem paradoxical. If suffering is virtue, then is it not impious to pray for divine intercession to put an end to that suffering? But the paradox is a worldly one that does not play out in the realm of conviction and belief. Suffering can be embraced as a sign of the sin of humanity, as a conduit for piety. To pray for a cure is compatible with an acceptance of this suffering. Ultimately, the reward for such suffering may be in the hereafter. Prayers cast to a loving but feared God in the name of suffering project forward beyond fleshly illness.

To make greater sense of this framing of pain, it is necessary to understand the general status of patience and disease and disability in a Christian context. In contemporary English, we readily separate out the concept of a medical patient and the quality of patience, but they are both rooted in suffering and suffering well. Patience, axiomatically, is a virtue. What is the nature of this virtue? To answer this, first it is necessary to understand the Christian context of suffering, its terminology and symbolism.[6] And to understand this, it is necessary to understand passion.

The detour takes my narrative back before Christianity, again to ancient Greece. Greek pain concepts conflated physical bodily pain with grief, anguish, rage, and vexation. But there is a broader context of suffering in the word 'pathos', which points to suffering in the most general terms. It includes the experience of pleasure, insofar as such a thing is produced outside of the person. Via the Greek πάσχω (*páskhō*), I undergo, or I experience, or I *suffer*, pathos finds its way into Latin as *passio*, and from there into English as *passion*. The modern English 'passion' does not indicate the richness of the history of this concept, or readily connect with the long context of suffering that it denotes. It might be thought of as an enthusiasm (a passion for collecting stamps, say), or a branch of romance (he's passionate), or an ill-fitting synonym for emotion. Yet the Passion of Christ still adorns countless churches. It is that context that will illuminate the problem of virtuous Christian suffering.

The Passion of Christ refers to the process of his suffering. Presented to the crowd by Pontius Pilate before being crucified, Christ becomes the emblem of endurance, a model to emulate. He is the *vir dolorum*, the *Schmerzensmann*, the man of pains or man of sorrows. What is the nature of his suffering in the Christian context? He is whipped, birched, cut by thorns, nailed to a cross, left to suffocate in physical agony. These physical wounds – the signs of bodily pain – are made to stand in for the deeper suffering of grief, of the context of sin. Since the fall of Eve, it was the human lot to suffer. (The biblical concept of 'labour', which in the case of women refers to the suffering of childbirth and in the case of men refers to the suffering of manual toil, are conceptually separated in modern English versions of the Bible, but were the same in the Latin Vulgate, Greek Septuagint, and Hebrew texts: *dolore*, λύπη (*lúpē*), and

בֶצֶע (*etzev*) respectively.) The physical signs of pain initiate a process of reflection about pain that is beyond the flesh. To the faithful, this aspect of suffering – the sight of Christ's Passion – is central to the practice of faith, central to the meaning of *piety* (which is itself a form of devout suffering, a commingling of the suffering or pity and the grief associated with *pietà*). To be like Christ – *imitatio Christi* – was to bear pain well, like Christ, and to understand and accept that suffering is the reward of sin, which is the mark of humanity. To suffer well, therefore, to be *patient*, was to be virtuous, Christlike, *pious*. Pain's meaningfulness lay in the capacity to bear its strain as an indication of a moral, good life.

To put pain into the world, in these terms, was to claim a stake in a certain understanding of humanity that centred the experience of suffering in the concept of the self.[7] In ascetic cultures, pain and suffering were actively sought: the mortification of the flesh was a channel of communion with the divine, the marks on the flesh a cypher for the tortured soul. Its signs were the hairshirt, starvation, and the marks of discipline. Such pursuits could result in a kind of ecstasy, their purpose being the erasure or occlusion of the world of flesh in search of a deeper understanding of suffering being. To pursue the suffering of Christ could, therefore, be both an everyday acceptance of worldly suffering and a deeply committed practice of embracing pain. To the extent that meaning is derived from expression, here we find that both silence and a kind of facial neutrality are the principal indications of tolerance and forbearance. The importance of immaterial pain – pain of the soul – had no distinct language of its own, only the metaphor of physical bodily pain and its associated imagery. Thus the depictions of Christ's pain – in a tradition of martyrology that echoes the virtuosity of painful death borne well – emphasize bodily disintegration combined with facial calm. The pain faces of the martyrs, if decontextualized from their bodies, do not usually look like pain faces at all. This series of passive countenances is indicative of divinity, of the capacity to undergo the most excruciating of bodily torments not without pain, but *as if* there is no pain.[8]

This was important, theologically. Christ on earth was a human and therefore could not endure his pain as God: that is, he could not be impervious to pain. If the lack of a pain expression was an indication of the absence of pain, then there could be no virtue in the apparent forbearance. Likewise, there could be no virtue in seeking an entirely pain-free existence. While it is not in question that people undergoing all different types of pain and disease in medieval and early modern Europe sought remedy for their ills, both spiritual and medicinal, they strove to endure the course of their sufferings in the right spirit. The most important scholar of medieval pain, Esther Cohen, has pointed to the functional logic of such a stance, much more prevalent prior to the creep of secular society, since there was no other way to square away an observable and lived experience of pain, everyday and everywhere, whether through illness or injury or war or disease or disability or age, with the existence of an omnipresent benign divinity.[9] Pain was a reward for sin, but to bear it well was to purchase a reduction in suffering after corporeal death: it was a process of purification; a path to heaven. Despite all this, there was no incongruity with hope and prayer for divine intercession to cure the diseased and disabled. Canonization records are packed with such miracles.[10] There are well-documented cases of those who appealed, sometimes *en masse*, to the images of suffering saints to put an end to disease.[11] To suffer well was to live with the belief in, but not the expectation of, such a possibility. Only armed with all this can one 'read' the Basilica Santa Maria Maggiore in Ravenna.

Such ways of making pain meaningful, of giving expression to it in a positive, extra-corporeal manner, are not limited to Christianity, but sit at the heart of many religions. Aside from the Islamic and Hindu examples given earlier, one could look to the tantric ascetics of medieval Kashmir, who followed Shaivist theology, seeking a transcendent state through a deep focus on physical pain; or one could look to the 'physical-emotional-mental-spiritual complex that defines the nature of human existence' in Buddhism, in which the right paths are to be followed to achieve a detachment from pain, rather than any kind of anaesthetic state.[12] Living with and through pain is a means to focus on the resistance of desire, which is both a strengthening and a cleansing process. Confucianism likewise has the experience of pain at its centre as a key indicator of the ways in which others suffer. It is a core quality of humanity. Without pain, one is not human.

In western culture, is such a view still possible? Perhaps, though it is hardly popular. Few would now try to defend it. C.S. Lewis (1898–1963) – of Narnia fame – tried to make a renewed claim for the existence of pain as a sign of God's love. In his 1940 book *The Problem of Pain*, he argued that if suffering was a sign of sin, then the blame lay not with God but with humanity itself. Pain's capacity to discipline, to improve humans at the level of the soul, made it an instrument of God's love. Therefore the embrace of pain was an act of piety. The signature line in Lewis's book is as follows: 'God ... shouts in our pains: it is His megaphone to rouse a dead world.'[13] If people prayed to God to reduce suffering, they were, in effect, praying to Him to reduce His divine love. In the context of the five years immediately following the publication of the work, with a world consumed by warfare, death, mutilation, pain, and suffering on an enormous scale, and amid a general decline in belief, the words rang hollow.

Those forces of secularization, of the state, of science and medicine, of industry and machines, of materialism and worldly philosophies, had grown throughout the nineteenth century and put a new emphasis on the question of the meaning of pain and how to put pain into the world. On the one hand, there was a rise of utilitarian thinking, from the late eighteenth century, that newly framed pain as an evil to be thwarted. The reduction of suffering occupied the centre of both philosophical and scientific endeavours in the nineteenth century and was a major part of political processes to boot. If pain was bad, meaningless, a blight on human progress (in stark contradiction to the foregoing view), then the emphasis had to shift to its removal or, failing that, its management. Alleviation, analgesia, anaesthesia, and social policies aimed at the reduction of suffering became the motifs of nineteenth-century civilization across Europe and America and were major conceptual components of the management of colonial and imperial projects of expansion and civilization. To express pain, in this context, was to signal the failure of modernity.

On the other hand, biological thinking in an evolutionary mode began to make sense of pain as a meaningful means of aiding survival, while at the same time doubling down on the rejection of a divine cosmology of meaningful pain. Nature red in tooth and claw, brutal, amoral, bloody, defined by screams and animal cries, could hardly be a sign of a benevolent God. But the idea of pain as a survival aid emerged through evolutionary thinking, justifying at least some painful experiences as both necessary and useful. These were limited to acute pains arising from injury – the pain that keeps a person from bearing weight on an injured leg, for example – but did nothing to explain those apparently pointless pains that endured. I will take each hand in turn.

Going Under

The anaesthetic properties of chloroform and ether were discovered in 1846–7. What was it like, at the point at which anaesthesia was a novelty, to be put under its influence? The philosopher, psychologist, and intellectual all-rounder Herbert Spencer (1820–1903) put the testimony of one of his correspondents on the record in *Popular Science Monthly* in 1878.[14] The correspondent, unnamed, might hardly be thought typical. Spencer made a note that, as a university graduate who had studied psychology and philosophy, he was able 'to see the meanings of his experiences', and that this character was 'extremely susceptible to female beauty'. His experience of chloroform for a dental extraction was one not of painlessness but of a kind of excruciating torture that seemed to be happening in the abstract. The self was erased by the chloroform, but not the pain, making the experience surreal. Yet the surrealism is situated. It is datable, contextually relevant to the times in which it took place. The form of the agony is inextricably bound to its context. The erasure of the self in the narrative seems to leave only context, of industry, of steam and pistons, of gothic horror, of modern physiological knowledge and modern physics, of an intellectual appreciation of the civilizational value of sympathy, as if context were itself definitive of the pain, which exists here in a tenuous relation to both body and mind. For these reasons, I offer a description and analysis of this rare experiential trip into the liminal zone between pain and painlessness, consciousness and unconsciousness, as evidence of the mind–body–world dynamics of expressing pain.

Eventually rendered insensible by the chloroform, the patient describes being 'terrified to such a wonderful extent as I would never before have guessed possible', of being unable to move, 'looking at nothing', 'alone in the dark'. He 'felt a force' on his arm, after which all senses of things external to himself disappeared. This disappearance of sensibility was not the disappearance of consciousness, however, but the elicitor of overwhelming 'panic', 'every air-cell struggling spasmodically against an awful pressure'. In 'universal racking torture', this 'iron pressure' settled into 'every nook and crevice of the scene'. His body was essentially gone; there was only this 'scene', filled with pain. His awareness was consumed by this 'isolated scene of torture, pervaded by a hitherto unknown sense of terror'. He began to recognize 'different parts' of his body, feeling pain in them in different ways, but as if they were not his own. His legs convulsed with increasing intensity, and then began the noise: 'innumerable drums began to beat far inside my ear, till the confusion presently came to a monstrous thudding, every thud of which wounded me like a club falling repeatedly on the same spot'. Thereafter, he forgets. The 'large fright that had seized me so entirely when I felt myself ensnared into dark suffocation' was gone, leaving only 'the huge thudding' and the 'terribly impetuous stroke of my heart'. It was almost elemental. Reduced to near nothingness, all that was left was the interoceptive awareness of a heartbeat and a banging pulse in the head, slowly diminishing in both volume and pain. As the drums receded his 'heart sprang out with a more vivid flash of sensation than any of those previous ones'.

The description to this point might have been difficult to date, save for the reference in passing to air-cells in his lungs, which put him in the age of physiological inquiry. But the metaphor for his painful experience takes a distinctly industrial, steam-age turn: 'The force of an express engine was straining there, and like a burning ball it leaped from side to side, faster and faster, hitting me with such a superhuman earnestness that I felt each time as if the iron had entered my soul, and it was all over with me forever.' He became the engine, his heart the piston. No longer an 'I' in any conventional sense, he was reduced to his 'burning-hot heart and the walled space in which it was making its strokes'. With every stroke there was 'exquisite pain on the flesh against which it beat glowing, and there was a radiation, as from a molten lump of metal between inclosures'. The burning centre of the industrial-age engine encapsulated a novel kind of torture. As the heat subsided and speed slackened, so the pain ended. The body, the 'I', was totally erased, but for warm vibration. This was followed by a 'fading sense of infinite leisure at last' before everything was 'hushed out of notice'.

Time passed, perhaps forever. Then the 'undisturbed, empty quiet' was marred by a 'stupid presence' that 'lay like a heavy intrusion *somewhere*'. I presume 'stupid' to mean insensible, which makes the phenomenon a contradiction in terms. Still, this presence became 'more inharmonious, more distinctly leaden' – more industrial imagery – and resolved into a 'heavier pressure' before suddenly looming out 'as something unspeakably cruel and woful'. The description here turns distinctly gothic, redolent of contemporary literary trends: 'For a bit there was nothing more than this profoundly cruel presence. ... It seemed unutterably monstrous in its nature, and I felt it like some superhuman injustice; but so entire had been the still rest all round before its shadow troubled me, that I had no notion of making the faintest remonstrance.' The idea of a cruel presence, of something malign, was compounded by a sense of 'injustice', a kind of cosmic unfairness that 'became so unbearable that I hardly could take it in', when it finally resolved into 'a massive, pulsating *pain*, and I was all over one tender wound, with this dense pain probing me to my deepest depths'. The gothic helplessness of an erased self, an immovable body in the presence of a cruel torturer, gave way to another contemporary simile, this time physical: 'I felt *one* sympathetic body of atoms, and at each probe of the pain every single atom was forced by a tremendous pressure into all the rest, while everyone one of them was acutely tender, and shrank from the wound – only there was nowhere to shrink.'[15]

The 'cruel element', previously felt, became a 'more crushing probe', forcing for a moment all the patient's 'atoms into one solid steel-mass of intense agony' (physics and industry again), which leads at last to a 'sense of reaction', a 'loosening', and he was 'urged into relief by uttering from [his] very depths what seemed not so much ... a piteous remonstrance as a piteous "expression" (like an imitation) of the pain'. He heard his own 'very low, infinitely genuine, moan' as if 'the sense of woe had got also *outside*', that he identified, at some level, with the pain itself, becoming it. Suddenly the pain that had been everywhere 'ran together (like quicksilver)', localized '*up on the right*', though no specific body yet existed. Still intensely painful, his moan 'was no longer a mere faithful representation out into the air of what was inside me' – this possibility is incongruous, given how much situated imagery surrounds the utterance of this moan – but a direct 'appeal for sympathy', without object. It is only fitting for a man of his class that he would look for sympathy as a salve, for the culture was deeply steeped in the idea that such sympathy was directly beneficial for the pained and wounded. Yet to ask, overtly cry out for it, was unbecoming, and likely to lead to the opposite effect. Thus, at this moment, just as he was about 'to utter a yet louder moan', a girl, 'that girl', appeared, with 'those lovely ankles' (pseudo-pornographic for the 1870s) and 'the graceful, Zingari brown stockings' (positively racy). He felt, in the presence of this girl – a 'young lady' he had seen in the railway carriage on his way to the dentist – 'that I would not make any cry, that it was not the thing'. Victorian feminine sensuality and the notion of a female presence aroused his masculine resolve to stiffen and endure.

The girl was extinguished by 'an agonizing, cold wrench' or three in 'hideously rough fashion', such that 'everything was tortured out of me but the darkness and the gigantic racking, swaying torture which was excruciating my right side'. The relentless, cruel industrial machine returned, an 'iron force, like a million-horse power', holds him, yet he himself was another such machine, 'another million-horse power which would *not* be pulled'. Suddenly, ascending through dense, vibrating agony, the 'I' returned, 'quivering, struggling, kicking out' through a 'convulsion of torture'. Light and air 'broke on the darkness' and he heard voices, words, and finally 'recognized that a "*tooth*" was being slowly twisted out' of his jaw. The body, the objects in the room, came back to his awareness as concepts, becoming more real as he continued to ascend, finally emerging 'out in bewildered light, just as the dentist threw away the second right molar from the upper jaw'.[16]

The piece is exemplary for its detail and its length, fitting with and characteristic of its times. There is, in this experience and its post facto remembrance, nothing of the divine, nothing of virtue, no point to the suffering. There is emptiness and darkness in the secular semi-slumber of chloroform, but it is no complete barrier against the pain in this case. Pain, when it comes, is a machine, or else some cruel presence: an evil in a moral-industrial metaphor of monstrosity. Yet it stalks its prey according to the physiological and physical imaginary, in which the self, depleted as it is, is little more than an assemblage of biological material. Pain, in the material world, is not in the realm of hell, but in the realm of the black scream of a giant piston in a factory – a place where this man of letters would likely never find himself. Thus, it does not, in this tangled literary trope, have any redeeming qualities at all.

It might be observed that this patient was hardly in a state of anaesthesia. Not only was the experience full of pain, but it was also memorable. Consciousness, which his correspondent Spencer was busy trying to unravel, was still present in various degrees. Imagine the dentist's point of view. The only outward signs of any awareness of pain in the patient would have come with the vocalization and in the final upward movement of the patient's body, back into a clear state of alertness. One could construct an argument about anaesthetic in an experimental era, where methods and particular ingredients and dosage were not completely worked out, to account for the Victorian patient's experience of liminal terror. One could call upon the testimony of noted psychiatrist George Savage, Medical Superintendent and Resident Physician at the famous Bethlem Royal Hospital in the 1880s, who made a case for the causal connection between the administration of different types of anaesthetic and the onset of insanity (especially in people with family histories of insanity and in 'hysterical' women).[17] Or one could look to the extended public and acrimonious wrangling about the phenomenological effect of different types of presumed anaesthetic agents used to benumb experimental animals in the physiological laboratory, arguments which also took place in the 1870s and 1880s. On the one hand, physiologists argued that physical movements and even screams were not reliable signs of the experience of pain, but might be mere reflex action. One could make the dead dance, given the correct stimulus.[18] On the other hand, many within the medical community and many more without warned against too easy an association between paralysis and painlessness. Just because a patient or experimental subject could *not* cry out or move did not mean they were not experiencing pain.[19] Anaesthesia focused the question of the reliability of the pain sign, and of the experience of pain in the absence of any pain sign. At times it was as if no gesture, word, scream, or lack thereof could be trusted as evidence of either pain or its absence. I will come back to this in chapter 5.

But to emphasize the vicissitudes of anaesthetic experience as historical artefacts is to overstate a notion of progress since those times. What happens when a patient goes under remains, to a great extent, a mystery, and as Kate Cole-Adams rightly argues, the medical practice of anaesthesiology quickly gives way to philosophical and phenomenological musings about the nature of consciousness and the extent to which this or that cocktail of drugs removes it. She offers up the testimony of a woman who regained consciousness during her caesarean operation in 1990. In some ways, it is remarkably similar to Spencer's dental patient in 1878, except the metaphors – the way of understanding the meaning of pain – had moved on. The pressure on her middle was 'as though a truck was driving back and forth, back and forth across it' and she 'thought she had been in a car accident'. While she claimed that she 'was just conscious of the pain', she was nonetheless conscious of it in figurative terms that precisely located her historically.[20] But she could neither move nor speak of the agony.

Cole-Adams points to a 1998 article about the connection between 'inadequate anaesthesia' and 'psychopathology'. It is not in the Victorian idiom of hysteria and heritable conditions of insanity, per Savage's intervention, but the parallel is striking given the interval of over a century. It was not so much the unexpected pain that led to mental trauma but the 'unexpected experience of complete paralysis'.[21] In a national survey of anaesthetists in the UK in 2013, to which more than 7,000 anaesthetists responded, only 132 of them (1.8 per cent) used monitoring equipment to assess the depth of anaesthesia during surgery. There had been a growth of scepticism about the value and reliability of such machinery, but previous studies had already shown that anaesthetists tended to underrate the incidence of patient awareness during surgery, despite a wealth of evidence that awareness under anaesthesia happens about 0.1 per cent of the time (which is one in every 1,000 patients).[22] Though the idiom of pain experience moves with the times, there is no doubt that painful experiences in situations where consciousness and mobility are inhibited, and where there is the promise of no pain whatsoever, remain deeply troubling, both in the moment and afterwards.

What is the flipside of this equation? What of the 99.9 per cent of patients who do not become conscious under anaesthesia during surgery? It is tempting to overstate the experience of the outlier, just as it is tempting to ignore it altogether because of a preponderance of success. The Victorian promise of anaesthesia had been an age of painlessness. For many, at least in the context of surgery, this has come to pass. The fear of the knife, which was a foreshadowing of the pain it would inflict, has been mitigated by the overwhelming expectation that all kinds of surgical procedures will be entirely painless. That promise is itself a salve. When it is broken, the experience and expression of extreme pain become all the more confounding.

Of Use and Uselessness

What about the second strand of secular worlding, to do with the evolutionary advantages of pain and its corresponding lack of broader cosmological meaning? I preface the discussion by reference, first, to Darwin and the wasp and, second, Darwin and utility. These dovetail into an emergent evolutionary interpretation of the meaning of pain and suffering. They have profound consequences for the ways in which pain could be put into the world.

In 1860, in the context of the spectacular success and critical reception of his seismic *On the Origin of Species*, Darwin corresponded with the noted American botanist Asa Gray (1810–88). The implications of Darwin's theory of evolution by natural selection had, by some critics, been presumed to be a thinly veiled promotion of atheism, insofar as it denied an understanding of the natural world according to intelligent design. Darwin wrote to Gray that the 'theological view' itself was 'painful' to him. Protestations to the contrary, he knew that he was entangling himself in a thorny theological problem but thought that the scientific idiom would be some shield against the opening of social and cultural battle lines upon which he did not feel equipped to fight. He admitted to Gray that

> I cannot see, as plainly as others do, & as I sh[oul]d wish to do, evidence of design & beneficence on all sides of us. There seems to me too much misery in the world. I cannot persuade myself that a beneficent & omnipotent God would have designedly created the Ichneumonidæ with the express intention of their feeding within the living bodies of caterpillars, or that a cat should play with mice.[23]

This is, once one starts to unpack it, an extremely complex statement about the reality of pain and suffering, in cosmological terms.

Darwin had written specifically about the ichneumon wasp (now, not without irony, known as the Darwin wasp) in the *Origin* in his discussion of utilitarian doctrine. For, he wrote, 'natural selection can and does often produce structures for the direct injury of other animals, as we see in the fang of the adder, and in the ovipositor of the ichneumon, by which its eggs are deposited in the living bodies of other insects'. The young subsequently eat the host from the inside out. In his conclusion, he returned to the subject, noting that natural selection removed the confusion and discomfort of marvelling at imperfection in nature, at the abhorrence of some forms of life.[24] Belief in intelligent design caused enormous problems in these cases because they compelled the witness to construct a positive argument for pain, misery, and suffering, tying themselves in intellectual knots for the sake of a prevailing theology. It was far easier, understanding natural selection as an ongoing process, to make sense of such imperfection if there were no intelligent designer. From this, Darwin's critics assumed that he was claiming there was no God, though his argument had not run to this length. Still, it shifted the terms of the cosmological discussion enormously.

The cat and mouse analogy was more of a philosophical trope in utilitarian thinking. Jeremy Bentham (1748–1832), the utilitarian whose mummified body remains on display at University College London, had famously claimed that he was afflicted with an equal love for the cat and the mouse, such that their eternal hostility presented a moral quandary.[25] What, in a secular world, was the meaning of suffering in nature? What should humans do with its presentations of suffering? While the basis of utilitarianism is that all suffering is bad, there are, nonetheless, different degrees of it. Bentham's intellectual descendant J.S. Mill (1806–73) was drawn into the subject of the exquisite quality of human pain, in contra-distinction to the more rudimentary sufferings of animals, and here the philosophy was caught in the natural historical weavings of the evolutionists. Because humans were more intellectually and sensorily complex, so their pleasures and pains were of a different quality. 'It is better to be a human being dissatisfied than a pig satisfied', goes Mill's famous axiom: 'A being of higher faculties requires more to make him happy, is capable probably of more acute suffering, and certainly accessible to it at more points, than one of an inferior type.'[26] Thus, even the utilitarians looked at 'nature' with a notion of scale or hierarchy, with the moral weight lying on the problem of human suffering rather than animal suffering. This adds a note of reassurance to the evolutionist's amoral appreciation of the apparent mercilessness of the natural world. At least, all things considered, *their* sufferings are not as bad as *ours*. Still, all of nature was predisposed to suffer, and both individual and collective practices were to be aimed at suffering's alleviation or diminution, according to the exquisiteness of the pain. What cats do to mice is, ultimately, a preoccupation neither for the evolutionist nor for the philosopher, though what humans do to cats and mice becomes an important question, to which I'll return. What is important for now is that the prevailing utilitarian understanding of humanity was checked and altered by the evolutionists, with a corresponding change in the way that pain was perceived and expressed in the world.

As Cathy Gere has argued, utilitarianism was fundamentally pessimistic about human nature, understanding the human desire for pleasure to be rooted in an animal, brutish and nasty – if I may mangle Hobbes – constitution. To govern on utilitarian principles was to restrain the human animal. But the utilitarian appreciation of the essential rapaciousness of the human animal was not grounded in biological thinking.[27] Rather, these biological assumptions were derived from an understanding of social and political behaviour, to which the utilitarians responded. The evolutionists, on the other hand, began with a far more optimistic understanding of biology in process, and of the emergence of restraints on behaviour through either public opinion or legislation as the product of social evolution. Evolutionist writing after 1859 assumed that 'civilized society' was a natural product of processes that began with innate communal morality.[28] If 'civilized' people concerned themselves with the surfeit of suffering in the world and wondered what to do about it, this sympathetic outlook was itself a part of the evolutionary process. Pain, in this view, afforded humanity with its fundamental beneficence, contra the utilitarians. If the utilitarians after Hobbes saw life as 'nasty, brutish and short', evolutionists allowed for a human alternative, based upon sympathy, kindness, and the relief of suffering. The practical result may have been roughly the same but prompted by opposed foundational principles.

If the positive meaning of pain was swept away by utilitarian thinking – if, in the end, to live was to suffer without purpose, and that the best anyone could do was to try to reduce the level of that suffering – then evolutionary thinking at least restored a *purpose* to pain that in turn could provide a different kind of meaning. Twenty years after Darwin had written to Asa Gray about the surfeit of misery in the world, he wrote to a different correspondent, young disciple George John Romanes (1848–94), about the reason for all this pain. Romanes had been trying to calculate the tree of mental evolution, understanding where each level of intelligence branched off from one kind of animal to another, working from the simplest organisms up to the high intelligence of humanity. Darwin, who basically excused himself from the whole subject of intelligence, nonetheless pointed Romanes towards the 'sense' of pain and pleasure. In essence, this was a utilitarian prompt, but the explanation was evolutionary in its impetus. The 'sense of pleasure & pain', he wrote, are among the 'most important steps in the development of mind'. What did he imagine this evolutionary progress to look like?

> a stimulus produced some effect at the point affected; & that the effect radiated at first in all directions, & then that certain definite advantageous, lines of transmission were acquired, inducing definite reaction in certain lines. Such transmission afterwards became associated in some unknown way with pleasure or pain. These sensations led at first to all sorts of violent action such as the wriggling of a worm, which was of some use. All the organs of sense would be at the same time excited. Afterwards definite lines of action would be found to be the most useful & would be practiced.[29]

Darwin noted that such notions were 'crude', but they are of a piece with his thinking at this time about the ways in which sensory reflexes transformed into inherited behaviours with specific meanings attached to them. The reference to the worm is telling in a context in which the meaning of such wriggling was being contested. His point, one that rang through his book on the expression of emotions in man and animals, was that bodily reactions to the perception of a painful stimulus could be useful in the story of survival of a species.[30] Darwin was back with Descartes's man with his foot in the fire, explaining the withdrawal of the foot as an evolutionary advantage, putting the pain bellpull into a cosmological, not simply mechanical, context.

From this point, we find a dominant medical-scientific orthodoxy that situates the meaning of pain in an evolutionary explanatory. It is not to say that the pain is in any way a good or positive experience, but that it is biologically *useful*. This marks the major break with utilitarianism, which could not find room – still cannot find room – for the utility of pain. In practical terms, what are the implications for the person putting their suffering into the world in these terms?

The first consequence is the renewed attention to lesion, automaticity, reflex, and mechanism. The ideas that a 'pain' signal causes withdrawal and that injury causes pain that instructs the sufferer to favour that injury to aid recovery (keeping the weight off a sprained ankle, for example) become dominant in western medical thinking about pain. They are the 'textbook' explanations for pain, reducing it to injury and defining a normative pain response according to a non-cognitive, mechanical, automatic explanatory. These foci define the appearance of pain and its purpose. The 'pain signal' mechanism did not originate with evolutionism, but evolutionism re-emphasized it with additional biological authority. The bellpull held good but with the force of evolutionary adaptation to make sense of it. For pain researchers who knew that the lesion focus was wrong, this became a source of frustration. Patrick Wall, writing in the late 1990s, lamented the fact that 'just about every high school biology text contains a diagram where a finger touches a saucepan and is rapidly withdrawn. It is used to "explain" pain as the method of avoiding injury run by a reflex mechanism consisting of sensory afferents that make motor nerves withdraw the hand.' One can almost feel Wall's fatigue as he continues: 'I despise that diagram for its triviality.'[31] Yet Descartes's man with his foot in the fire, which is essentially the same thing, appears thirty pages earlier in Wall's book, presented far more neutrally in a discussion of the problems of dualist thinking. It is, he points out, 'precisely the same formal structure of a sensory signaling system that many accept today'.[32] However unhelpful such an image is when thinking about the causes, experience, and treatment of pain, its major critics could not help but include it.

For the person in pain, the whole experience of therapy becomes defined by what the experience of the injury *should* be like, according to the evolutionary explanatory. The appearance of what look like exaggerated experiences of pain or, conversely, a strange absence of pain could therefore be ascribed to mental problems. Pain outside of the lesion idiom therefore becomes an 'all in the mind' problem, fit neither for pain doctors nor for pain medication. Chronic pain has no obvious recourse to this evolutionary explanation and is therefore invalidated or relegated as psychosomatic. Sufferers in these categories find themselves politicized out of the medical system and into the thorny administration of psychological assessment and disability claims. The cry of pain transforms into a plea to be *believed*. Where the pain does not fit the injury, or where there is no injury, there is suspicion. Expressive options are cut off. The pain experience is silenced in the official records, or else diverted into evidence of pain expressions being used as a cypher for deeper, underlying problems of character, mind, constitution, weakness. For the sufferer, this new pain regime only makes the experience worse.

Dualism had its apogee with evolutionary mechanics, despite early attempts to connect the evolution of forms with the evolution of mind. The resolution of this reflex explanation into behaviourism fundamentally altered the status of the affective experience of pain and its contextual situatedness.[33] Nowhere has this been clearer than in the pain and emotions of infants and women in childbirth. Under a behaviourist rubric, the cry of an infant does not automatically indicate pain, and insofar as pain measurement has addressed the face, it did not address the pain face of the neonate until the 1980s, as shown in chapter 2.[34] In fact, for much of later modern history, the expressions of infants, perforce non-verbal, have been discounted as immaterial to their experience. Either infants could not experience pain at all because they could not reflexively conceptualize or communicate it, or because their nervous systems were not fully developed, or else their pain was meaningless, short-lived, and had no long-term consequences. This contrasts with earlier strands of thought that understood infants to be *more* sensitive to pain.[35] While most people would now readily admit that infants can suffer pain, there is still no means of accessing their experience of it without projecting the meanings attached to pain after the acquisition of verbal and cultural concepts and forms of expression. The infant cry, a subject of debate on ever-shifting ground, either has indicated an unhappiness in excess of 'a criminal in irons', or has been of no more significance than the writhing of a worm.[36] The question of precisely how infants world their pain remains open, but the answer lies not in an isolated focus on the infant but in an understanding of the infant in social relation. An expression of pain in the world is only effective if others can see, hear, and otherwise sense it, and the infant likely learns how to put pain in the world through the responses of adults.[37] Worlding requires a world.

Medicalized ambivalence to pain expressions is dehumanizing. While acknowledging the presence of pain, painful procedures are still routinely carried out on small children without anaesthetic, such as circumcision and frenotomy, despite a clear ethical demand to err on the side of caution.[38] There are clear procedural guidelines, at least in the Anglophone world of medical ethics, for minimizing risk and guaranteeing painlessness. Nonetheless, an article in the *British Journal of Midwifery* boasted of a new clinic that specialized in infant tongue-tie and breastfeeding problems that had performed 220 tongue-tie divisions over a sixteen-month period without anaesthetic. The article reflected that 'infants do perceive pain, seemingly more keenly than adults, as their descending inhibitory pain pathways are immature', but operators used facial-expression monitoring as evidence that the procedure caused no pain.[39] Others simply state that the procedure can be done without anaesthesia or analgesics.[40] A more recent article shunned such practices, noting that 'surgery without anaesthesia in paediatric patients seems unethical'.[41] For circumcision, there have been a number of recent calls for regulatory guidelines for painful surgeries to be observed, on the understanding that such guidelines are still not followed.[42] As late as 1999, anaesthetic was still 'not typically administered' in American hospitals because of 'a lack of familiarity' and concern about 'risk', with the background of the myth of infant painlessness still firmly in living memory.[43]

The debates are still alive, driven in part by concern about the effects on cognitive development and stress response of neonatal exposure to anaesthetics.[44] While hardly a decisive intervention, I submit that few adults would agree to such a surgery without any form of anaesthetic and therefore underscore a question about the assumptions being made about infants being able to somehow take the pain. Moreover, there are significant causes for concern about the long-term effects of infant pain. Recent research has shown that infants exposed to pain undergo changes in the central nervous system and changes in the biological stress response that manifest in adulthood. Early exposure to pain is connected to a greater sensitivity to pain in later life. According to Gale Page, who has researched the biobehavioural effects of infant pain, such people are more likely to become hypervigilant as adults, with a correspondingly more acute sensitivity to painful stimuli, such that one may speculate on the relationship between the inchoate conceptual processing of the experience of pain in infancy and the more concrete social conceptualizations of fear, anxiety, and sensitivity in adulthood.[45]

If the pain of infants has been dismissed, the pain of bringing them into the world has had its own historical vicissitudes along the lines of use and uselessness. Having been part of Christian religious lore for centuries, the gradual removal of childbirth from community-based systems of folk knowledge and midwifery changed both the experience of pain and its meaningfulness. From the point of view of western medical authority, nineteenth- and twentieth-century pain in child-birth came increasingly to be seen as an unnecessary (and pointless) part of the process, with corresponding moves to eliminate it.[46] This represents a shift of the conceptualization of childbirth, from natural process to medical process, with a corresponding shift in the reading of women's expressions of pain from meaningful to untrustworthy (and unnecessary). While not making an argument for the pleasurable quality of labour pain, many women now assert its meaningfulness, resisting medical intervention, and historians have tried to assess whether childbirth prior to the administration of anaesthetics (epidural or general) was less frightening and the pain more bearable. Findings from Puerto Rico and the US in general, to Canada, to the Sahel region of Africa, to Congo, to Japan have repeatedly shown that the medicalization of childbirth, with its specific aim to reduce or eliminate pain, has resulted in lost knowledge, with corresponding increased feelings of loss of control, fear, and anxiety. Without the framework of folk knowledge of parturition, and without community-based birthing practices, women lost control, to various degrees, of their ability to world labour pain in a meaningful way.[47] Most analyses understand this as a patriarchal imposition. In the African examples, medicalization was often seen as a form of colonial control, adding an extra dose of disempowerment to the process. All of which is to say that the pain of labour is no less situated, no less political, than any other pain, and that its experience is related not directly to a physical or physiological condition, but to the conditions of possibility afforded by its framing: whose pain is it, what use is it, what is it for? Sometimes, medical interventions that block the worlding of pain directly impose themselves upon meaningful experience, especially where there is no choice. The secular, positivist, evolutionary explanation of pain impoverishes pain as a meaningful category and, in many ways, makes it more unbearable.

Worlding through Art

Is pain in this context more difficult to express? Elaine Scarry's argument about the 'world destroying' effect of pain in the context of torture has been taken by some and extended, as if it had stated that *all* pain were world destroying and there are no adequate words for *any* pain. The history of the experience of pain does not bear this out. Moreover, why should pain expression (or the expression of any emotion) be limited to the verbal utterance, to the word? If there is an inadequacy of words, there is nonetheless an abundance of artistic outpourings in many media that, while perhaps highlighting the difficulty of finding a language of pain in strictly verbal utterances, demonstrate the communicability and shareability of pain and suffering. They are themselves a medium of expression that shows that there is more to the language of pain than words.[48]

To demonstrate this, there are endless possibilities. I have already discussed the importance of artistic expressions of pain and suffering in an earlier Christian context, especially in the medieval and early modern periods. Now I turn to artistic suffering in a secular context (which is not to say that religion has no bearing on it). My selections here exemplify the historical, situated, and contextualized worlding of pain in modernity. I begin with Edvard Munch's *Despair* (1892).[49]

Munch (1863–1944) had embraced Søren Kierkegaard (1813–55), the nineteenth-century Danish philosopher and theologian, and in some respects painted through those philosophies. Kierkegaard's book *Begrebet Angest* (1844) has been variously translated as *The Concept of Dread*, *The Concept of Anxiety*, and *The Concept of Angst*, but it is Munch's reading of it, and its transfiguration of it into art, that interests me. In Munch's series of paintings in the 1890s that made up his *Frieze of Life*, angst plays a central role. Angst, be it in German or, as here, Norwegian, translates poorly into 'anxiety', though it is often the translation of choice. I would not translate it directly into 'pain' – just as loose – because it denotes a particular kind of *suffering*. As with other situated concepts, my preference is to leave the word in the original language and try to explicate it in such a way as to show the complexity of its signification. In short, the answer to the question 'What is *angst*?' is '*angst*'.

There is a genealogy of imagery here. Munch painted *Evening on Karl Johan Street* in 1892, showing a crowd making its way in dour fashion up the street towards the viewer. This grouping was then split up, part of it reappearing in *Angst* (1894). The grouping in *Angst* occupies the same position on the same street as Munch's more famous painting *Scream* (1893). One figure ommitted from *Angst* had been given a canvas almost entirely to himself in the first iteration of *Despair*, and the compositional elements of that painting were again repeated in a different *Despair* from 1893–4. All these paintings form part of the *Frieze*, and all of them speak to an understanding of pain or suffering that is not exactly embodied, but nonetheless present and all-consuming. All of them are connected to Munch's reflection, having been walking in the spot in Oslo, on Ekebergåsen, on suddenly being alone.[50]

The preparatory sketch for *Despair* (1892) has an accompanying text (Fig. 14). An edited version of this text would appear in Munch's diary (entry no. 34). The text disappears as the painting's composition takes place, such that the painting may be said to convey these words even in their absence. At the least, one can glean a clear sense of the artist's intention and context from this accompanying commentary. Before analysing it, let it be said that the painting is a *response* to pain. It is a form of expression, a way of getting things *out*. Beset by grief caused by the death of his father in 1889, and disturbed by the poverty into which that death had plunged his family, Munch grappled with suicidal thoughts. This was in the context of a history of family 'madness' and the stalking presence of tuberculosis, which had accounted for the lives of his mother and one of his sisters. The father figure loomed large. Munch had described him as 'temperamentally nervous and obsessively religious' and concluded that from his father he had 'inherited the seeds of madness. The angels of fear, sorrow and death stood by my side since the day I was born … threatening me with death, hell, and eternal damnation.' This 'worm-eaten' youth was in a diseased state, propagated by his father.[51] He described this madness as syphilis, giving a formal pathology to the inheritance: a morbid metaphor of pain, disease, and disintegration. Falling away from Lutheranism into a complex entanglement of the fear of eternal damnation and worldly bourgeois pursuits of the flesh, Munch was stalked by his demons. The Norwegian *fortvilelse*, here translated as despair, includes the notion of giving up completely, or of violent grief. Such is the context of *Despair*.

Figure 14. Edvard Munch, study for *Fortvilelse* (1892). (Munch Museum.)

The text that Munch wrote alongside his preparatory sketch is oft-quoted (though usually not in the context of this image) because it is understood to be the conceptual origin of the painting *Scream* (1893). That painting is itself commonly misunderstood, as if the figure in it were the screamer, not the one *hearing* the scream. By falling back to *Despair*, it becomes easier to see how the heard scream is a reflection of the internal cry of anguish, the silent scream of the despondent. Below I give the transcription of the text accompanying the sketch of *Despair*, with line-by-line translation in English.[52] Munch wrote:

Jeg gik bortover	I was walking along
veien med to	the road with two
venner – så gik	friends when went
solen ned	the sun down

Himmelen ble	The sky became
pludseli blodi rø	suddenly blood red
~~– og jeg følte~~	~~– and I felt~~
~~et pust af vemod~~	~~a breath of melancholy~~
~~– en sugende smerte~~	~~– a sucking pain~~
~~under hjertet~~	~~under the heart –~~
Jeg standset, lænet	I paused, leant
mig til gjæret træt	against the fence tired
til døden – over den	to death – over the
blåsorte fjor og by	blue-black fjord and city
lå blod ildtunger	lay blood in flaming tongues
Mine venner gikk	My friends walked
videre og jeg sto	on and I stayed
igjen skjælvende	again shaking
af angest –	with angst –
og jeg følte det gik et	and I felt a
stort uenneligt	huge endless
skrik gennem naturen	scream through nature

Before dissecting this, it is important to add the wider context of Munch's diary entry no. 34 if the paintings are to be successfully read, for in it is found the recapitulation of the imagery of cosmic pain and anguish. Munch recounts walking with comrades at 'a time when life had ripped my soul open'. The setting sun 'was like a flaming sword of blood slicing through the concave of heaven. The sky was like blood – sliced with strips of fire.' He noted the 'exploding bloody red – on the path and hand railing'. Then he 'felt a great scream' and 'heard, yes, a great scream'.[53] The paintings, *Despair, Scream, Angst,* and the later *Despair* are all expressions of these descriptions but left to stand without written form.

The way that Munch establishes the context for the situated meaning of *angst* is crucial. Life – circumstance – had ripped open *his* soul. The account of this despair, this *angst*, began with his pain. The lines struck out in the text accompanying the image are therefore a curious erasure. Here were his feelings, his breath of melancholy, his pain under the heart, but by deleting them the impression is that deathly fatigue, the shaking, the *angst*, emanate from nature itself, turning to flaming blood, licking the sky, such that the experience is of the scream of *nature*. In the English translation of Munch's lines on the Munch Museum website, those struck-through notes that locate the pain in the body of Munch are simply omitted. To consider them seriously is to connect the personal, the soul, and the cosmic, nature. The scream – this anguish, pain, despair – is everywhere. *Angst*, in this context, is a profound admixture of personal emotional and physical pain, bound with a rupture at the cosmic level. It cannot be reduced or displaced to anxiety or dread or fear. It is far more profound than that.

With the text removed, one might search in vain for these meanings in the painting itself. But there is an erasure in the picture that parallels the erasure in the text. The face of the figure who leans over the railing is literally blank. There are no features at all. The pain face, if you will, is not just an absence of expression, but a nothingness where a face should be: not a mask or covering, but an erasure. The origin point of this experience of overwhelming pain is transferred to the sky, suggesting not the impossibility of the communication of pain in the faceless individual, but the accessibility of pain to anyone who deigns to look up. This scream of nature, this renting of the sky, erases the personal aspect of subjective suffering and places it everywhere. The realization of the final painting, which has no text save for its title, is sufficient to give expression to this sense of cosmic angst. The more famous *Scream* and other associated paintings all build on precisely this expression of painful despair rooted in all of nature.

For the Croatian artist Mladen Stilinović (1947–2016), pain was rooted in power, or rather powerlessness, though he may have rejected my attempt to analyse his pain works. Compared with the 'cynicism of power', he wrote in 1994, 'art was nothing, absolutely nothing. I am convinced that art is nothing. Nothing, pain.' This concordance of nothingness/powerlessness/pain is key. Art was a 'manifestation of powerlessness, visionlessness, a blindness, deafness, … a pain that lasts … in zero'. Pain is, in a sense, annihilation of everything except itself. The context Stilinović gives is of the way power removes the capacity for subjectivity but leaves the pain: 'In the middle of the day it (power) says good night and looks me in the eyes and I feel ashamed for it. I know that one day I shall repeat good night (for one learns by repetition even unconsciously), but through repetition one does not learn only to repeat but also to forget.' Day is night. White is black. You are not you. In an earlier work, from 1977, prior to the socialist state's collapse, Stilinović conceives of a game of pain, for one player, played with a single die. On each side of the die is the word *Bol*, which in Croatian (and in a host of other Slavic languages) means pain, grief, anguish, misery, affliction, and so on. As with so many other languages, the vernacular conception of pain emphasizes its everythingness, which Stilinović roots in the nothingness of everything else. The player can play the game of pain, but every result is pain. Winning is pain; losing is pain. The game is rigged from the outset. 'When I say pain, questions are immediately raised,' he wrote in 1994: 'what pain, whose pain, wherefrom the pain, as if pain had to be explained, analyzed. There's nothing to be explained … the pain is there.'[54]

Yet for all the simplicity or reductionism of such a statement, the bleakness of this powerless surrender to the nothingness of pain, Stilinović was explicitly engaging in his pain work with Ludwig Wittgenstein's 'private language argument' and with Peter Handke's reading of Wittgenstein in the 1967 play *Kaspar*.[55] All of this, in addition, was being filtered through a particular context of artistic production, after the collapse of Yugoslavia and the subsequent descent into war in 1991. Wittgenstein had explored the essential unknowability of the other's pain, while confirming the certainty of one's own subjective claims to be experiencing pain. The observation is explained by the beetle-in-a-box analogy, where we are asked to imagine that everyone has a box with a beetle inside but where nobody is allowed to see any beetle but their own. How does one know what a 'beetle' is beyond the knowledge of the form of one's own beetle? Perhaps each 'beetle' designates a different thing to each person, based on what is in their own box. The answer lies in the irrelevance of the content of the box, compared with the public experience of the subjective experience of those contents. In other words, the box contents are publicly known only through what can be shared in language, and this is therefore the only relevant field. Substitute the box for the body and the beetle for pain, or for sensation more generally, and the analogy plays out as follows: what pain *is* is irrelevant; only what is designated as pain in a shared language is relevant. This is as near as one can come to knowing the pain of another, and while one may know one's own pain, one is similarly limited by the available 'language game' in sharing it.[56]

Stilinović contorts Wittgenstein's logic, for he understands the language not simply to be about pain, without approaching its object, but rather as inflicting pain, for in powerlessness all language is imposed. Here he confronts Wittgenstein with Handke's character Kaspar:

> Words that you hear inflict pain and the words that you pronounce. Nothing hurts, because you do not know what it means to feel pain, and everything hurts, for you do not know the meaning of anything. Since you do not know the name of anything, everything inflicts pain, although you do not know that it hurts, for you do not know what the phrase 'to feel pain' means.[57]

The paradox suggests an inability to understand the meaning of experience, caused by the violence of words, and an inability to understand the meaning of words, because of the lack of an experiential frame of reference. Pain is everything and nothing, inaccessible, unutterable, ubiquitous, and in every word. These lines, expressing a conceptual ambiguity about the state of being in pain and about the capacity to express pain, can only assert the nothingness of the sufferer and implicate the inflictor of pain – power – and its instrument: language. These lines introduce Stilinović's work *Dictionary – Pain* (1994), which were later given full realization as a physical dictionary, its pages individually displayed, the definition of each word having been whited out and replaced, in hand-written block capitals, with the word 'PAIN' (Fig. 15). Pain is literally the definition of every word. At one and the same time, pain inheres in language as the meaning of everything and, paradoxically, becomes meaningless.

The effect, however, is profound. I first encountered it at a massive and eclectic exhibition simply entitled *Schmerz* at Hamburger Bahnhof in Berlin in 2006 (see also the epilogue).[58] In this monumental display of circular reference (a dictionary separated and displayed as individual pages takes up a lot of wall space), we see both the intended nothingness and an inescapable *magnitude* of suffering. Expression through words is cut off, perhaps, but in the assemblage of this contradictory expansive reduction, pain takes up a physical space, acquires materiality. While Stilinović claimed that art was nothing in the face of power, the irony of this particular expression of it is that in raising awareness of this nothingness it is, in itself, a political statement. In denying

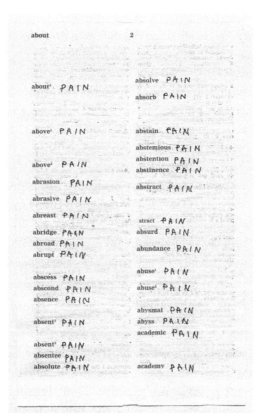

Figure 15. Mladen Stilinović's *Dictionary – Pain* (2000–3). (Reproduced with permission of the artist's estate.)

the expressibility and experience of pain, it suggests an approach to confronting the instruments of power in such a way as to find an expression of pain.

This is an analysis that I think would have resonated with Louise Bourgeois (1911–2010), the French-American sculptor, who understood that the practice of artistic creation was in itself an act of expression that could give 'voice' to the otherwise unsayable. She remarked on this in relation to the production of a small sculpture, sitting in the middle of a table:

I became uneasy, progressively anxious, terrified. The pain was physical, and yet it was so deep within the sculpture. What was wrong with the sculpture was what was wrong with me. Knowing what was wrong with the sculpture would enlighten me. To effectuate this shift from the sculpture to the person, you have to feel very loose, very accepting and humble.

This humility, which in Stilinović became a nothingness, in Bourgeois becomes a source of power. To an extent, she became the sculpture, pursuing an incoherent volley of images that amounted to a memory or foreboding of pain:

> What crept into my mind was that the sculpture had nothing to stand on, no relation to the floor. One half of its being was cut off by the table. I had this feeling that I might be cut in half myself. There was this terrific, intense identification with the sculpture. I felt cut in two. I visualized the caryatid or a woman cut in two. I thought of the kitchen cleaver, and of the fear of the cleaver, which would cut me in half. I had an identification with an animal I put into the cooking pot. I had this tension around my waist and I relived this fear of a little child.

These images, however, are recognized *as* images, as phantoms of suffering: 'But I kept thinking, "You're not a caryatid, you're not an animal, you're not passive. You're active. Don't let this happen to you. Just do it to someone else."' Thus the initial identity with the art becomes a power to express this pain without embodying this pain. The completion of the work depends upon the process of making a feeling conscious and then letting it go, doing it to the thing: 'The compulsion subsided. I rebuilt the sculpture from the floor up.' Bourgeois stated that such an 'experience' was 'very tiring'.[59]

Not for nothing did Bourgeois famously claim that the 'subject of pain is the business I am in. To give meaning and shape to frustration and suffering. What happens to my body has to be given a formal aspect. So you might say, pain is the ransom of formalism.'[60] I return to a long-held interest in Bourgeois's *Arch of Hysteria* (1993), analysing it as a formal expression of pain (Fig. 16).[61] It shares a formal identification with the other works I have focused upon here, insofar as it eschews any notion of the relation of pain to the face. In addition, it upturns gendered stereotypes about the experience of pain, directing us specifically to the wracked but apparently neutered body. There are numerous

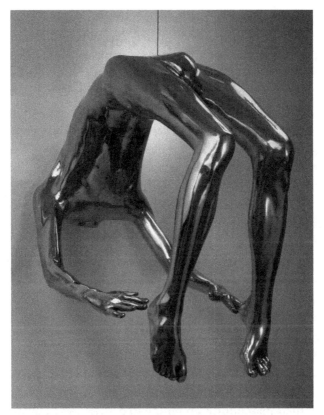

Figure 16. Louise Bourgeois, *The Arch of Hysteria* (1993). (© The Easton Foundation/ VAGA at ARS, NY and DACS, London 2022. Photograph courtesy of Galeria Soledad Lorenzo, Madrid, Spain © Album/Scala, Florence. Reproduced with permission.)

different versions of the work, but the one I have personally examined is in highly polished bronze. A headless male body is suspended from a single point. The body has no genitalia. It takes the form of the *arc-en-circle*, or the hysterical arch, made famous by Jean-Martin Charcot through his studies of hysteria at the Salpêtrière hospital in Paris in the nineteenth century. Charcot's hysterical patients would fall obligingly into this pose, arching the back such as to make a painful contortion, mimicking the classical presentation of tetanus.

Why Charcot's patients did this (men as well as women, though the women received more attention, both clinically and historiographi- cally), and how the hysterical arch came to be seen as a symptom of hysteria that was specific to a certain historical period, have been well documented.[62] Responsibility ultimately lay in Charcot himself, as the suggester of this pose. As he was a progenitor of psychoanalysis, it can be said that the problem of suggestion is as old as analysis itself. Even if Charcot's suggestion is accepted as fact, it was clear that this circular presentation of hysteria started to appear far and wide, among patients who had never been in his care. Even if these cases can be enfolded into the suggestion argument, on the basis that knowledge of this esoteric posture spread as the sign of a certain kind of trauma, a question still hangs over *why* people would so readily fall into it. Does it make sense to load the answer entirely on the hypnotic power of the doctor? The hysterical arch afforded men and women suffering from pain and trauma that did not readily fit any situated diagnostic category a means of giving expression to their pain.[63] Hysteria, especially in the nineteenth and first half of the twentieth century, was a broad church. Any number of psychological and psychosomatic complaints could be housed under its capacious conceptual roof. To be sure, women were more likely to be diagnosed as hysterical because their sexual organs were thought to be a primary cause of mysterious maladies, from emotional excess to fatigue and languishing, and to a general state of sentimental irrationality. But men were not immune from hysterical attacks (though such attacks often impugned their masculinity), pointing to deficiencies in character, moral fibre, and so on. What often gets lost in *looking* at hysterics from these periods – for they are abundantly photographed, drawn, and otherwise depicted – is the possibility of genuine experiences of pain and suffering and trauma that these expressive postures represent.

The *arc-en-circle* gave undiagnosed and undiagnosable trauma a route towards validation by medical authority. At the least, it garnered medical attention. Often, this validation was sufficient to effect the beginning of an appropriate therapeutic course. Thus, though born of clinical suggestion, the hysterical arch served a real purpose as an expression of pain. This is not to say that hysterical patients *performed* the arch in the sense of deliberate and wilful acting. It is, rather, to point to the process of cultural script writing and cultural script reading, such that the *performative* of the hysterical arch happens *as if* unconsciously and *as if* naturally. Hysterics were not (or not usually) fakes. A new expression had been created for a range of conditions that did not, at that point, have more viable diagnostic explanations, presentations, or treatments.

Bourgeois was long in(to) psychoanalysis, long aware of the ways in which hysteria was made central to psychoanalytic discourse, and long aware of the extent to which this centred on 'problematic' women under the gaze of men.[64] But, in her view, Freud was 'barking up the wrong tree' and 'did nothing for the artist', unlike, perhaps, Charcot, who was 'modest. He was only a scientist and not a theorist.'[65] To put the hysterical arch in the body of a man was already to subvert the orthodoxy of the hysterical imaginary.[66] To effectively neuter that body was to draw attention to the ways in which masculinity and femininity are valued and disrupted by the ways in which they handle and signal suffering. To decapitate the figure was to de-centre the brain, the psyche, as well as the face, and focus the viewer's attention on the experiential locus of pain: the body. It is also armless. In the words of Bourgeois, 'No arms means you cannot defend yourself.'[67] Armlessness equals helplessness. Moreover, by means of its highly polished surface, what viewers see in this crescent of suffering, this plea for help, is themselves. Bourgeois could tap her own pain, her own emotions, but her field was pain and trauma as conditions of humanity. Pain was obviously shareable. As she said of Francis Bacon's art: 'I sympathize. His suffering communicates. ... I feel for Bacon even though his emotions are not mine.'[68] To view this suspended, agonized body, gently rotating at a fixed point, is to view the self, distorted. To give Bourgeois the last word: 'The hysterical arch speaks of suffering but also of expression, of illness but also of communication.'[69]

FOUR

Suffering

Chronicity and Pain Syndromes

The artistic endeavours at the core of the last chapter have spoken, implicitly, not to pain as an acute event, but to pain that endures, even if they have not been couched explicitly in the language of chronic pain. Chronic pain is a modern category, but that should not be a barrier to an analysis of pain syndromes in the past. The modernity of 'chronicity' should be a clue to the ways in which painful experiences are defined and re-defined, and usually not by sufferers themselves. Recently, the concept of chronicity has been co-opted by historians of disability and the experience of chronic pain has been theorized from the patient point of view, using theoretical concepts such as 'crip time' to explain the political and experiential distance between those in pain and those they encounter. In this chapter, I'll show the usefulness of such innovation, and the limits of it. I am sceptical of projecting a diagnostic category of chronic pain into a past that did not know it, and instead favour an understanding of sustained painful experiences in the context in which those experiences were made meaningful to the sufferer. This is not simply rhetorical juggling and handwringing (if the two are possible at the same time), but a commitment to the historicity of experience. In the balance is the changing field of chronic pain knowledge against the background of shifting meanings associated with pain, and transformations of social relations. Changes in the knowledge status of pain butt up against changing concepts of the value of pain: the shifting understanding, both expert and lay, of the purpose pain serves. In many ways, chronic pain stumps modern medicine in its uselessness, but past actors have found ways to account for and even to make virtuous meaning out of their sustained agonies. Yet by equal measure, many sufferers, failing to convince medical authorities of the validity of their pain, which may have been dismissed as a figment of the mind, or a mere emotional disorder, or a defect of character, became lost in the endless meaninglessness of a pain that did not fit any script. Within the recent historical script of chronic pain, there are special particularities. How, for example, can one begin to make sense of a category of suffering that affects perhaps 40 per cent of all adults on the planet? It is a problem so enormous, so grotesque, that it is easily dismissed as 'normal' suffering, or else it is evaluated only for its economic costs: chronic pain is an inefficiency in the labour market, a cause of lost days and lost revenue. Can it be addressed in capital terms like this? Can it be solved in such terms?

Making Chronic Pain Knowledge

This book began with the instability of definitions and a series of knowledge scripts through which the medical science of pain was constructed. Most of the modern historical explanations of pain do not apply to modern experiences of chronic pain. It is much easier to see how interrupted flows, whether of blood or of other humours or of *qi*, might endure and cause pain that did not end. Those older scripts much more readily accommodated the conflation of physical acute pains caused by bodily injuries and lasting pains that were more redolent of disease, in terms of the suffering that they implied at both bodily and emotional levels. But such enduring pain in antiquity, or in medieval Europe or Persia, or in Han Dynasty China, would not be readily understood as a *syndrome* as the category of chronic pain is now defined. The causes, practices, expressions, meanings, and treatment of chronic pain syndrome – a modern understanding of pain as a disease – are specific to its modern iteration.[1] This does not cut off the study of pre-modern chronic pain experience (on the contrary, it encourages it), but it does cause some procedural difficulties in disambiguating the problem of chronic pain as it has been understood, especially from the twentieth century onwards, from other historical examples of pain that endures.

The main problem, analytically, centres on the erasure of subjectivity as useful diagnostic or therapeutic information in the pain science that bloomed in the nineteenth century. Not only did medicine erase the importance of patients' testimony about their own experiences of pain, but the framing of pain as a mechanical or electronic process, with evolutionary value, stunted the phenomenological language of pain that did not fit into this framing explanatory. When pain patients did not fit scientific formulations, it was often deemed that there must be something wrong with the patient rather than something wrong with the science. Much of the recent critical work on chronic pain, therefore, has been about putting patient experience back into medical knowledge of what chronic pain is, including experiences of the body, of time, of associated mental states such as depression, anxiety, and suicidality, as well as feelings of shame, guilt, anger, frustration, and isolation. Insofar as I can digest medical-scientific knowledge to summarize what medical authorities now understand to be 'the problem' in chronic pain, it is unfathomable without understanding this encompassing picture of disability that forms through and around chronic pain. It is this summation of the experience of chronic pain that amounts to the problem to be tackled on medical, social, political, and cultural levels, for a neurophysiological understanding of chronic pain is neither an adequate framing nor an adequate basis for therapy. In many cases, it seems as if chronic pain disorders are caused by the context of social and community fracture, by capitalist temporal logics and negative emotions. Viewed from this perspective, the problem of chronic pain is a problem of society itself. Its cure cannot, therefore, be sought on an individual bodily or psychological basis. Nevertheless, this is precisely the idiom of much medical research, even when it aggregates pained bodies to form a meta-analytical idea of the scale of the problem. Those bodies, understood as problem bodies, locate the problem in the individual human nervous system, not in the world occupied by the people who house those nervous systems.

Despite the instruction of the IASP in 2020 that 'Pain and nociception are different phenomena', and that 'Pain cannot be inferred solely from activity in sensory neurons', many pain specialists still think primarily in terms of nociception and still search for the cause of chronic pain in the idiom of nociception. While the definitional shift has been coming for some time, chronic pain research remains, to some extent, on a divergent course. An extremely influential article in *Science*, for example, understood the emergence of chronic pain, bracketed as 'pain hypersensitivity', as being related to 'neuronal plasticity', within a framework of pain knowledge that was limited to physiological, inflammatory, and neuropathic types. According to this model, neurons change according to the ways in which they are activated, modulated, and modified, constituting 'a continuum encompassing the diverse reactions of neurons to changes in their activity or environment', which 'determine the gain in the system'. Despite the reference to the 'environment', it is only the 'mechanism' that provides interest.[2] In a similar vein, a 2016 article developed the concept of nociplastic pain, 'defined as pain that arises from the altered nociception with sensitisation as the major underlying mechanism', which was put forward as a likely cause of chronic pain, commonly seen among patients with fibromyalgia, chronic fatigue syndrome, Ehlers–Danlos syndrome, migraine, and so on.[3] This was to complement the two prevailing understandings of physical pain: nociceptive pain ('pain caused by damage to non-neural tissue') and neuropathic pain ('pain caused by a lesion or a disease of the nervous system').[4] This concept of 'sensitization' of the central nervous system therefore does the work for chronic pain that 'damage' and 'lesion' and 'disease' do for more acute pains, even though it is mobilized precisely in the name of pain without damage or lesion. Pain of all kinds is still being understood in sensory and mechanistic terms, through the idiom of nociception, and on the understanding of a failure of the messaging system between the periphery and the centre (the spinal cord and the brain): a physical, biological problem. In a major *Lancet* review from 2021, it is suggested that central sensitization might be caused and maintained by 'nociceptive inputs arising from peripheral tissues', such that therapies aimed at this peripheral damage 'can potentially attenuate central sensitisation'.[5] This is a circular argument that takes chronic pain therapy back to the search for peripheral damage. It is not applied to every case, but it is indicative of an ongoing tendency to divide the study of chronic pain between what it *is* and its social and emotional *effects*, where the *is* of pain is rooted in bare physiology, devoid of meaning-making or worlding or conceptual framing. Central sensitization does not amount to pain, for it still needs to be made meaningful and meaning-making processes still take place in dynamic relation between brain-body and world.

I posit, therefore, that there is no theoretical justification to persist with this division of chronic pain according to *is/effect*. An examination of the experience of pain according to historical frames suggests that it is far more fruitful to understand the experiential framing of chronic pain as constitutive of chronic pain itself. Central sensitization is no less situated in the world than pain from a cut or a broken leg. The fact of its existence does not amount to an explanation of chronic pain. In a letter to the editor of the journal *Pain* by Lars-Petter Granan from the Department of Pain Management and Research at Oslo University Hospital, in response to the 2016 article that proposed nociplastic pain as a 'third mechanistic descriptor for chronic pain', there was already a strong rejection of the continued quest for mechanistic research. 'In virtually all cases of persistent pain,' he wrote, 'central changes (networks, gray matter reduction) have been reported. The problem is that these changes help little to explain why the pain arises; they are so far just structural correlates of persistent pain.' The same applies to nociception, for 'nociceptor activity or activity in pathways and cortical networks are not pain' because pain 'is a feeling experienced by a person', and that feeling cannot be reduced to a mechanism in the brain, the spinal cord, or the peripheral nerves.[6]

Other studies with a greater sensitivity to the context of the onset of chronic pain bear this out. A 2017 study that tried to find the causes of the onset of chronic musculoskeletal pain in children, for example, concluded that the presence of 'depressive symptoms' along with the onset of pain could be a predictor for the development of chronic pain, furthering a link between the 'ability to cope' and the amplification of pain by 'negative mood'.[7] Over many years there have been clear indications of a link between depression and chronic pain, where depression precedes the onset of the pain syndrome.[8] These are compounded by other studies that show the relation in pain syndromes between lasting pain and pain-related fear and pain catastrophizing – an emotional outlook that induces withdrawal and inactivity and so enhances and extends the experience of pain.[9] Such scholarship should direct chronic pain research into the context of enduring pain, to the conditions in which depression, fear, anxiety, despair, and loneliness are produced, sustained, and reproduced, and to the situated historical circumstances of the development and practices of those emotional and affective concepts. There is good reason to argue that chronic pain is a modern historical phenomenon of such enormity because of its connections to other modern experiential phenomena. Since depression and other psychological 'traumas' are so central to an understanding of chronic pain, the historical conditions that have produced these phenomena should be squarely in view. In historical contexts where mental illness was not conceived or experienced in the same way, it is unlikely that chronic pain states were lived in the same way either. This is not to erase histories of mental illness and chronic pain that existed, as it were, *avant la lettre*. Rather, it is to insist that the meaningful experience of such things can only be understood in context, according to the practical, material, and conceptual framework of a time and place, and according to situated knowledge, beliefs, and social configurations.

The immediate context of modern chronic pain is inescapably capitalist and corporate, insofar as the ways in which chronic pain is measured frame it as a productivity or efficiency problem. When chronic pain is measured at the population level, what purpose does the measurement serve? In expressing the magnitude of collective suffering (which is to say, of millions of people suffering alone), suffering is somehow erased. Judy Foreman compiled the statistics for chronic pain sufferers for the United States and found that 'one hundred million American adults live in chronic pain'. The figure comes from a report by the Institute of Medicine and is corroborated by other studies.[10] Similar numbers are found in other nations, ranging from 35 per cent for the UK, to anything between 18 and 50 per cent for Australia.[11] The numbers are, from a certain perspective, astounding, for they indicate a problem of such scale that no system seems able even to conceive of helping it. Insofar as this great wave of continuous suffering is turned into a political problem, a policy problem, an institutional problem, or is seen as a drain on profitability, productivity, workplace satisfaction, or, perhaps most cynically, as a problem that hinders *compliance*, then chronic pain is displaced into logics and rhetoric that only address the suffering indirectly. So long as the debates about the problem of chronic pain go on, as political debates tend to do, so the experience of those *in* pain continues unchecked, unreached.

For the person in pain, it is doubtful that it helps to hear that there are millions in the same position and that the problem is structural. The problem is often measured in terms of 'cost': time off work, cost per person per year for the healthcare system, unemployment, payment of benefits, and so on, to the point that it seems that the motivation for solving or salving chronic pain is to keep people in labour and to reduce costs. Chronic pain is a social burden to be eliminated not primarily out of compassion for suffering, but for economic and social efficiency and political expediency. Patients are *expensive*.[12] As one 2014 study found, tracking outpatient visits over eight years, the cost for pain medication annually in the United States was \$17.8 billion.[13] A programme for the reduction of suffering is a means to economic ends.

I do not think that the framing of the problem or burden of chronic pain as economic or social suffering is purposely tangential to the experience of chronic pain in the individual. On the contrary, this framing of chronic pain is formational of the experience of chronic pain for sufferers, for it expresses, usually fruitlessly, the structural frustration that compounds their difficulties. After all, the scholarly presentation of the economic costs of chronic pain has been presented in a similar way for decades. In the late 1970s, Steven Brena referred to the 'staggering cost of chronic pain', and such formulations seem to have taken off after that.[14] In 1981, the National Institute of Drug Abuse in the United States published a book that tallied 700 million lost work-days a year, with costs for healthcare and 'payments for compensation, litigation, and quackery' at almost \$60 billion annually.[15] While one could point to structural and treatment improvements in various directions since then, the problem is larger than it was. Chronic pain is now bound up in a politics of well-being and happiness, compounded with structural problems of community breakdown, a perceived epidemic of loneliness, and a loss of social support.[16] The apparent availability of access to healthcare and essentially meaningless statistics suggesting that national happiness can be measured are offered as a rhetorical fillip to the reality of austerity politics, with growing poverty rates, social isolation, rising suicidality, and a systemic frustration of the expression of pain. According to one recent study, more than 20 per cent of Europeans will wish themselves dead during their lives.[17] It is difficult to isolate, within that number, who these people are. But it is certain that chronic pain and associated conditions like generalized anxiety disorder increase the likelihood of suicide ideation and suicide attempts.[18] The true 'cost' of chronic pain is encapsulated by the silent and silenced suffering of so many millions suffering alone.

The Subjectivity Gap: MPQ

So far, the connection between the language of pain used by sufferers and the metaphorical framing of the knowledge of pain by authorities has only been loosely elaborated. I referred in the previous section to the silence – a silence at the social and political level – in which chronic pain is endured, but individual sufferers do encounter healthcare workers and medical authorities and they do speak. What do they say? What was the twentieth-century solution to the subjectivity gap that medicine had itself created? My argument is that people in chronic pain have, since the 1970s, been directly and consciously *supplied* with the language of pain by medical authorities. The medical-scientific realization that the language used by people in pain is useful, from a diagnostic and a management point of view, has been applied to organize and standardize the ways in which such language is understood. This kind of intent is understandable, even if it is fraught with difficulty. People do make sense of their own pain through figurative language, and the value they find in so doing stems from such language being readily understood by others. The potential gap – of class, perhaps, or education, or of standard language use as opposed to dialectical expression – between patient and doctor, however, often means that an effective means of communicating a problem to a friend or family member is rendered useless, even misleading, when used with a medical authority. What the patient means by their description of how their pain feels might, therefore, be missed. A growing sense of consciousness among medical personnel, in the second half of the twentieth century, that the subjective testimony of patients might be materially helpful crystallized the problem of how to interpret, in a schematic way, patient metaphors for pain. This was the impetus behind the McGill Pain Questionnaire (MPQ), developed by Ronald Melzack and Warren Torgerson in 1971.

The idea was to give physicians much more appropriate diagnostic and therapeutic guidance than could be inferred from a scale of intensity. The corollary effect, in allowing patients to give testimony about the specific quality of their chronic pain, was to put control of the experience of pain back in their hands, allowing them effectively to guide the doctor to a correct assessment and treatment of their problem. Designed specifically to better understand the experience of chronic pain, the MPQ collated common adjectival and metaphorical pain descriptors, ranking them according to the intensity they indicated, and grouping them according to type: sensation, affect, evaluation, miscellaneous. Information about other symptoms and the patient's lifestyle were included. The patient would locate their pain on a schematic drawing of a human body, thus providing the doctor with a complete picture of their pain, from its physical manifestation and location to the way it felt and the experience of enduring it. The premise in making the MPQ – a premise formed through clinical experience – was that patients tended to describe their pain in similar ways. The systematic collection and interpretation of this kind of testimony promised the advantage of a more uniform response to patient testimony, with diagnosis and treatment being made more consistent through the recognition of types and intensities of pain tropes.

Undergirding this attempt was a wholesale rejection of the fundamental guiding principles in pain knowledge in modern western history. Melzack and Wall's Gate Control Theory had already provided the means for a new understanding of how sensory information from the body reached the brain, and how pain was produced as a *response* to this signalling, rather than being intrinsic to the signal itself. Now Melzack and Torgerson threw out the whole notion of a 'conceptual nervous system in which "pain impulses" are transmitted from specific pain receptors directly to a pain center in the brain, so that stimulation of the receptors must give rise to pain and pain only as though it comprised a single, specific quality of experience'. Instead, whatever tactile, thermal, or chemical impulses were transmitted from the periphery, the central nervous system was selective in handling the 'upward' flowing information. Pain resided not in the 'sensation', but rather in 'an endless variety of qualities' according to the way that information was handled and processed. That they assumed the signs of this variety to be linguistic was to make a great intuitive leap. For while there was an implicit assumption that the linguistic categories would be uniform and universal – such is the impetus behind all attempts to elaborate a metric – Melzack and Torgerson were nonetheless inspired by specific cultural insights. They observed how an 'evening of radio, television or newspaper commercials makes us aware of the splitting, pounding qualities of headaches, the gnawing, nagging pain of rheumatism and arthritis, the cramping, heavy qualities of menstrual pain, and the smarting itching qualities apparently well-known to sufferers of piles'.[19] Pain research turned explicitly, therefore, to metaphor; but the metaphorical landscape in question was North American and Anglophone of a particular vintage. What common tropes might they have discovered if they had looked elsewhere?

The specific words that were tested for inclusion in the MPQ did not only come from popular media sources. Melzack and Torgerson turned to much older studies that had attempted to categorize and label types and qualities of pain. The first act was to remove those words that they 'considered inappropriate' (they do not say why) and then to augment the list 'by examining the medical literature' (they do not provide any references on this point). They arrived, after this, at a list of 102 words that were chosen, it seems, according to no standard beyond their own judgement. The words were then organized into sensory, affective, and evaluative categories, each of which was further subdivided according to different types or intensities of pain. The list was subsequently presented to twenty university-educated test subjects who would confirm or reject the inclusion of each word in its assigned category. It is important to note, before proceeding further with the analysis of the MPQ, that one significant methodological problem was 'baked in' from the beginning. No people who were experiencing pain were canvassed with respect to their actual language use. Rather, the list of descriptors was entirely generated by expert insight and confirmed by a single class of test subjects. Whatever clinical use the MPQ would thereafter be put to, therefore, it would inevitably *suggest* to pain patients the range of qualitative language that the physician was prepared to measure or entertain for the purposes of diagnosis and therapy. The risk was the delimitation of the qualities of experience that were the object of the study, and even of the exclusion of many varieties of pain experience that simply found no place among the expert-produced lexicon. As with many measuring devices before this one, the MPQ reproduced the implicit ideology of its creators. This was compounded by the field testing of the words to find a way of ranking intensity within the subdivided categories. Of 180 test subjects, only twenty were patients and all of them were 'white, English-speaking Protestants belonging to the lower-class income group' who 'attended a special poor-people's clinic set up in a Montreal slum area'.[20] They were not supplying their own language of pain, but merely responding to and ranking the language that was provided to them. In terms of probing the specific qualitative values of pain through language use, therefore, the study was limited. That the MPQ emerged from this study and became a globally important diagnostic and pain management tool is, therefore, surprising. This was not the primary aim of the original study.

That aim, and its implications, were extremely significant. The aim was to shift the study of pain away from a simple metric of sensory intensity. The broad agreement on the meaning and rating of the words deployed in the study allowed Melzack and Torgerson to assert that the logic of pain research was faulty. For if a researcher 'contends that A delta fibers carry pricking pain and C fibers carry burning pain', then it was incumbent upon them to 'find fibers for cramping, crushing or wrenching pain'. If the researcher 'contends that the different pains simply represent fusion with pressure fiber impulses, then he must find fibers for punctate, incisive, constrictive and traction pressures'. This was a mechanistic wild goose chase. 'It is far more likely', the authors argued, 'that the varieties of pain experience are subserved by different nerve impulse patterns from the periphery, modulated by central mechanisms.' If the analysis was still in the mechanical idiom, its own logical inertia took it into a different realm of metaphor. Burning pain, for example, did not necessarily have to have anything to do with an actual burn. Likewise, a 'splitting headache' was not a description, usually, of a fractured skull. 'It obviously represents a figure of speech, meant to convey some property of the total pain experience – that the pain feels *as if* the head were being split open.' The formal medical journey to the *as if* had begun. While the MPQ would implicitly limit the range of possibilities for taking seriously pain metaphor as a reliable indicator of pain experience, the principle of the research shattered the logics of hundreds of years of mechanistic and objective intent. Melzack and Torgerson had filed both sensory-discriminative and motivational-affective dimensions of pain under the vagaries of 'higher central nervous system processes': pain experience, ultimately, was a product of 'attention, past experience, and the meaning of the situation'.[21] No wonder it seemed so variable and contingent.

Still, the original study did conclude by proposing its mobilization into a questionnaire, which could then be used to gauge the efficacy of analgesics. The collection of large quantities of questionnaire data, analysed comparatively by computer over time to assess the effect of drugs on the pain experience, was a major implication. So, having opened up the study of pain to the vicissitudes of subjectivity in all its richness, the MPQ encircled that subjectivity with a lexicon that was not, ultimately, of the patient's own choosing. The language of pain, the importance of which Melzack and Torgerson had set out to demonstrate, would ultimately be the language of the psychologist and the language of the physician. As the MPQ spread, the problem of this imposed language constraint would be compounded.

The problem was realized as early as 1975, when Melzack first presented the MPQ to the scientific world. It was 'important', Melzack wrote, 'that the patients understand the meaning of the words. Some of them may be beyond the patient's vocabulary and may need to be defined.' The language of pain, even in the relatively uniform setting of an Anglophone research hospital in Montreal, was perforce the investigator's language. Melzack did not necessarily see it as a major structural impediment to the use of the questionnaire. On the contrary, he noted that 'Patients are grateful to be provided with words to describe their pain; these kinds of words are used infrequently, and the word lists save the patient from having to grope for words to communicate with the physician.'[22] There is no reason to doubt Melzack's testimony that many patients were relieved to light upon words that they 'use to describe their pain to family and friends', for these were patients in Melzack's own cultural setting. But the implication was present from the beginning that many would struggle to match their experience to the available words. Patients were provided with a prescribed list of ways to express how they felt. They were given no choice but to locate how they felt within this category. For some, it would have been easy, and satisfaction would have been felt, both by the patient and by the doctor. For others, the process would have been confusing, disorientating, and exclusionary. Prescribed categories of feeling, when delivered by an authority figure in the context of institutional power, force a negotiation at the level of experience. Those patients whose feelings did not fit may have had their suffering exacerbated or altered in an unproductive way.

Implicit in the above is the fact that the MPQ was useful primarily as a tool for helping with pain syndromes of various description. Of the 297 patients whom Melzack used to compile his 1975 study, all suffered from pain that endured, whether that pain was caused by arthritis, cancer, phantom limb, or a host of other complaints. Thus, the effectiveness of the questionnaire could be tracked over time, and the consistency of pain experience monitored. While Melzack was aware of the relief that patients might derive from 'finding' their own subjective pain language in a clinical setting, the purpose and value of the MPQ lay 'in its ability to provide useful research data'.[23] Various therapeutic techniques and drugs could be empirically tested by comparing pain data before treatment and after. It was, at that point, 'only a rough instrument': a staging post on the way towards the 'measurement of clinical pain' that permitted 'research on the effects of experimental and therapeutic procedures on pain in clinical rather than laboratory conditions'.[24] Yet Melzack seriously entertained the idea, despite the conscious resort to the realm of metaphor, that a refinement of the MPQ could lead to 'universal tools for the measurement and assessment of pain'.[25] As the fame of the MPQ grew, it seemed as if many were prepared to accept the first step on the way as the destination itself.

At the core of the MPQ was the wound metaphor. As it made its way around the world, researchers and clinicians began with the notion of translation, as if the particular meaning-making trope of the devastating effects of weaponry could be finessed into any cultural linguistic repertoire. It has become increasingly clear that the attempt to fix and universalize the qualitative language of pain experience does not reflect the variance in the way pain is conceptualized in different cultures and through different rhetoric. The problems caused by the imposition of pain language created or curated by the pain expert have been repeated. The inadequacy of Anglophone metaphors in other languages has confounded researchers and patients alike. Even the purpose of the MPQ, for the study of pain syndromes, has unravelled as it has been adapted to other locations.

In Japan, even though researchers have claimed that the MPQ is valid and useful, more than one of its core values was thrown into doubt. The 'different qualitative aspects of pain' were poorly discriminated in Japanese. A general pain score could be arrived at, but discrimination, say, between sensory and affective measures was confounded. Moreover, and confirming earlier observations, researchers observed that 'it is difficult to rank the intensity of Japanese pain descriptors ... because almost all the descriptors are assessed as being of moderate intensity'.[26] Meanwhile, the translation into Arabic in Kuwait altered the way in which the MPQ was used. The language used by sufferers of chronic pain was discounted because it was 'systematically' different to the descriptions of those 'experiencing acute pain'. The reports of educated Kuwaitis were discounted as being too 'esoteric'. English words defined as 'sensory' fitted better, in translation, in 'affective' or 'evaluative' categories. It was concluded, 'There is good reason to suppose that pain categories may vary from culture to culture.'[27] Such a conclusion implies a corresponding variability in pain experience, from culture to culture. Translators of the MPQ into Finnish similarly struggled, for 'no dictionary contains satisfactorily meaningful category/intensity equivalents. ... [B]oth attribute meanings and intensity scales defy translation.' Finns could not associate pain with punishment 'for some real or imagined sin', for example, but 'two distinctly different subgroups manifested themselves' in relation to the 'temporal' and 'brightness' sensory classes of pain, which were entirely absent in the English-language studies.[28] German translators were more sanguine about the possibilities of translation, noting especially that German cancer sufferers corresponded to Melzack's patients in describing 'shooting' pain, while nonetheless conceding that a 'literal translation ... is, of course, impossible'.[29] Meanwhile, the Italians found no shooting pain at all (while dismissing chronic pain patients from their purview), but listed under the category of 'shooting' the phrase '*E' come una molla che scatta*', like the snap of a spring. The Italian translators consciously eschewed the methodology of the other questionnaires, resorting to a group 'not affected by a professional knowledge of the topic'. While they kept the 'subdivision into classes and subclasses proposed by Melzack and Torgerson', they did so in the knowledge that the 'pain experience' is 'strongly affected not only by individual factors but also by ethnical, religious and social factors'.[30] A stronger conclusion, perhaps, is that language and metaphor are at the heart of experience. It is therefore of great consequence to know who provides the language of pain and by what means. The pain questionnaire is unavoidably political.

In a 2009 study carried out by the George Institute for International Health in Sydney, the MPQ was found to have been translated into twenty-nine languages, using anything from forty-two to 176 pain descriptors. While its authors warned that the translations were poorly tested, and that 'non-English versions' should be used 'with caution', it seems clear that no less caution should be applied to the use of the English version.[31] Its status as 'the original' does not answer for its own deficiencies. As I have shown with other strategies for the measurement of pain, it is impossible to standardize the experiences of pain through a standardized tool. Inasmuch as the MPQ sought to give voice to subjective experience of pain, it provided the language and, by extension, influenced that experience.

Memory and Re-experienced Pain

The eminent Victorian sociologist Harriet Martineau (1802–76) may have originated the idea of the evanescence of pain. It has been oft repeated. Martineau could enumerate a short list of the exact times when she was not in pain or suffering, over the course of years, but nevertheless claimed that the individual or discrete moments of pain, as they passed, were 'destroyed so utterly, that even memory can lay no hold upon them'. It is an unusual claim, since Martineau's work does so much to preserve the experience of pain. Yet the claim is reinforced by a further qualification, which pits mind against senses. For the 'sensations themselves cannot be retained, nor recalled, nor revived. ... Sensations are unimaginable to those who are most familiar with them.' To be sure, the 'concomitants' of these painful sensations can be recalled, and they can 'excite emotions' at later points, but the 'sensations themselves cannot be conceived of when absent'.[32]

It seems remarkable that, for all the richness of the language of pain, Martineau felt able only to navigate discursively around it. Each experience of it was 'new every time', such that there was no repository of pain knowledge to draw on. Even though she claimed to be in pain at the time of writing about it, she did not describe it. It was present, soon to be gone, irrecoverable. Yet pain was formative of the human soul, a formation to last forever.[33]

The apparent paradox between a moment of pain (an acute experience) and the memory of it (an unstable, shifting, but in some way fixed experience) is further complicated by pains that are not momentary but enduring. People who have lived large periods of their lives in constant pain exist within its trauma. The precipitating 'event', if one can be identified, may have passed, but it lives on regardless in the memory. It is not that the pain of the 'event' is re-experienced so much as it is experienced anew. The pain associated with it is not an aspect of then, but a lived reality of now, yet remains connected to the past through the particular formations of its expression. The experience of chronic pain such as this exists outside of the confines of post-traumatic stress diagnostic logics, especially when they are either from a period before the formalization of this diagnosis or from a place or linguistic context where it does not register. Situated accounts of the connection between trauma and memory and, flowing the opposite way, memory and trauma can in any case function without or beyond the medical gaze.

When the traumatizing event is war, it may be that there is a collective memory that conjoins with a collective experience of long-term suffering. Instances of pain connect with a politics of expression when linked to other sufferers who associate their pain with loss, fear, and injustice. Thus, Hanna Kienzler writes of Kosovo women's collective struggles with their health, in the context of the aftermath of Serbia's war with Kosovo in 1998–9, as the mobilization of a shared political language of suffering, whereby bodily symptoms of physical pain and distress became expressions of 'intimate feelings of loneliness, sadness, loss, and hurt as well as yearning for a past associated with solidarity, wellbeing, and celebrations of life', in addition to expressing 'dissent with dominating historical and political constructions of reality, the iatrogenic effects of well-meaning humanitarian aid, and competition for scarce resources among persons with equal needs and desires'. To function as such, 'the meaning of symptoms' had to be unravelled, through interpersonal narrative, into something other than mere 'ill health', to be *about* history, about 'socially contentious issues'. The physical symptoms themselves are rooted in the historical, social, economic, and political context. They were caused by the war and they serve as a living memory, which is to say, an active experience of it.[34] In part, at least, this is predicated on the rejection of engagement with medical authorities that would tidy ongoing symptoms away into the category of PTSD.

In other contexts, it is difficult to find such communal sharing of pain in the aftermath of collective trauma. The reason is straightforward enough: especially in the context of warfare in the first half of the twentieth century, combat trauma (which was not called as such) was common but not necessarily shared. To compound its plural individuation, it was not infrequently medicalized as having something to do with inherent weakness of the individual. Nonetheless, Ville Kivimäki has documented the extent to which many patients in Finnish psychiatric hospitals in the early 1940s were triggered by 'troubling war-related memories' or were 'disturbed by ... earlier war experiences', augmenting this highly situated view with compelling evidence of traumatic memories appearing in dreams, sometimes for decades after the war, as 'brutal repetitions of the traumatic event'. The key factor is that this relation between trauma and memory, while taking place both before and outside of the medical politics of PTSD, nevertheless shares some elements of that diagnosis. But in culturally and histori-cally situating the ways in which post-traumatic memories play out, the experience of that enduring trauma can and should be understood on its own terms, through situated diagnostic frameworks, situated treat-ments (and lack thereof), communications and languages of pain (and the failure thereof).[35] The meaning-making repertoire for pain in the individual and in the collective, when it endures, is subject to temporal diachronic processes, such that the memory of pain, or re-experience of pain, shares of both the past and the present. This is to say something rather more complex than that pain is evanescent. Rather, the pain that recurs evokes the original trauma, but it is nonetheless a present pain, even though it may fall into an ongoing construction of a narrative, perhaps without end.

Outing Pain

If the artists in the previous chapter could put their pain, or pain in general, into the world in the ways they did, is there anything to stop everyone else from so doing? I want to begin to address this question obliquely, starting with self-harm as a practice of outing pain, exploring its cultural weight and experiential function, before asking if art therapy does not follow a similar rationale, but displacing the body. In this I am inspired by the work of Deborah Padfield, who bridges the divide between the experiences of patients in pain and the politics of medical orthodoxies for the treatment of pain, directly intervening as an artistic mediator of pain that affords patients new potential outlets of expression and therapy and, potentially, affords doctors new means of access and management to the pain of their patients. In *Perceptions of Pain*, Padfield describes the intention to give patients 'control' of their pain, how it is 'seen and understood', by searching for an appropriate visual language.[36] Particularly striking is the account of Helen Lowe, who produced a photograph of her own arm, covered in scars from self-harming, and a separate image of words that form around the shape of the same arm, working in tandem with the image. A chronic pain sufferer, Lowe explains that she used 'self-harm as a way to control the pain', putting on the visual surface of the body the invisible pain that dwelled within it. To exhibit these marks of pain in public, in a photograph, extended the reach of the expression of pain, alerting the viewer at once to the experience of anguish and to the pain of being disbelieved. The scars are 'what the pain made me do. It says to me that is how I expressed my pain. It was the only way I could express it at the time.' To make it public was to share it and allow others to recognize themselves in it, displacing the need to cut. In the text that accompanies the image of the scarred arm, Lowe writes: 'The pain is invisible, people think I'm making it up. Even doctors told me that I didn't look like I was in pain. What am I supposed to look like?' The scarring provides this missing expression, this missing *look* of pain.[37] Researchers have correspondingly argued, both before and since, that self-harm, much pathologized as a psychological defect, may be 'better construed as a meaningful, embodied emotional practice, bound up in social (mis)understandings of psychological pain and how best to attend to such pain'. They suggest that self-harm is a performance of 'socially situated acts of healing, survival, and self-creation in a physical attempt to retell complex, fragmented stories of abuse, existential angst, trauma, and loss of self'. It is a practice of putting pain into the world.[38]

Padfield's photographic interventions would suggest that artistic expressions can work in much the same way to 'out' pain in a non-normative (from a medical point of view) but nonetheless effective way, without the need for self-harm to be part of the art.[39] It is not directly about seeking relief, but the successful expression of pain may itself feel like a relief, however temporarily. If, thereafter, the creation leads toward a better understanding of the experience of pain, for patients and their doctors, it may lead to a better form of treatment and management. The expansion of Padfield's project, which always involved both medical practitioners and their patients, has led to a small bloom of scholarship and cultural awareness on the positive value of worlding pain through art.[40]

This kind of worlding is far from new, even if it is an innovation within formal channels of pain management and therapy. Katherine Foxhall has documented the artistic endeavours of a collective of migraine sufferers, whose response to calls from the British Migraine Association to illustrate their pain in the 1980s has made an extensive archive – some 600 works – of a particular form of painful experience. The archive depicts experience in specific worlds, providing some sense of a community of suffering, as well as underscoring the subjective isolation of a person with their pain.[41] For Lisa Olstein, who recently wrote of her long-term suffering with migraines, pain was acute-chronic. A migraine could be any time, any day, and last a brief period or for days. When a migraine strikes, the experience of it does not seem to be reducible to pain, or, put another way, the concept of pain would have to become extremely expansive to accommodate all the sensory and other bodily effects that migraine brings with it. But it is also bodily pain, of such violence that for Olstein the experiential aspect of migraine and the pain of migraine seem to be separate. Pain is, for her, a *thing*, not a meaningful experience, not a vehicle for literature, not something you can get at by deriving its meanings. Yet, not without irony, it is all these things, conveyed as it is in this case through literature, through situated frames of reference that Olstein carefully selects and applies to her pain. For the pain *is*, in fact, all those sensory and bodily experiences; it is the life and the world of the sufferer, whose moments out of pain are nevertheless interwoven around her moments of pain. *Vide*:

> [M]igraine is a space you enter and are enveloped by and it is a different version of the world in there, where perception itself is an identifiable orchestration in full swing, and all the familiar and all the strange, the invented and the reflected and the revealed take up their parts and, like music, unfold in time, but a form of time contained by the architecture of certain stabilities so you can not quite rewind or repeat but continue playing or step back into the playing, which is always playing until you step back out of it and in some ways it stops and in other ways it keeps going.[41]

Some pain scientists might find this frustrating, but the tensions among chronic pain patients between belonging and not belonging, between a world commonly recognizable and a pain-world, like Olstein's, that seems surreal, are a major phenomenological aspect of the experience. The attempt to flatten out or reduce an aggregation of experience to an essential ingredient or mechanistic explanation tends simply to miss the point. For in whatever sense chronic pain sufferers share their experience, they nevertheless usually suffer with their pain alone. Its immediate presence, the 'absolute private certainty' of pain from the point of view of the sufferer, is often a source of doubt to the observer.[43] As Daniel Goldberg has said, pain 'encourages silence because of typical reactions to pain behavior, which tend to stigmatize the pain sufferer'.[44] And silence, in turn, isolates. Social exclusion, painful in and of itself, compounds the pain syndrome.[45] The artistic expression, or what might in other artistic forms be called a poetics, of pain[46] serves much as the scar as indicative of self-harm: they register the pain in a material form that may mitigate such frustrations, sharing, collectivizing, pluralizing. Sometimes. But can the relation between suffering and the experience of time be accessed? Can it be shared?

Fronto's Crip Time?

'Of pain: that which is unbearable, kills us; that which endures, is bearable.' This famous aphorism about pain from Marcus Aurelius (121-80 CE) is not as straightforward as many have made it. I have been inclined towards the *Meditations* precisely because I knew Marcus Aurelius to have talked about lasting or chronic pain. The operative word (translated as 'endures') is χρονίζον (*chronizon*), in which we see the stem of the word for time. It reads like a clear statement of the fact of chronic pain, that it must be borne, for it endures but does not lead us out of life. But it is not as simple as this. For starters, the focus on the enduring quality of pain has neglected to interrogate whether Marcus was talking about pain at all. In other passages, he references suffering (πάσχει· – *páshkei*) and the faculty of pain (λυπούμενον – *lupoumenon*) in terms that are readily recognizable as being directly about these subjects.[47] But in the reference to chronic pain, the subject is πόνος (*pónos*), which refers to labour and the consequences thereof, including suffering. It is clear that there is a relationship between toil and pain, labour and suffering, and that the two overlap in their meaning, but the word choice here does not readily translate to 'pain' in the limited, modern sense. Labour which is unbearable does us in; labour that endures is bearable. There is, in this re-translation, a greater sense of process, of effort and suffering.

Staying with ancient Rome affords a potentially fascinating entry point to the problem of experience and time, especially when couched in a Stoic philosophical context. The Stoic experience of such suffering is difficult to grasp, for while suffering endured, the 'mind safeguards its own calm by withdrawing itself, and the Ruling reason takes no hurt'.[48] In saying this, Marcus is consistent with his earlier passages that were more explicitly about pain. Reason can only be upset by that which emanates from itself, which puts the body's sufferings outside of it. He says that the body, *if it can*, should take 'thought for itself' and, if it suffers, 'proclaim the fact' – as if bodily expression, where it is available, occurs outside of reason and 'speaks' not of it.[49] His mind refuses, therefore, to suffer, irrespective of what his body may 'say'.[50]

This would seem to parcel off the body from the mind. The distancing perspective, from a philosophical point of view, is not concerned with worldly time or effort or suffering, for it contemplates greater matters than this. It is, as it were, out of time. The notion, drawn from Plato, follows shortly after the aphorism on labour.[51] But philosophizing aside, what was Marcus's lived experience of chronic suffering, his own and others'? Does his practice stack up against his Stoic claims?

For this I turn to Marcus's tutor and lover, Marcus Cornelius Fronto (100–70 CE), from Cirta, North Africa, and the correspondence between them, with Marcus in his mid-twenties–thirties and Fronto in his mid-forties–fifties. Both Marcus and Fronto have been subjected to scholarly scrutiny pertaining to their illnesses, pains, and complaints.[52] Fronto is responsible for the preponderance of these complaints, but Marcus also talks about his problems a good deal. The letters make for fascinating reading, though they are fragmentary and of uncertain dates.[53] I interrogate them for what they say about the experience of suffering that endures, despite and perhaps in contradistinction to professions of Stoicism, and use them, afterwards, to say something about the possibilities of the experience of time for those in chronic pain. One could scarcely imagine a richer set of primary sources from antiquity.

In about 144–5 CE, Marcus writes to Fronto that he longs for him to come, 'if only your health will allow of it, for I hope that the sight of you may do something for my health also'.[54] The sensory appreciation of a friend acts directly to assuage suffering, for, quoting Euripides, 'Sweet 'tis to look into a friend's kind eyes.' The body does speak for itself, for

Marcus suggests his condition cand be measured by 'the shakiness of my handwriting'. He notes that the pain in his chest has gone, and that his strength is returning, but still complains of 'the ulcer ... the trachea'. He is 'under treatment and taking every care that nothing militates against its success'. He feels that his 'protracted illness can be made more bearable only by a consciousness of unfailing care and strict obedience to the doctors' orders'. So much for the resort to the unsuffering mind and to reason. Marcus is subject to doctors' orders! He follows with this, which seems almost ironic: 'Besides, it were shame, indeed, that a disease of the body should outlast a determination of the mind to recover health.' Stoicism sounds like a hollow philosophy when put to the test of an actual illness.

Fronto, for his part, conveys his own problems. Scholars ancient and modern have debated what his condition was, whether gout, arthritis, or rheumatism, but the diagnosis is less important for my purposes than the experience of the symptoms.[55] He is 'troubled ... in the night with widespread pains' in his 'shoulder and elbow and knee and ankle'. He adds: 'In fact, I have not been able to convey this very news to you in my own writing.' Fronto is in worse shape than Marcus, for while Marcus's hand trembles, Fronto cannot even hold the pen. Fronto's pains keep him from writing, experienced by Marcus as a slowing of time and an increase in longing. The longing increases as the promise of seeing Fronto nears, only for hopes to be dashed as illness again intercedes. Fronto is 'seized with pain in the knee', which increases in violence, after which he succumbs to an illness (*imbecillus*). The news of Fronto's health directly disturbs the health of his student. Marcus complains of having experienced 'immense anxiety and intense distress, most acute pain and burning fever, so that I have no heart to sup or sleep or even study'. The body, even for the Stoic, was master of the mind. Marcus is 'in pain because you [Fronto] ... are in pain' (*doleo quod interim doles*). He concludes that Fronto's health will in turn assure his own health. To Marcus, time is marked by incidents and accidents, other people's injuries and pains, and a scorpion in his bed. Fronto teases Marcus with his Stoicism, noting that while he, Fronto, would have been shocked by the scorpion, he is sure that Marcus would have been unperturbed by such a discovery. This Fronto follows with the announcement of a new pain in the neck, which causes new anxiety for Marcus, who is suffering himself with a cold. It is as if a competition is playing out in which Marcus's minor tribulations pail in comparison to Fronto's debilitations. Each tells the other that the other's convalescence would ease their own troubles, but while Marcus appears to do better, Fronto's pain in the neck persists. Marcus ups the ante, writing in a way that makes it seem as if he has taken a sudden turn for the worse, when he is actually writing about his wife. This startles Fronto, who reflects on the meaning of the initial shock at thinking Marcus was in danger, followed by the relief that it was not he. As Marcus later reassures Fronto that his wife is recovered, Fronto returns with 'pain in the toes' of his left foot, frustrating further personal meetings with additional pains 'in the elbow and neck'. Schedules, plans, good intentions, all go asunder. While Fronto more fulsomely elaborates his love, and his consciousness of the drain on Marcus's time with the 'superfluous trouble and burden' of having to answer his letters daily, these elaborate flights are bathetically crushed by 'very severe pain in the groin'. Marcus reassures, hopes that the passage of time will have brought a remedy, only to be told that 'I have been seized with very severe pains again in the other side of the groin.' So it goes. The passage of time, for Fronto, just means more of the same.

Fronto summarizes his condition to Antoninus Pius, the emperor and Marcus's adoptive father. Celebrating the anniversary of his accession, Fronto says he counted it the 'birthday of my own health, reputation, and safety', but nevertheless bemoans 'severe pain in my shoulder, and much more severe pain in my neck', which have 'so crippled' him that he is 'scarcely able to bend, sit upright, or turn'. The memory of health and prosperity, some ten years past, is directly confronted with the reality of pain in the present. To what does Fronto aspire or hope for the future? Very little. Time is, ultimately, displaced to the other. Fronto claims to own health 'of body and mind, happiness, prosperity', so long as Marcus has these things, for in reality Fronto does not have them. Only the health and prospects of the other allow him to 'cling to life, in spite of my ill-health'. 'Apart from you,' Fronto writes to Marcus, 'I have had enough and to spare of life and toil, of profession and fame, but of pains and infirmities something more than enough and to spare.' The rhetorical effort to displace himself into the health of another's body and mind is yet beset by the grind of pain that, despite its chronicity, is not, in fact bearable. Futurity, in this state, cannot be conceived. The only way to live with the pain is to put life at a stage of remove, in a proxy. Time collapses. Hope, he tells Antoninus Pius, 'had been illusory'. When struck by a 'choleric attack' (not cholera, but a humoral disease), Fronto passes out, barely alive, thought dead. Slowly revived, he writes to Marcus that 'Only when I see you shall I live.'

Given Marcus's own not infrequent allusions to his ill health and to his understanding that it was important to be a good patient, as well as his repeated statements that his own bearing, both mental and physical, depended on the good health of his beloved, it is somewhat surprising to find him dismissing the effect of pain on reason, some years later, in the writing of the *Meditations*. His Stoicism as a philosophical ideal had not been lived out in practical adherence in his earlier years. Moreover, his awareness of the debilitating effects of pain that endured in his master Fronto gave him an intimate and oft-repeated insight into the relationship of bodily enfeeblement and the capacity to work. For all that he wrote that 'the mind safeguards its own calm by withdrawing itself', his experience of Fronto's chronic pain was that Fronto displaced his mind and body into that of Marcus to try to establish a rhetorical withdrawal. Yet all the while the pain served as a constant reminder of Fronto's situation in his own body.

How, then, to re-read Marcus's aphorism 'of pain'? Per the above, I think it should be reformulated to be about labour and suffering, and it might be understood through the vicarious experience of Fronto. For while Fronto could mark time and bear his suffering, he existed. When the suffering became unbearable, he did not immediately die, but the perception of futurity collapsed, along with his capacity to work and to write. The capacity to move according to the expectations of his associates, as well as his capacity to take himself anywhere, ceased. Hope became a phantom. Focus was turned inward to the always present – the constant but forever *now* – pain. A sense of chronicity – of the passage from a before to a now to a yet to come – collapsed. In this sense, Fronto was *destroyed* by unbearable pain, long before his death. The relation, to keep it in Marcus's terms, between chronicity and bearability is bidirectional. For the bearability of suffering and the capacity of the sufferer to mark time are each other's guarantee. When futurity – hope that there might, sometime, be wellness – ends, it is a sign that pain has destroyed the sufferer; when pain becomes unbearable, it is a sign that the capacity to endure is over.

This is not to say that this is *the* experience of the relation between suffering and chronicity. Whatever structural observations one can make about the relation of pain and experience that may apply more broadly, Marcus and Fronto were nonetheless situated. They were highly privileged: Fronto was carried to bathe by his servants (even if he did bemoan being dropped by them when doing so), and the two men mixed their intimate accounts of bodily functions and dysfunctions with high politics and philosophy. Their lives were duly framed, their feelings duly directed.

Still, wherever one looks in the historical record, one can find this kind of relationship between pain that endures and the collapse of both normative movement according to others' expectations of timing and the subjective experience of the passage of time from past to future. Andrea Marculescu, for example, has documented how the pained characters of medieval French dramas lived within 'crip time', where 'the future is dislocated, and the attention is oriented towards the present'.[56] A sense of diachronicity is replaced by a continuum of sameness, of a singularity of focus on the body and what it does. Crip time is a useful concept for beginning to think about how chronic pain alters the whole experience of life beyond or through the fact of pain, but it does not (or should not) predetermine what that experience is. As Emma Sheppard has written, 'there are multiple ways of moving through crip time, and multiple ways of living crip lives', which will produce situated coping and managing strategies, on the one hand, but situated confusions, conflicts, and invalidations, on the other. As Sheppard notes, 'ableist expectations of "normal" orientations and timespans are part of the construction of disability', so it is of great moment to try to reconstruct the shifting boundaries of the meaning of normalcy and of the ways in which disability sits in relation to them.[57] These are not boundaries that can be taken for granted, as shown by Karen McCluskey and others in relation to the representation of people with disabilities in medieval art. For while impairment might have been thought a mark of sin, so all pain was a reminder of sin, and at the same time a vehicle for piety and an approach to the divine. In an examination of the pictorial *vitae* of *Beata* Fina in fifteenth-century San Gimignano, the authors found that 'impairment was ... a key text to explain an ideal of Christian living and a vehicle for understanding the Christian journey toward union with Christ and, ultimately, salvation'. Impairment doubtless had its particularities of temporal experience, but insofar as these earthly disablements allowed for 'spiritual fulfilment', they were 'enabling'.[58]

This positive stance is echoed in contemporary literature with calls to validate the meaning-making processes of crip time.[59] But the contextual challenges are great. Compare the medieval example to the contemporary account of Ellen Samuels, for whom 'crip time' is *time travel*. 'Some of us', she writes,

> contend with the impairments of old age while still young; some of us are treated like children no matter how old we get. The medical language of illness tries to reimpose the linear, speaking in terms of the chronic, the progressive, and the terminal, of relapses and stages. But we who occupy the bodies of crip time know that we are never linear, and we rage silently … at the calm straightforwardness of those who live in the sheltered space of normative time.[60]

There are so many situated concepts in play in this description of the experience of crip time, which, in contradistinction to medieval and early modern examples, is framed by an entirely earth-bound, secular notion of the life course, of the possible future. Moreover, there is the specific subjective experience of the individual in crip time, which is often the thing denied to the historian. As Samuels says, the contempt for those who have lived through 'decades of proper health' mounts to hatred. These feelings and experiences, which arise from a painful condition, are framed and delimited by what is possible and impossible in a given world, and by the politics of medicine and by politics in general: by the imposition of naturalized norms that are, in the breach, revealed as not natural at all. Living in chronic pain, living in crip time, reveals what is wrong with the world. Chronic pain does not create social injustice, invalidity, inaccessibility, and so on, but casts the pre-existence of these things into relief. Insofar as norms are retained and reinforced such that the experience of chronic pain lies outside of them, so the suffering of chronic pain will be compounded by them. Statistically speaking, there is a high likelihood that everyone who reads this book will, at some point, suffer from a chronic pain syndrome. Given the extent of the problem, the time for agitation about justice, validity, and accessibility, about the rigours and logics of the capitalist clock, is not at the moment that *you* experience chronic pain. It is now.

FIVE

Commiserating

Sensing, Feeling, and Witnessing the Other in Pain

Could Marcus, intimate as he was with Fronto, know Fronto's pain? How does anyone know the suffering of another person, or another animal, in pain? What if we get it wrong? What if we put feelings in the wrong place? Here I review some recent research on empathy, which has been on a quest to find the mechanisms by which people know the minds and bodies of other people, before subjecting the importance of this concept to a rigorous critique. Those looking for empathy in the brain will not find it because there is no *it* to find. Empathy is biocul-turally constructed, not biologically in-built, and as such it is but the latest technique of the self in reaching for the experience of other selves. Failure to regard the pain of others, as Susan Sontag (1933–2004) put it, is a social and cultural problem, not simply a biological dysfunction.[1] This critical passage takes us back to other historical formulations of fellow-feeling, from ancient forms of pity to Enlightenment ideas of sympathy, compassion, mercy, and humanity, then returning to that strain of biologism beginning in the nineteenth century that debated the pain face and other pain signs, and the potential disassociation between such signs and the actual experience of pain. I want to make explicit and lay bare the mutability of the senses and the emotions in accessing the other body in pain to show that knowing the pain of others, whether we respond to it or not, is always a situated, always a political, act.

For all the debates about the shareability or relative privacy of subjective pain experiences, the focus has for decades been on pain language. The Wittgensteinian view that pain is 'an interactional phenomenon' – not so much a sensational experience, but a linguistic one – has afforded claims about the inherent accessibility of pain through translations of sensation into utterances, such that pain might be said to exist 'between' people, not inhere in them.[2] But if it is to be a starting point, the linguistic view is an obstacle to extra-linguistic approaches to shareability, especially in cases where language seems to be impossible. That is therefore where I begin.

The Animal in Pain?

If it is difficult to access the pain experience of another person, with whom one can communicate in a common language and according to a conceptual repertoire that both understand, how much more difficult is it to access or assess the pain experience of a non-human animal, which can neither talk nor signify its suffering in ways that are transparent to humans? The temptation – a temptation that has itself a long history – is to make assumptions according to the degree that an animal is considered human-like. It is a slippery category, this human-likeness, for it does not necessarily follow taxonomic lines. Many within the scientific world and in opposition to the scientific world have tried to draw lines of connection according to various markers of similarity, from sensitivity to intelligence; from bodily signs of anguish to the apparently universal pain face, be it of mice or men; from the mere presence of a spine to the number of nerve endings in the skin. The allure of anthropomorphism, and the attractive fallacy of logical inference between species, has coloured ethical debates about pain for hundreds, if not thousands, of years. Understanding this fallacy is crucial to understanding a rich history of mistaken ideas about the other body and the other animal in pain. It unfolds only in the light of recent empirical research in both history – the history of emotions and senses in particular – and neuroscience, in its social, predictive processing, and enactivist forms.

Central to the findings of both is the claim that concepts – principally but not exclusively linguistic concepts – are central to the development of emotional and sensory experiences. The brain is formed in dynamic relation to its environment – they co-constitute each other – and one of the key components is the conceptual repertoire: what things are called, how they are identified, what they specifically *mean* in a particular time and place. The concepts that give pain meaning are abundant. They have risen and fallen along with changes in political, cultural, and religious histories, and the ways in which brains have formed and developed and made meaning has changed accordingly, responding to and feeding such transformations in context. What pain means, and therefore how pain is experienced, is always therefore unstable. Yet, despite this, every epoch has been marked by its desire to pin pain down; to define it, objectify it, understand it in concrete, absolute terms, be they spiritual, positivist, or mechanical. Wherever and whenever such theories and declarations emerge, and especially when they emerge and are sanctioned by great authorities, whether religious or scientific (or both), the question inevitably arises as to the extent to which animal pain is like human pain, which is to ask: to what extent are *they* like *us*?[3] In some cases, the impetus is to distance animals from humans, often on the basis of the nature of the soul, but sometimes on the basis of differences in anatomy, physiology, brain size, and function. The human experience is projected onto animals in such a way that it does not reflect back. In many other cases, the impetus is to project what is 'known' about human pain onto animals, based on some individual or collective quality or function that is thought to be similar or analogous to the human. This projection is then reflected from the animal as if the animal is, through some expressive or reflexive means or another, intelligibly communicating its pain. Whichever way this goes, ethical considerations and politics immediately follow.

A fallacy of logical inference is alive in every case. They all presuppose a form of knowledge or a state of being that is rooted in essential qualities pertaining to the bodily or spiritual qualities of the human, and from this the quality of non-human animals is determined. If we understand animals as more like automata – clocks, in the famous allusion of Descartes – then their cries and grimaces become meaningless. If we begin, as some utilitarians did, with the view that it is possible easily to sort out who or what suffers and what does not, then suffering *potentially* assumes a horizontal aspect, morally and ethically alike across all species capable of experiencing it.[4] And then there are the animals that do not seem to be like humans at all, taxonomically, physiologically, intellectually, or sensitively. How does one enter the pains of an octopus, or an oyster? I do not intend to supply the answer (I am not altogether convinced that this is even possible), but I can gesture at the knots that have been tied by historical figures who tried to supply such an answer.

At the same time as photography was being used to capture, in a new way, the static face of pain and suggest its universality, there was a parallel development in scientific ethics that seemed to put a science of pain at odds with this proposition. As physiological research bloomed, especially from the 1860s onwards, many critics raised the question of whether safeguards were necessary to prevent scientists from inflicting unnecessary pain on experimental animals, thereby risking both their own moral fibre and, if sufficiently extensive across the scientific community, the moral fabric of civilized society.[5] How did one know if an animal was in pain?

Earlier in the nineteenth century, an argument had been made that there was no great mystery in decoding the violent expressions of any animal to access their experience. One anonymous proponent of 'comparative psychology' from 1820 noted that since the 'language of action which animated all beings' was not subject to 'volition', there was no problem in connecting 'the feelings and their natural expressions', and that this 'natural system of signs belongs to the whole animal kingdom'. Thus, the 'writhing of the worm when trodden upon' – a nineteenth-century meme, if ever there was one – 'is as clearly indicative of the pain it experiences, as the gesticulations of the happiest actor'.[6] But if writhing was an obvious sign in 1820 and a typical expression for Darwin in 1872, for the remainder of the century such expressions were far less transparent.

The question of how to know if an animal was in pain became the purview not of psychologists, but of physiologists. The scientists responsible for experimenting on animals were, they thought, the best placed to provide pain answers, so the lack of certainty they evinced was a cause for concern. By the 1870s, most experiments were predicated on the use of anaesthetics, so that the pain equation was usually completely removed, but doubts remained about both the experience of anaesthesia and what, precisely, constituted an anaesthetic substance. It had become increasingly clear that the substance curare, which had been used as an anaesthetic, was only a paralysing agent. Under its power, the experimental subject could no longer move, but it could still feel. Curare gave the lie to the universal pain face, for it was possible to imagine extreme pain in an experimental setting in which the animal undergoing pain made no facial expression and no sound at all. The lack of a pain sign could not be taken as evidence of the lack of pain. Where animals did exhibit a pain face, it could scarcely be trusted. As Gerald Yeo reflected at the high point of controversy over the question of vivisection in 1883, writing under the auspices of the Association for the Advancement of Medicine by Research, the human insight into the pain of others could only come from 'what we have ourselves suffered'.[7]

How could one interpret animals' expressions? There was nothing to indicate that their cries or grimaces stemmed from consciousness or came close to superficially similar human expressions.[8] All the physiologists who had been studying motor function and reflex, whether concerning muscular action or cerebral localization, knew that it was possible to *forge* an expression or to make the dead or disembodied move. The early experiments with galvanism had put pained grimaces on the face of a corpse, to the horror of the assembled audience.[9] Wasn't this precisely what Duchenne had proven with his galvanically produced expressions? They indicated, by accident of a flawed methodology, not the universality of expression as communication, but the utter unreliability of expression as a sign of any kind of affective experience. If expressions could not be trusted under these conditions, for what reason could they be trusted under normal conditions? The West Riding Asylum neurologist James Crichton-Browne remarked in 1875 that it was uncomplicated to make animals *appear* to be in pain even when they were in 'the deepest state of anaesthesia' or had had their brains removed. All one needed to do was to stimulate the 'motor centre'. The observation was based on common practice. One could produce a countenance that indicated 'intense and protracted agony' that was in fact indicative of no more pain than that felt by a 'pianoforte when its keys are struck'.[10]

Many attempts to understand the pain of others have played upon points of connection and disconnection between animals and humans. The fallacy is that there is something intrinsic in human nervous systems or human brains that can describe pain as an objective phenomenon. Since we know that there is no objective or predictable correlation between a sensory stimulus and an experience – that a gunshot wound may not hurt at all, but the stroke of a feather might be excruciating – we cannot extrapolate anything from mere sensory or nervous mechanics about the pain experience of animals. Among humans, there is a dependence upon the way pain is communicated to understand its experience. This is inadequate, full of potential for misunderstanding, under-treatment or over-treatment, invalidation and exclusion, cruelty and excesses of curiosity, but the rich repertoire of human pain concepts at least provides a basis for sharing and comprehension, where there is a will and, crucially, a common framework. I cannot feel your pain, but I might be able to arrive at a reasonable understanding of what your pain is like, based on the degree to which you communicated your pain to fall within my own experience of what pain is like, and according to the cultural framework we share. Then again, your pain might be so agonizing as to be beyond my ken. If you are from a different culture, or speak a different language to me, or – the historian's particular problem – if you are already long dead and speaking, as it were, through the archive, then I may struggle to understand. With other animals, all the advantages of conceptual accessibility disappear. We are left with speculation, conjecture, probability, and, if one is to be honest, a large dose of ignorance.

Anthropomorphism rears its head at every juncture, sometimes hitched to and sometimes derided by scientific inquiry; sometimes validated and often invalidated. Whatever the case may be, it is nonetheless generally agreed that projection of human states onto the perceived expressions of non-humans is not *proof* of shared meaning and does not in any way afford access to the substance of experience. Moreover, anthropomorphic projections have at their core an assumption that there is an essential human referent to which all humans have access. What pain is, for example, or what fear is, only work as anthropomorphic projections when they are rooted not in culture, linguistic concepts, historical context, and so on, but in bare biology. Nervous systems and physiology can be directly compared, but it should be clear enough by now that the experience of pain cannot be found in these essentials.[11] Nevertheless, the evidence of animal emotion and animal pain is still derived through situated projections and essentializations of human experience, and still lies at the heart of certain scientific orthodoxies among evolutionary biologists and animal behaviourists.[12]

The rise, across the sciences and humanities, of knowledge about the human as plastic, dynamically formed, contextually contingent, affectively unstable, changes all of this. We can still claim to know ourselves, but not as Linnaeus intended. To a certain extent, one could inscribe this as a return of logocentrism: a way of thinking about humanity that foregrounds the importance of linguistic concepts as functional parts of both brain and world development. They are uttered, yes, performed, after a certain definition of that term, and embodied, as both makers and markers of experience. But it is not only linguistic concepts that are important here. Humans maintain highly situated non-linguistic concepts in bodily gestures, facial expressions, embodied signs, and the material culture that they build around them. The practices of meaning-making involve all these things. Often, these non-linguistic concepts are assigned a linguistic concept that further enhances or deepens their meaningfulness. Whether linguistic or not, all these conceptual signs, used in common among people in their specific context, are lived, practised, and shared in such a way as to continually make and re-make experience in the ever-forming brain. At the same time, this aggregation of meaning-making processes – this accumulation of experiences that help to predict what new experiences will be like – is subject to checks, changes, novelties, and uncertainties. Apparent stasis in the conceptual framework of experience is always, *always*, beset by the possibility of instability, disruption, and change. What does this knowledge, which includes knowledge about what it means to experience pain, do to our ability to make projections onto other animals? We do not know – cannot know – their conceptual worlds. If, from the similarity of brain and physiological function, we make similar conclusions about animal cognition and animal experience, then we *must* have the courage to say that we *cannot* know their experience, be it emotional, sensory, or their pain.

I am drawing heavily here on recent bioconstructionist theories of emotion, though in embracing certain principles of social neuroscience I am critically disrupting them through the lens of the humanities. The key, with Lisa Feldman Barrett, is that 'emotion is perceiver dependent, so questions about the nature of emotion must include a perceiver'.[13] If the perceiver is a human, then through shared conceptual repertoires and a lot of effort, a sort of common understanding of the other *might* be reached. Across time, across space, the effort required might be more and the possibilities of success might be reduced. But where the perceiver is non-human, what is the point of access? As I have said elsewhere, with Mark Smith, to 'infer from human concepts ... the emotional and experiential life of non-humans is to engage in a fallacy of logical inference. It is straightforward to say that animals have affective experiences, but far from straightforward to say that these experiences can be understood through a modern conceptual framework in the English language.'[14] As Barrett puts it, the human perception of 'fear in the fly' can be researched scientifically, but this will say something about humans, not flies. Flies do not feel 'fear' because the concept 'fear' is a human linguistic concept. As soon as one starts to essentialize what 'fear' is to allow for the possibility of it in the fly, one is no longer dealing in fear at all. Barrett is explicit that this is not a denial of emotion in animals, but rather a denial of human capacity effectively to tap animal experiences of it.[15] I am arguing the same thing about pain, built on an understanding that pain is a meaningful, situated experience predicated on context, concepts, attention, and emotion. Since the conceptual and emotional world of non-human animals is inaccessible, so there is no accessible world of pain. This is not my way of saying that animals do not feel pain, but my way of saying that whatever pain they may have, an increase in perspiration, heart rate, hormonal production, or skin reactivity will not tell me what their pain experience feels like, just as such dolorimetric readings were fruitless for measuring human pain. I have no access to meaning in the animal, and without meaning there is no account of pain.[16]

There is great moment to the claim that we cannot know something. Politically and ethically, the limits of human actions concerning the pain of others have been set according to what is known or can be known. To reformulate a philosophical position, based upon historical, anthropological, and neuroscientific empiricism, that we cannot know destabilizes the bases for the ethical treatment of other humans and other animals. Some would worry, I think, that the embrace of epistemological and ontological ignorance concerning the pain of other animals would lead inexorably to monstrous excess. Animals would once again become the victims of all kinds of horrific abuse, the subject of the worst human whim and caprice, populating ghastly kitchens and bloodied fields like the nightmares of a Georgian romantic. But this is to confuse not knowing with not caring. It implies that the ethical status of animals and animal pain always inhered in *them*, when their ethical status, now as ever, resides in 'us'. By 'us', I refer not to you, the reader I identify with myself, but to the ever-shifting human collective that ascribes the labels 'we' and 'us' as a politics of distinction and difference from other beings that are, for whatever reasons, excluded.[17] As with the original coinage of agnosticism, which Thomas Henry Huxley (1825–95) put forward to express not a denial of God's existence but a fundamental block in the way of proving it, here I propose that not knowing does not excuse humans from ethical practices. Where non-human animals are concerned, not knowing their experiences of pain might lead us to take every care in our practices with them *in case* we cause them to suffer. Just as agnosticism was the antidote to arrogant atheistic evangelism among the most radical adopters of evolutionism in the late Victorian period (though it did not work for long), so might the admission of epistemo-logical and ontological limits in the case of human capacities to know the experience of animal pain serve to reinforce ethical standards. It might put scientists on an intellectual footing that is, for a want of concrete and positivist knowledge, more honest and more enduring.

According to the Human Thing

So what about the human in pain? Wherever one looks in the historical record, one finds proclamations, sometimes personal, often political, about the universality of the human experience of pain. The need to reach out and connect one's pain to the pain of others, in other places and in other times, is enduring. A unity in pain is an attractive idea. It can connect the suffering, the oppressed, the grieving, the unjustly punished. It services the notion of a common humanity, a means of understanding human experience at an elemental, essential level. Such a position obviously has political heft. Yet the evidence concerning painful experiences strongly negates the universalist view. This points us to a different kind of universalism: a universal breach in the experiences of sympathy, compassion, pity, humanity, mercy, empathy, and a discon-nection between the witness of power and the suffering of the oppressed or the excluded. For the great historical variety of concepts that have tried to capture the human capacity for entering and understanding the pain of others, what if humans are far more likely to misunder-stand, to misread, and to misinterpret suffering in other people? What if the politics of pain universalism are in the way of empathy, whatever empathy is?

I call this the 'human thing' after a much debated and misunderstood passage in Thucydides' *Peloponnesian War*, in which the idea of a universal is continually adapted to changing circumstances to service the rhetorical convenience of the notion that things stay the same.[18] Humans change all the time, save for this one 'human thing' that seems to universally attract them to the idea of constancy. If we analyse both popular and expert accounts of pain throughout the ages, we find this plot: it is the great universal of pain that grants us access to understanding the pain of past sufferers, just as my knowledge of my own pain allows me to commiserate with yours. It is a great convenience, but it should be clear by now that it is not correct. Repeated claims about the universality of pain are appealed to *despite* historical and cultural differences in the experience of pain, the knowledge of what it is, and the way in which it is encountered by the sympathizing other.

It is the sympathizing other – the pitier, the consoler, the empathizer – who then looms large. What permits one person access to another person's pain, whether they are proximate or call out across the centuries? In what ways has commiseration changed, and why? Here one must dig deeply into the cultural politics of feeling with others and into the practices that are associated with suffering by proxy. There is a history of humanitarianism in this, defined by shifting definitions of the deserving and the valid, that places witnessing, acknowledging, and acting upon the pain of others within the analytical frameworks of class, race, gender, age, and the contexts of social, imperial, and military history.

A simple question to begin: what is sympathy? I have asked this elsewhere and attempted to provide some situated answers.[19] Here I preface a targeted account of sympathy's vagaries with a list of dubious synonyms: pity, compassion, mercy, humanity, fellow-feeling, empathy. Each label has its own wrinkles of distinction, its own dynamics and expressions of power relations and social configurations. All of them imply a relationship to another's suffering. Sympathy, from the Greek, is literally *with* (*sym*) *suffering* (*pathe*). At the core of all these terms is a particular construction that frames interpersonal feeling by a politics of identification. If one person can feel another's pain, it is because, on some level – particular, fundamental, or essential – the other and the witness are alike. If the witness cannot feel the other's pain, or chooses to ignore it, eschew it, or even relish it, it is because the pain seems wrong, exaggerated, irrelevant, unlike anything the witness can see in themselves, or else because it has become routine, mundane, *unimportant*. The pain of an enemy may, if there is identification, arouse the mercy of the antagonist; where the enemy is an object of indifference, there is no mercy.

There are degrees of identification. David Konstan has shown that 'pity' for the ancient Greeks and Romans – Ἔλεος (*Eleos*) or οἶκτος (*oiktos*) in Greek, *misericordia* in Latin – presupposed a distance between the pitier and the pitied. Aristotle claimed that pity did not apply to close kin.[20] In this respect, the dynamics of pity were hierarchical, but they were still predicated on an identification at a more fundamental level. To pity was to acknowledge kinship at the level of being, even if it denied kinship in a more personal way.

The refinement of this position found its expression in the Scottish Enlightenment, especially in the works of Adam Smith and David Hume. In approaching the suffering of the other, the other's differences are removed in favour of a more essential set of similarities. As Smith put it, 'By the imagination we place ourselves in his situation, we conceive ourselves enduring all the same torments, we enter as it were into his body, and become in some measure the same person with him, and thence form some idea of his sensations.'[21] Yet for all the universalism of Enlightenment humanity, it is explicit that this quality of the imagination was limited to men of civilized society. While some would quickly point out that women ought to be included in the purview of civilization – that they were the physical embodiment, the biological preservers, of this quality of sympathy – few contemporaries made the same leap for the 'uncivilized', for indigenous populations of colonized spaces, for the enslaved, or for the non-human animal.

The problem was elaborated by nineteenth-century utilitarians, who sought to understand how to approach the suffering other when the suffering other could not effectively communicate that suffering for themselves. Beginning with Jeremy Bentham's oft-misunderstood line, 'the question is not, can they reason?, nor can they talk? but, can they suffer?', asked in 1789 but popularized only decades later, a means of assessing the capacity to suffer in the other (other being, other person, other thing) increased in importance. Bentham, contra popular present-day opinion, understood human suffering to be of greater weight and greater moral concern than animal suffering, and thereby signed off on things like vivisection because, in the balance of suffering, the benefit to humanity outweighed the harm done to animals.[22] But how, among others distant from the civilized self, could the weight of suffering be measured?

In the previous chapter, I mentioned this problem in brief. J.S. Mill perceived a far greater degree of suffering in the philosopher than in the fool or the pig and noted that 'if the fool, or the pig, is of a different opinion, it is because they only know their own side of the question'.[23] In a nutshell, this was the problem for everyone trying to understand pain in another.[24] Edmund Gurney, psychologist, dabbler in the paranormal, and utilitarian writer, understood pain to be the principal ethical consideration, noting that only the degree of suffering in any being was important: *'nothing but that counts'*. But even for Gurney, the essential problem of the suffering other presented an insurmountable object: '[T]he sole means to the conscientious estimation of others' suffering, which is a prime element in the reckoning, lie in imagining it as one's own.'[25] This might be a source of identification with a common group, but it was equally likely to lead to the gross misunderstanding of someone or something else's suffering. The sympathy at the heart of civilized society was ultimately limited by the powers of the imagination. Unsurprisingly, therefore, it tended to mirror existing lines of exclusion: the pains of racial others, women, working men, and animals fitted only uncomfortably with the imagination of the civilized man's own pain. In the process, the pains of those others were either transfigured or else denied.

As this tightly limited yet paradoxically 'universal' sympathy was adapted by biologists in the nineteenth century, it paid little more than lip service to the idea of expanding its compass. The fundamental quality of nature, for both the utilitarians and the evolutionists, was suffering. To live was to suffer, to know pain, in its varying degrees, apportioned by God or by nature according to the status of the animal in question: refinement of nerves, of voice, of brain, of culture, or whatever mark of distinction. The capacity to alleviate suffering, for both the calculating philosopher of the happiness of the greatest number and the expansive scientist who saw the tree of life extending in time in both directions, was uniquely human. To whom this capacity should be applied, and under what conditions it should be withheld, was therefore of great moment. The utilitarians, assuming the base human life to be fundamentally nasty, sought to limit the ways in which suffering could afflict populations; the arch-evolutionist Darwin, assuming the human to be fundamentally good, sought ways to extend the moral qualities of the best of civilization through the instruments of public opinion. The upshot was about the same, in principle: spread humanity and sympathy to alleviate suffering, beginning at home, extending to all society, then to all peoples, and finally to all animals. The capacity to end suffering was the pseudo-romantic goal, however mired in dubious statistical innovations and anthropometric databases. As Darwin's followers took up the baton, the end of human suffering found its ultimate expression in eugenics: the logical nadir for a universal sympathy that could not, as Darwin wished, include everyone and everything. If to live was to suffer, but to suffer least was to be the most civilized, most evolved, most cultured, most *rational*, then would it not be better to let those who did not make the grade not live at all?[26]

Care is thus required when conjuring with sympathy and correlates of fellow-feeling. Historically, they have excluded far more than they have included. Strikingly, Xine Yao has recently pointed out that even those who sought to extend the compass of sympathy to women and people of colour in the nineteenth century did so as an instrument of white supremacy.[27] The key to the doors of civilization was acceptance of a human 'universal' constructed in explicitly white male terms. To reject such terms was, in effect, to reject the definition of humanity supplied by the colonizer, the slave owner, the white male authority: to refuse the terms upon which sympathy was enacted. Yao has shown the extent to which this refusal can be an act of resistance: a way to feel (or not feel) in resistance to external expectations; a conscious political withholding of sympathy as a means of not falling into line with dominant and dominating emotional practices of white power. The refusal to sympathize with or validate white tears is a salient example.

Others have long since pointed out that sympathy, to be effected, had to be relatively low effort. To console another in pain, or another group in pain, involves not merely the act of inclusion, however condescendingly, but also the means of enacting sympathy without huge cost to the self. Circumstance had to make sympathy both morally compelling *and* easy to do. By such reasoning, Thomas Haskell explained why the well-to-do in the late eighteenth century sought to alleviate the suffering of the enslaved while leaving the suffering of the working-class poor in the East End of London untouched.[28] By extension, one could thus explain why societies for the prevention of cruelty to animals preceded similar societies for the protection of children. But too much pain could cut sympathy short. Susan Sontag zoomed in on the problem of compassion fatigue in her classic text *Regarding the Pain of Others* (2003). Constant exposure to people in pain through distancing media – television, photography, social media – renders the witness bored, indifferent, hardened. Such imagery becomes entangled with the unreal, the stuff of entertainment in adjacent contexts of storytelling and filmic production values. These things are designed to move, maybe, but only in passing, and not in any way to discomfit the viewer on their couch. The sight of pain might well be a cause of pain, but how many times can the same kinds of suffering be witnessed before they become sources of indifference or, worse, entertainment? The imagery of others in pain has long been purposely designed to engage the viewer emotionally in specific, situated, political ways.[29] There is not and has never been an automatic, essential response to the sight or sound of the pained body, even if many of those intentional designs would have people believe the opposite.

In any case, all of this has a nebulous intellectual quality to it. What does or did sympathy with another's pain and suffering mean in practice to the sufferer? How did one go about sympathizing with pain? What difference did it make? The answer will depend on the when and the who of the acts of sympathizer and sympathized, but I will offer a small case study of the inefficacy of sympathy in the sick-room in the mid-nineteenth century. All the tropes, all the rhetorical devices, are there, known by the ill person and the sympathizer alike: a script to read and perform according to the standards of the day. But in the sufferer's private account, sympathy is far more likely to identify the selfish indulgences of the sympathizer than any real attempt to succour the pained. I do not wish to belittle or deny the value of having fellow-travellers in pain, one way or another, but simply point out some of its practical limitations. As an exemplary case, I offer up the attitude of the aforementioned Victorian thinker Harriet Martineau.

Sympathy in the Sick-Room?

Martineau was an important writer and thinker in her own lifetime, even if today her influence has waned. Known for her sociological theorizing, she was an early influence on Darwin, but her intellectual, social, and political ambitions were checked by a uterine tumour diagnosis in

1839. It would see her retreat to invalidity and solitude, but she asserted control over the conditions of her illness in a way that has since been seen as a disruption of the typical authority of medicine over the sick. She recorded this in her illness narrative, *Life in the Sick-Room* (1844), which has been well studied, but not as an article on human sympathy. Yet it is eminently valuable for precisely this.[30]

The chronic sufferer has more opportunity than most to see the vagaries and varieties of sympathetic intent and action. 'If all sorrow teaches us that nothing is more universal than sympathy, long and irremediable sickness proves plainly, that nothing is more various than its kinds and degrees,' Martineau wrote.[31] If sympathy is actively sought by the sufferer, finding it may be 'heavenly solace', but the conditional is important.[32] Sympathy is not always sought, and often says more of the attitude of the witness to pain than about any particular experience or wish of the person in pain. Sympathy, insofar as it is prompted by pain, is itself a kind of pain, a suffering caused by suffering. The desire to end *this* suffering is often the prompt for practices and stratagems to solve the original source of the pain. According to Martineau, 'the pain of sympathy in the hearts of friends impels them to cast about for relief, and tempts them to speak of hope to the sufferer who has no hope, or none compatible with the kind of consolation they attempt'. This is 'disguised selfishness', evident to the sufferer, and unpalatable.[33] The compulsion to invoke 'hope' is met by Martineau with the affective calculation of the ancient Greeks. To surrender to hope when reason, circumstance, and probability suggest there is none is to enter self-delusion. It is to trust in the passive intercession of God or gods, nature, the cosmos, fate – what you will – and therefore, especially in the mind of a materialist such as Martineau, to set oneself up for crushing disappointment *on top* of the ever-present suffering. Hope, instrument of the sympathizer, has a long tradition among the educated of being an unwelcome and unjustifiable indulgence: a portent of certain ruin. Don't, Martineau exhorted, look out 'wistfully' for hope, but rather try to endure.[34] She wrote of a sweet spot between blind hope and compassion fatigue. 'It is a comfortable season', she said, 'when one's friends have ceased to hope unreasonably, and not "grown tired of despairing".'[35] What is the behaviour of one's friends in such a 'season'? Solidarity in despair? Perhaps. Solidarity in the reality of the experience of suffering might be nearer the mark.

Martineau complained of another selfish indulgence of the sympathizer in denying or 'disallowing' 'pain and a sad prospect'. Chin up, turn that frown upside down, think positive thoughts. What do platitudes do? According to Martineau, 'the tendency' of the sufferer 'to make the worst of bodily complaints … is much aggravated, if not generally caused by the tendency in the healthy and happy' to deploy them.[36] The sufferer is much more likely, in Martineau's estimation, to be pleased and soothed by 'speaking the truth in love': 'Let the nurse avow that the medicine is nauseous. Let the physician declare that the treatment will be painful. Let sister, or brother, or friend, tell me that I must never look to be well. When the time approaches that I am to die, let me be told that I am to die, and when.'[37] But, and this is something seldom acknowledged in the history of sympathy, for the most part let there be nothing, no one, no words, no practices.

The most sympathetic course is to accede to the sufferer's own wishes. For Martineau, this meant solitude. 'I cannot but wish that more consideration was given to the comfort of being alone in illness,' she wrote.

> This is so far from being understood, that, though the cases are numerous
> of sufferers who prefer, and earnestly endeavor to procure solitude, they are,
> if not resisted, wondered at, and humored for a supposed peculiarity, rather
> than seen to be reasonable; whereas, if they are listened to as the best judges
> of their own comforts, it may be found that they have reason on their side.[38]

Does such a sentiment now make for uncomfortable reading? Loneliness has become a social pathology: a phenomenon that makes pain worse.[39] Martineau likely had no access to such a concept, which is evidently a product of late modernity. She expressed a problem of too many people, whose reasons for keeping company were, on face value, to ease suffering, but on reflection were about meeting obligations and easing their own sense of suffering. Sympathy itself is pathological, a pain. Why cannot the 'invalid' herself declare the terms of sympathetic company? The 'invalid whose burden is for life' finds it 'best and happiest to admit our friends only in our easiest hours, when we can enjoy their society, and feel ourselves least of a burden'.[40]

It makes sense. Why not enjoy company when it is mutually able to enjoy yours? Moreover, Martineau found it 'indispensable to our peace of mind to be alone when in pain'. The connection of these terms, of being alone and in pain and with peace of mind, may seem like contradictions in terms. But Martineau is referring to the social burden of exhibiting pain to loved ones and friends, which in turn makes the suffering worse. 'Where welfare of body is out of the question, peace of mind becomes an object of supreme importance,' she wrote, 'and this is unattainable when we see any whom we love suffering, in our sufferings, even more than we do.'[41] Remember the veiling of Achilles, as much to protect others as to shield himself. Here, Martineau's veil was withdrawal into isolation, the closed door. This, by a stunning reversal, is the practice of sympathy. As in so many other respects, Martineau asserts the right to take control of her own experience of illness, against the rhetorical, practical, embodied, or professional claims of others. The realization that her suffering is the cause of suffering – her pain is the cause of pain – allows her to assume the role of sympathizer: not a passive object of well-wishing concern, but an active agent in protecting loved ones from an illness that is more straightforwardly endured in private.

Martineau did not look back on her own account of her days of invalidism with fondness. In her own times and afterwards, the narrative of her life was one of resignation to a life-long illness that, suddenly, went away, only for another spell of invalidism to thwart her, though not her spirit, towards the end of her life. Medical authorities with skin in the game were quick to point out, after Martineau's death, that her narrative was false: the illness that caused her death in 1876 was the same illness that had blighted her in the early 1840s, an ovarian cyst. The passage from invalidism, constant pain and suffering, and a raft of other symptoms to remission and reprieve, followed by new symptoms of discomfort and disease in later life, was all part of the natural progression and growth of the cyst. Martineau had bucked the authority of medical opinion, especially in the 'cure' she eventually found in Mesmerism, as well as bucking the authority of received accounts of the function and necessity of sympathy in a civilized society. The self-congratulatory conceit of those medical men who were quick to point out they were right all along, against the headstrong hysterical woman (the fact of a pathology of the ovary only served the argument that Martineau's behaviour was somehow connected to the essentially inescapable pathology of being female), now looks like bad taste.[42] But Martineau's extraordinary self-reliance, and the assertion of control of the terms of sympathy for pain, and its limits, now look prophetic. Hers is, in many ways, a model of the modern autopathography: an autonomous grasp of the control of an illness narrative, and a defence against the easy platitudes and practices of the obligated bearer of deepest sympathy.[43]

Empathy

Does an object feel pain? The answer is obviously 'no'. In that case why do people put pain into objects? I am standing in front of a faithful copy of *Venerina*, by Clemente Susini (1754–1814). at the Palazzo Poggi in Bologna (Fig. 17). Crafted in 1782, it is a full-size anatomical model of the human female, which can be disassembled. Yet *it* somehow does not seem to capture what this object is. *She* lies prone, abdominally skinned, not alive but nonetheless representing something not dead. The experience is uncanny. The museum in which she lies describes her as being in 'agony', at the very moment at which she 'abandons herself to death'. Yet this abandonment is undergone 'voluptuously'. The description card, suggestively, references the 'alienating effect', attributing it to a combination of 'anatomical detail, crude and repulsive', and 'a harmonious and sensual litheness', made consciously to express the 'sensitivity' of matter, the 'core' of the human. The anatomical Venus seems, while motionless, to *writhe*. Her head is thrown back, evoking the abandoned joy of Gian Lorenzo Bernini's *Teresa* (see chapter 6). The index and second fingers of her left hand seem to extend, as if to reach out. If she is in agony, it seems ecstatic.

She is sculpted, from wax, from a real model. She is, essentially, modelled after death. There have even been attempts, back-working from the wax, on the understanding that it was cast from 'life', to diagnose the cause of the woman's death.[44] Be that as it may, the model's agony, represented by the artist, does not exist. If I feel it, what is the status of that feeling? One could scarcely call it empathy, or, at least, not by contemporary definitions of that term. So what purpose does this serve?

My own experience is not evidence of how any historical actor might have felt faced with the anatomical Venus, or any other medical moulage, for that matter. As Jessica Adkins puts it, 'We are not accustomed to art, beauty, and science being part of the same project.'[45] Those who

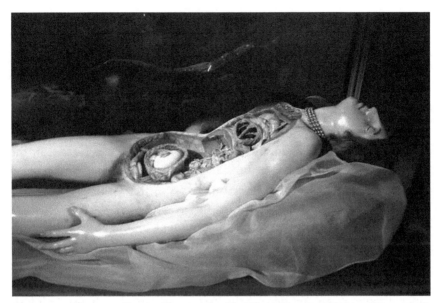

Figure 17. Clemente Susini, *Venerina* (1782), Palazzo Poggi, Bologna. (Photograph by Lisa Rocaille.)

have studied such things have documented a changing reaction to the sight of or encounter with anatomical waxworks over time, from fascination to fear to disgust.[46] Throughout the nineteenth century, critics increasingly worried that exposure to the sight of pain (even when it was mere depiction or model) benumbed the viewer to the reality of suffering in real people. Such a view lay at the heart of the campaigns against vivisection and the spectacle of blood sports.[47] In addition, critics worried that overly sentimental reactions to literary fictions – the death of Little Nell in Dickens' *The Old Curiosity Shop* (1841) being the exemplar here – would render readers unfit morally and emotionally to face real life. There was, among certain intellectual trains of nineteenth-century thought, a steadily growing conviction that it was irrational to perceive any emotion or pain emanating from inanimate objects, and that they could be borne with a passive tolerance predicated on the knowledge that there was no pain in a wax model, any more than there was pain in an anaesthetized experimental animal.[48] To think and to feel otherwise was, so the argument went, a corruption of pity through the excesses of sentimentality. Others thought that exposure to such sights was to risk their moral fibre, fully committed to the unavoidable effect of the sight of pain or blood. Such people – that is, those the rational intellects accused of having already succumbed to sentimental wallowing – simply wished for the removal or prohibition of such sights and activities. Even those intellects who stood against the sentimentalists occasionally allowed that it was only through their superior powers of mind that they could beat down both sympathy and revulsion for essentially 'dead' things.[49]

The concern betrays an admission: pain was readily perceived in the inanimate other. It still is. The specific quality of that perception changed over time, but the essence of the experience – that feeling is perceived to inhere within or emanate from an *object* – endures. Herbert Spencer called it the 'luxury of pity': an embellishment of tender and 'maternal' instincts that projected the need to nurture into the inanimate and observed the need for nurture to emanate from the inanimate. Like the child's affection for a doll, such a feeling was written off as child-like – an uncivilized atavism. Yet despite the best intentions of early psychologists and evolutionists to spirit such sentimentalism away, it persisted. New explanations were required.

Thus, the strange feelings aroused by such things as the anatomical Venus became part of the initial definition and development of the concept of 'empathy' in aesthetic theory. Fashioned into English Greek from the German *Einfühlung* – feeling into – based on the psychological investigations of Theodor Lipps (1851–1914) and the philosophical distinctions of Max Scheler (1874–1928), the original definition of empathy was 'The quality or power of projecting one's personality into or mentally identifying oneself with an object of contemplation, and so fully understanding or appreciating it.'[50] The notion of empathy as the reading or feeling of another person's emotions or experience did not arise until after the Second World War and was not popularized until much later than that. Empathy, as translated by the English psychologist Edward Titchener (1867–1927) in 1909, was a power of the subject to understand the world through a process of projection and reflection, where what came back from objects of contemplation were not the qualities intrinsic to that object, but some comprehensible aspect of the self that had been extended to the object in question.[51] *Einfühlung* was pursued, at the end of the nineteenth century, by Vernon Lee (born Violet Paget; 1856–1935) and Kit Anstruther-Thomson (1857–1921), who combined art historical and aesthetic theory with carefully studied and selected themes from a rapidly expanding field of psychological expertise. Adopting the term 'empathy' after Titchener's translation, Lee would come to understand access to the beautiful as deriving from movement. The mental response to an image was achieved through a physical response: a muscular, even visceral, attempt, however involuntary, to define the movement perceived in the picture. To understand such fleeting or micro movements, a studied introspection was employed to make the unconscious conscious. Importantly, following the physiological insights of William James (1842–1910), the way the body changed in the presence of an object, including respiratory and cardiac changes, was 'not merely a *reaction* to the form of the object but rather *constituted* the perception of form'.[52] Perception, irrespective of the rhetoric of positivity or objectivity, was *subjective*.[53] If this kind of perception applied to line, geometry, and form, why should it not apply to the line, geometry, and form of the face and the body of others? It seems as if these qualities have their own force, but it is put there by the viewer, based on what they know, at the level of feeling. For all the nineteenth-century anatomical declarations that had injected material positivism into the various faces of pain, from compassion to anguish, the theory of empathy had the capacity to upend the meaning of such faces, for they were known to the perceiver not by anything intrinsic to the movement of the pained face, but only through the subjective experience of the movements – muscular, internal, visceral – of the viewer.

I am extrapolating. The first few decades of empathy research did not make the logical extensions that I am making. Rather, the concept of empathy remained largely confined to aesthetic theory, whether among psychologists or the art world. I put it forward because it seems to afford a plausible model of understanding why pain seems, still, to emanate from objects and works of art, and how, in the end, humans can recognize pain in other beings. It would seem unwise to assign the process by which people experience the pain of objects a different explanation to the process by which they experience the pain of other people and animals. In short, it would be productive to take what is now commonly understood by the term 'empathy' and re-cast it according to the ways in which the human sense of the pain of others is a 'sticky' projection of the self.

It is necessary to take seriously the status of material objects in the history of sensation and experience. An object – it does not matter what it is, whether a book, a shoe, a sculpture, a chair, a sword, a cup – has significance insofar as it forms part of a meaningful and practical mode of existence with and among people. Objects do not, of themselves, have intrinsic value or meaning. Even the most elaborate machine or painting is just crude stuff, considered purely physically or chemically. It can be analysed for its properties and qualities utterly beyond the realm of meaning or signification. But that is not how people generally think and have thought about elaborate machines and paintings, their clothes, possessions, and the material culture all around them. Even food and drink are replete with ritual and symbolism that augment bare nourishment with cultural significance. Still, these objects cannot be reduced to their cultural presence. They exist. They have matter, and the matter matters.

The matter matters, fundamentally, in its relationality. Humans touch stuff. Their stuff touches other stuff. To service a well-known metaphor, in the process of this physical, embodied encounter, which goes beyond the haptic to include all the other senses (we touch with our eyes, we evaluate by smell, taste, sound), human feelings *stick*. On the most simplistic level, this might account for personal relationships with physical things. People put their own pain into a doll, a painting, an instrument, a bottle, and then recognize it coming *from* the place it was put. Moreover, other people can see it too, if appropriately directed. This is inherently neither harmful nor helpful, but it could be both. Recent experimental pain therapeutics have emphasized a conscious enhancement of the meaningfulness of objects that are associated with or embody a patient's pain. It might be that the patient creates an object – a sculpture, a painting, a photograph – that puts their pain into an object. Once there, the patient, struggling otherwise to communicate their experience of pain, can *see* it *stuck* there, and, in conjunction with others, can explain it. Then again, the same rationale lies behind some practices of self-harm, where the blade, the blood, the wound, and the patchwork of scars all amount to the locus of pain that is otherwise locked away, unexpressed. It is a process of sticking the pain to things, such that the things give it presence.

Taking a more complex view, conjuring with Sara Ahmed's development of the notion of stickiness, the emotions, sensations, meanings, and associations that have been stuck to an object stay stuck there.[54] For once shared, the feelings stuck to a thing remain associated with it, among the collective that has agreed that said feelings are associated with it. Moreover, the stickiness endures over time – not without slippage – such that objects 'speak' of past associations in the present. Insofar as objects become woven into the cultural fabric over time, their meaning seems to come prior to an actual encounter with them. They seem to suggest the nature of the experience to be had in the encounter. Thus, the wax anatomical Venus in Bologna was something I knew about; it was something I had wanted to see; its effect on me was, to some extent, prescribed. The Venus would 'speak' to me of her pain, her ecstasy, her humanity, just as I would be prepared to meet these expressions with bewilderment, in the knowledge that no such things exist.

This is part cultural memory, part academic memory, stuck to the Venus. It does not afford me access to the experience of the past, but it is at least suggestive of (a) an artistic and scientific attempt to put an expression of anguish, or something similar, into an object and of (b) a collective wilful attempt to keep it there, in some way, even through those efforts to hide the object from public view. To insist on an object's offensiveness is to reify it.

Humans are unlikely to stop this behaviour. If I may riff a little further on Ahmed's words, pain 'sticks to objects' and therefore pain becomes 'an approach to objects'.[55] It is something we know by moving towards those things associated with pain, such that we recognize it there. Moreover, I think this is the same process as occurs among people and other animals in pain. Humans do not, ultimately, *feel* the pain of others. They recognize the signs of pain stuck to others and experience only what they already know of pain themselves. Thinking now with Monique Scheer, if we understand people to be 'supremely practiced at the subtleties of movement, posture, gesture, and expression that connect them with others', and that these practices 'adhere to a learned repertoire that positions a person in a social field', then we have a similar account, for society and social relations, of the ways in which associations get *stuck*.[56] A pain face, a pain posture or movement, a pain word, said in a pained tone, with pained timbre, are practices of pain that both come from and contribute to the 'social field' that Scheer describes. These seemingly 'natural' expressions, written on the body or the face, or inhering in the word or the metaphor, or in the pitch or intonation, are no less a part of the cultural fabric of memory than the pain signs stuck to the anatomical Venus. The ability to command these expressions is related to the capacity of those around to read them. While they change over time, disrupted by the fault lines of politics and the way status is accorded along racial, gender, class, and age lines, and in keeping with the status and shifting parameters of medical knowledge, the stickiness nevertheless ensures a presence of the past in the present. Whether that presence is readable – whether the stickiness wears off or endures – depends on the extent to which a person's or group's positionality within a social field permits them to see and acknowledge the pain that is there. The experience of the pain of another, ultimately, depends on the extent to which the objects of that pain – including the body and the face and the words of the pained subject – can find an accord with the 'supremely practiced ... subtleties' of the observer. Every time, therefore, that the historical record throws up evidence of pains overlooked, pains ignored, pains underrated, or pains amplified or over-treated, it is to this that the historian must refer. It is, ultimately, political. Humans see pain in others only where it fits with a well-honed understanding and feeling of their own experience. As such, humans can put pain into inanimate things and see it there. They can discount the pain in people where their own associations with the sight, sound, and feel of pain do not appear to be stuck to the face, the voice, or the body, or where the body itself is a body with which they do not identify.

Empathy is a practice of the self, not access to the other, and it therefore has no intrinsic relation with altruism or the capacity for goodness. Insofar as the empathizer must recognize what is stuck to the expressions of others – the associations and signs of pain – it is necessarily limited in terms of its reach, though, as I have tried to show, oddly extended in its implications. However much it can be conclusively demonstrated that human brains respond, like a mirror, to the motor functions they see in others, it can be equally demonstrated that humans need to understand the movements they see to be able to take the perspective of making them themselves.[57] Moreover, they need to accord these movements sufficient attention to attach meaning to them and therefore to feel something in response to them. In addition, empathy research makes an all-too-easy association between motor function (movement) and access to emotion, as if what works for the movement of limbs also works for the movement of faces into grimaces and aspects of despair. This is predicated, in turn, on an understanding of a 1:1 relationship between the emotional expression that is written on the face and the experience of the emotion identified by that expression. Such a relationship has been seriously questioned, not least by historians of emotion.[58] Thinking back to the figural face, no face automatically, or by some timeless natural law, tells us what the emotion *behind* it is. If it were true, then the pained faces, and the pain objects for that matter, of the past would be immediately transparent to us. They are self-evidently not transparent. Again, thinking with Scheer, if expressions and gestures and postures and language are all learned and practised behaviour, and if it is the practices themselves that give shape and meaning to the feelings that needs must be expressed, then it is from the context alone that anyone can derive the pain experience of another. If I can empathize with you, just as I may empathize with the fictional injuries of an actor in a film, or with the childhood teddy bear who has lost an eye, it is not because of something intrinsically and transcendentally human about me; it is not because of some ancient system of mirrors in the brain. On the contrary, it is because I am situated in such a way as to share these signs of pain.

The lesson to be derived from *stuff* is that such sharing, a coherence around something mutually sticking us together, is fallible. I might be wrong about your pain. If I empathize with an injured doll, maybe it confirms me as human, but I am in error. If, on the other hand, I express my pain in sculpture, sticking it there, and you do not see it, then perhaps you are in error. If I readily see the pain of an historical actor and feel I have empathic access to it, I *might* be in error again. I cannot assume that the social field in which I understand the signs of pain is the same as the social field of any given past. It may turn out to be remarkably similar. It may not. To understand pain in the past, just as to understand pain in the present, is to acquaint oneself with those 'supremely practiced ... subtleties'. Like learning to play a musical instrument from scratch, accustoming oneself to the subtleties of another social field's intricate gestures and expressions can be disturbing, disorientating, difficult. Whether pain is easily recognized or readily dismissed, it would be as well to test why phenomena are so straightforwardly categorized. Speaking historically, I know I am on the right track when I am, metaphorically, all fingers and thumbs with the pain of others.

There are huge risks in not adopting such a stance. Empathy, on face value, might be no less an exclusionary and violent practice than was the universal sympathy of the eighteenth and nineteenth centuries. For me to recognize your pain is a projection, on my part, that you are *like* me, or at the very least understandable to me. You conform to my experiences, my judgement, the context of my own possibilities. To fail to recognize your pain or, worse, to deny your pain is, at least in potential, a choice to put you outside of the context of my own possibilities and therefore to dehumanize or invalidate your experiences. In contemporary parlance, this is often expressed as 'belief'. When someone makes a claim of having suffered, some dismiss those claims and others say 'I believe you.' To believe is not necessarily to understand. It does not imply feeling with. It does not equate to empathy. It acknowledges that, perhaps, there is suffering beyond my ken. Someone is expressing it and that is sufficient. If we rely on empathy, whether we are reading the present or the past, we might, in the process of finding emotions and experiences with which we can identify, render invisible or irrelevant those emotions and experiences with which we cannot.

SIX

Contextualizing
Pleasure and Punishment

If pain is subjective and mutable, unpredictable and unreliable, is it possible to go further in demonstrating this, to take a measure of pain's inherent immeasurability? There is the testimony of the injured and diseased: a cut, a pinch, or a burn feels differently to different people and even differently to the same people at different times. Context, attention, experience, and emotion all mediate the meanings that humans make of sensory input. It may be useful to think of pain not as a sensory experience at all, but as an experience that is sometimes produced as a result of the situated processing and evaluation of sensory information. When a painful experience is produced, it is not necessarily a negative experience; sometimes, pain is the height of ecstasy, be it religious or sexual. Sometimes, painful experience is laden with such terror that it serves as a gruesome means of administering punishment, or of extracting confessions. This chapter weighs all of this in the balance, looking at the extremes of contextual difference in pain states, from torture and corporal punishment and disciplinary pedagogy (learning by the rod) to sadomasochism, to the conquering of the 'pain barrier' in sport. The aim is to show that pain can never be essentialized as a negative experience without understanding the ways in which contextual and political framing superadd fear, anxiety, repression, punishment, and intentionality to the essence of what pain is. For the same reasons, this affords the possibility that pain can be ecstasy or joy.

Torture Worlds

Elaine Scarry's famous treatise on torture begins with a distinction I feel I must collapse: that between 'real' pain and its 'felt experience'. In torture, she says, 'Real pain, agonizing pain, is inflicted on a person; but torture, which contains specific acts of inflicting pain, is also itself a demonstration and magnification of the felt-experience of pain.' Here she refers to the ways in which the production of bodily pain

> bestows visibility on the structure and enormity of what is usually private and incommunicable, contained within the boundaries of the sufferer's body. It then goes on to deny, to falsify, the reality of the very thing it has itself objectified by a perceptual shift which converts the vision of suffering into the wholly illusory but, to the torturers and the regime they represent, wholly convincing spectacles of power.[1]

The 'conversion of absolute pain into the fiction of absolute power' is part of torture's aim, according to Scarry, thus transforming the experience of 'real pain' into something else, something more. Not only does Scarry's account seem to rest on the inherent relationship of the wound and bodily pain, but it also rests on the preservation of the distinction between physical and psychological pain. For, she says, 'Physical pain is able to obliterate psychological pain because it obliterates all psychological content, painful, pleasurable, and neutral.' It has the 'power to end all aspects of self and world'.[2] Later, Scarry insists that 'physical pain' is 'exceptional in the whole fabric of psychic, somatic, and perceptual states for being the only one that has no object ... in the external world'.[3]

It is clear from many different disciplinary accounts that the premises of Scarry's argument must be wrong, for there is no direct relation between physical injury and the feeling of pain, just as there is no separation of bodily pain from psychological pain. In fact, one might strongly argue that there is no bodily pain *without* psychological involvement. The distinction between 'real' pain – that is, the production in the body of a sensation entirely and only in relation to its injuries – and the experience of pain is a false one. There is no such thing as 'physical pain' without an 'object in the external world', because physical pain is inseparable from the fear, anxiety, despair, and so on, that make it meaningful. These things, as Scarry herself points out, are intentional – they do have objects in the world. Pain is nothing if it has no meaning associated with it. The pain experienced in torture is so terrible precisely because of its contextual, emotional, and political framing. It is not so much world-destroying as insistent that all experience must be filtered through the world it creates, which is not to say it is meaningless, but rather it is richly meaningful in the strictest coercive terms. Were it not for this psychological coercion – the power, the fear – the infliction of bodily injury would not amount to torture at all. It is only the context that separates medieval torture from medieval surgery, but that *only* is of great moment. It defines the quality of fear, of despair or hope, and the political framing of help and harm, recoverability and obliteration, sympathy and hostility. Scarry's argument can be turned on its head. Torture is itself of the world, and it expresses a specific context and imposes it on the victim. The victim, whether in submission or resistance, partakes of that world and makes their own place in it, or outside it. There is no worldless place, no place or space or time that is context-free. Torture is no exception.

Pain in torture is therefore mutable. It is richly meaningful for the victim, but this meaningfulness is contextual, changeable, and perforce political. In re-visiting the subject, I want to show how in certain situations the torture victim is distinctly aware of the world possibilities beyond the specific expression of power of the torturers. I also want to show that the symbolic representation of the pains of torture become contestable within the world in which they are represented. Think back to the example of St Agatha and the symbolism of her torture. Compelled to give up her faith, she resisted. The show of power and authority that inhered in the wounds that were administered to her became the evidence of a higher power: faith. The marks of injury and the experience of suffering torture re-focus the piety of the victim, and they become outward cultural symbols of the virtue that inheres in forbearance. Worldly power and fleshly power are defeated time and again in martyrological representation, as the disfigurement of the body under torture comes to stand for the failure of pain as a coercive device. Instead, the signs of pain are intentionalized precisely towards the thing that is supposed to be rejected: God.

Wherever one looks in the annals of history, one finds similar stories of the ineffectiveness of torture for changing convictions and beliefs, political as well as spiritual. Contra the plotline of George Orwell's *1984*, perhaps the modern archetypal myth of torture's effectiveness, in which torture is used as the instrument of conformity and the means to effecting a betrayal of self and those one loves, the reality of torture is that it galvanizes or tempers convictions. Fire may burn the flesh, but it may harden precisely that part of the spirit it is designed to break.[4] This is not to say that torture does not do great harm. Those who survive torture are often condemned to live with the memory of the trauma, a lifelong pain that can unravel the seams of existence.[5] But this is neither the intention nor a desirable goal of torture.

Despite this, for much of history, torture was considered necessary, acceptable, and effective by those authorities that employed it. From antiquity to the early modern period in Europe, a guiding assumption was that pain was a medium of truth, for it would purify sin. The principle was thought to work in questions of earthly penal law as well as in a spiritual sense. To confess was meant to be painful, both in terms of the process of confession and in the *penance* that followed from it. Confession in narrowly legal terms was also thought to be better through the medium of pain.[6] In other parts of the world, as in China, similar assumptions meant torture occupied a central place in the justice system over millennia.[7] Yet, despite the longevity of this view, it was always fraught with the possibility of reversal. For, as is now known, torture is more likely to produce false information and false confession than it is to reveal the truth. For all that torture may have confirmed *a priori* assumptions about guilt, the conviction with which it could be thought to have proven guilt remained shaky. There were additional risks. In the case of heretics and others tortured for their beliefs, the conviction that torture would reveal the truth would be tested by those who would not betray their faith. An unchanged or perhaps a more radical heretic, after torture, might be evidence that they, not their torturers, were on the right side. As for the torture of criminals, a failure to elicit a confession, or any valid intelligence, risked the whole logic and penal rationale of torture. If those presumed to be guilty prior to torture did not reveal their guilt in the process of torture, they may not have been considered less guilty, but the authority of the system was undermined.

These paradoxes of the wielding of pain as an instrument of power and the power of pain to undermine that same power were central historical structural elements of the experience of pain throughout the medieval period in Europe.[8] Esther Cohen attests that 'As early as the second century there ran the thread of uncomfortable knowledge that some (or most) people would say anything their questioner wanted to hear in order to free themselves from torture.'[9] As such, despite a general view that it was 'common' at all times, Cohen has shown that most medieval trials were resolved without having recourse to torture.[10]

Discipline and Punish

Pain has often been promised as the reward of non-compliance. It is the knowledge of what lies in store that keeps people on the straight and narrow, or so the logic runs. But to have this knowledge, one must have the example of the punishment in question, which means that the deterrent cannot be too successful lest it be forgot. The archives are over-stuffed with accounts of corporal punishment, which shows the place of pain in the upholding of justice, but just as often the fortitude of those who sought justice irrespective of the promise of pain. For while there are many types and degrees of corporal punishment, the need to employ them is often suggestive of an authority that cannot justify itself on its own terms, resorting therefore to fear, shame, and suffering to keep people in line. To that extent, the existence of corporal punishment is suggestive of weakness. That so many took the risk of being subjected to penal retribution suggests that, while terrible, pain knowledge did not necessarily stand in the way of a good cause. There is a central contra-diction to the notion of corporal punishment, especially as a public spectacle, in an historical context that otherwise valorized the experience of pain and fortitude in the face of suffering as pious virtues. The public spectacle, designed as both warning, expression of power, and enter-tainment, risked falling into standard martyrological tropes, especially if the victim seemed to bear the punishment well. A theological logic would suggest that the infliction of bodily pain, especially over matters of conscience, was to reward the 'criminal'.[11]

All of which is not to say that corporal punishment was always unjust, for in situated terms it was duly meted out to those who transgressed just laws, in full knowledge that this was a consequence if caught. Contextual notions of justice must be given their due, but that does not mean that they are not subject to analytical interrogation. The history of corporal punishment that was designed to repress, humiliate, and otherwise denigrate certain types of people can be explored in some depth. The options here are distressingly abundant, from the corporal abuse of slaves on American plantations, to the imposition of *peine forte et dure* on those who refused to submit to what they perceived to be the illegitimacy of worldly courts for matters of conscience and belief, to the cane, strap, or rod that was a standard of English schooling until well into the second half of the twentieth century.[12] I choose, through the material grotesqueness of an instrument of punishment, to focus on the subjection of women in early modern Europe.

The scold's bridle or branks is an ugly affair. Its image was designed to ridicule the wearer and strike fear into those who saw it, who might themselves be subjected to it. The example here (Fig. 18) is German, but the practice was widespread. The mask is of iron and surrounds the head. Missing from this example is the mouth bit, a common feature across all types of bridle design. Usually also of iron, the bit served as gag and torture device. Often, these bits had sharp points or nails in them to pierce the tongue. The purpose, simply, was to painfully prevent a woman, castigated as a 'scold' or 'shrew', from speaking. More broadly, the purpose was to keep women from speaking against authority, or from assuming for themselves a status beyond their sex. It was an instrument of patriarchal enforcement that showed to all who saw it being worn that women had no stake in society, no stake in politics, no stake in the way things worked. Ralph Gardiner (b. 1625), writing from prison to petition Oliver Cromwell, documented its use in Newcastle in 1655, reporting an eyewitness account of Ann Bidlestone being driven through the streets by an Officer of the Corporation,

> holding a rope in his hand, the other end fastened to an Engine called the Branks, which is like a Crown, it being of Iron, which was musled over the head and face, with a great gap or tongue of Iron forced into the mouth, which forced the blood out. And that is the punishment which the Magistrates do inflict upon chiding, and scoulding women

– noting that the witness had 'often seen the like done to others'.[13] While Lynda Boose could not find many formal records of the scold being used as punishment, she speculated that this was because, in England at any rate, the courts knew it was not legal. It was, in effect, an illegal instrument of torture employed by magistrates. Despite this official blank in the records, plenty of bridles exist, as well as cultural references thereto, such that Boose could find it in use in 'at least five English

Figure 18. Scold's bridle (sixteenth–eighteenth century), Science Museum, London. (Wellcome Collection.)

counties' as well as across Scotland in the sixteenth and seventeenth centuries. She asserts, reasonably, that the bridle's 'use and notoriety were widespread enough for it to have been an agent in the historical production of women's silence'.[14] The bridle itself, therefore, represents the pain inflicted in the space where women's voices should have been.

There are precious few first-hand accounts of the experience of having to wear a scold's bridle, but one is provided by Dorothy Waugh in 1656. She was a follower of the Quaker martyr James Parnell (1636–56) and had had the temerity to speak in public, in Carlisle, against 'deceit and ungodly practices'.[15] She was summarily removed to a prison and visited by the mayor, who reacted furiously to Waugh's obstinacy, calling for the bridle to be worn for three hours. Waugh does not relate the pain, but the weight, the size, and the violence of the procedure. The bridle was like a steel cap, and my hat being violently plucked off, which was pinned to my head, whereby they tore my clothes to put on their bridle, as they called it, which was a stone weight of iron ... and three bars of iron to come over my face, and a piece of it was put in my mouth, which was unreasonable big a thing for that place, as cannot be well related, which was locked to my head, and so I stood their time with my hands bound behind me with the stone weight of iron on my head, and the bit in my mouth to keep me from speaking.

The attempted effect was to shame her, for she recounts that the 'mayor said he would make me an example to all that should ever come in that name', but it seems she had the pity of her witnesses, who 'were broken into tears' to see her 'so violently abused'. The mayor chided their '*foolish pity*', and the jailer charged every visitor two-pence admission. Later she was forced to wear the bridle again to be sent home, 'whipped' through the streets (it is unclear if this is a literal whipping), under the 'vile and unsavoury words' of the mayor. Again, the description is not of pain, but of the attempt to shame.[16]

The silence about pain is curious, for there can be little doubt that considerable suffering would have been the result for most people entrapped in such a device. But it is the context in which the device comes to be on the head that is key, for here is the physical infliction of authority – the binding of the limbs to prevent resistance, the forcible removal of headwear and clothing, the violent procedure of getting the bridle over the head and the bit into the mouth – which must have induced considerable alarm. Whatever physical pain may have been caused by the weight, by the iron on the skin, by the spiked bit in the mouth, would have been part of an atmosphere designed to create both shame and fearful obedience. To whatever extent the physical pain may have been endured, it was part of an atmosphere of fierce resistance. Either way, the bridle was a sign at once of the power and fragility of patriarchy, a sign of pain and a sign of resistance to pain, a sign of what happened to women who spoke out of turn and a sign of the just.

The allure of such a corporeal nightmare endured in practice into the nineteenth century, and thereafter some British writers congratulated themselves with titillating popular essays on the muzzling of 'ladies', even in the name of celebrating modern civilization's progress.[17] But the practical use of the bridle had already endured beyond early modern Europe, having been picked up in plantations as an effective means of marking the status of slaves. As Robin Blackburn has put it, 'The slave condition could also be understood within the terms of patriarchal ideology as one which was emasculated and "feminized"; the "scold's bridle" used to gag impertinent women was to reappear on the plantations, as did ducking or burning as weapons of "correction" or terror.'[18] What is most striking, considering the extent of the use of the bridle and the long period of its employment, is just how rare first-hand testimony of the experience of the bridle is. Waugh's account stands alone as a piece of writing produced after she had been forcibly silenced. We must accept the overwhelming silence of the archive not as a reason to speculate on whether or not the widespread use of the bridle has been exaggerated, but as a sign of a great unvoiced howl of pain and suffering, in contexts of fear, shame, injustice, and repression.

Agony and Ecstasy

The centrality of context to experience is exemplified by the case of corporal punishment as a pedagogical aid. The word *discipline* as a means of using punishment as a specific training aid refers explicitly to the whip used to flagellate the buttocks and stems from the ascetic practices of certain monastic orders. Per the previous discussion about the virtuosity of pain as a practice of piety, this fits in. But the transference of *discipline* to pedagogical spaces is predicated on the notion that pain is itself pedagogically useful, both in terms of memory and learning and in terms of guiding behaviour. The overwhelming result of the use of the cane, rod, birch, and paddle in the corporal punishment of children has been lasting psychological trauma, itself played out in situated ways, that has, in some cases, affected entire communities and cultures. Yet it was only in 1979 that Sweden became the first country completely to ban the corporal punishment of children and to collapse any distinction between punishment and abuse.[19] As corporal punishment came under increasing scrutiny and prohibition across the world, scholars attempted to come up with frameworks for understanding the traumatic effect of school abuse of children, noting situational differences in cultural tolerance of the infliction of pain.[20] Since then, the floodgates have opened on the lasting and intergenerational harm done in Residential Schools in Canada, amounting to cultural genocide, as part of a colonialist vision of nation and civilization building.[21] The abuse was not only physical, though this physicality was ever present.[22] Research from across the world has testified to a late modern awareness of the unavoidable damage done by corporal punishment.[23] For the centuries in which it went unremarked or unchallenged, the damage done has to be enfolded into interpretations of silence, silencing, cultural justification, and recapitulation. Pain and trauma inflicted deliberately and wilfully on children are part of the cultural-historical fabric, existing, by and large, outside of the framework of pain and trauma studies.

Despite all this trauma, there is nonetheless a counter-narrative of the experience of pleasurable discipline. But context is key. Here I focus not on the abuses of school-based discipline (the debased pleasures of the administrator of pain in children) but on the consensual (if nonetheless subversive) sexology of discipline and the experience of pleasure in the receipt of pain.[24] The relation of pain and pleasure through sex is ancient, though not in fixed terms. The *Kama Sutra* famously states that 'all the places that can be kissed are also the places that can be bitten'.[25] But to get to the bottom of what is sometimes known as the 'English vice', I turn first to *The Virtuoso*, a play from 1676 by Thomas Shadwell (1642–92). It is, according to Lesley Hall, possibly the first account of pain and sexual pleasure specific to pedagogical 'discipline'. The experience of the rod at school is carried forward by the character Snarl into adulthood as a fetish. Thereafter, the allusion to sexual pleasure derived through pain from the rod or cane became a common feature of English literary and artistic culture. In his genre-defining *Fanny Hill* (1748/9), for example, John Cleland (1709–89) portrays Mr Barville's enjoyment of sex as dependent upon the whip, with the explicit allusion to school culture. He was 'condemned to have his pleasure lashed into him, as boys have their learning'.[26] Here and elsewhere, as in *A Harlot's Progress* (1731–2) by William Hogarth (1697–1764), in which the whip appears as an accoutrement of the life of a prostitute, there is a clear tension between the representation of perversity, with the places and practices of social and moral transgression that encapsulate it, and the givenness of the relationship between sexual pleasure and pain, as if this 'vice' needed no further explanation.

Nonetheless, it received numerous attempts at explanation, beginning in the seventeenth century with an account by Johann Heinrich Meibom (1590–1655) of sexual flagellation, buried in the respectability of Latin in 1629, translated into English in 1761 as *A Treatise of the Use of Flogging in Venereal Affairs.* He gives the practice ancient roots and thus accounts for it being customary, but ultimately offers a functional, physiological explanation relating to the kidneys, the production of semen, and the transference of heat. While this is the province of the 'perverse and frenzical appetite', it is comprehended through a common biology, or perhaps animality would be nearer the mark.[27] The allusion to the beast would endure into the formalization of sexology at the turn of the twentieth century, the most prominent English exponent of which was Havelock Ellis (1859–1939). Inspired in part by Richard von Krafft-Ebing and Albert Moll, Ellis's 1903 work *Love and Pain* referred to animality undergirding humanity as an explanation of the 'intimate and inevitable association ... of combat ... with the process of courtship', in turn an explanation of the relationship of sex and pain.[28] Civilization, according to this view, corrupted animality, for the violent expression of male power was indulged at the expense of female pleasure. Nonetheless, Ellis could imagine the derivation of pleasure from submission, and he understood that pain was a normative part of many acts of love. It was not ultimately power that activated the ecstasy of sadomasochists, but pain itself, because pain 'is the most powerful of all methods for arousing emotion'. The association of anger and fear with pain states were what made pain meaningful and, looking again to the animal world and to the logics of evolution, Ellis saw that these were integral to sexual selection. There were boundaries here of normal sexual behaviour and transgression, but it is noteworthy that anger in the male and fear in the female constituted normative dispositions for Ellis in the act of physical love, activated for both parties through pain. The transgression of this boundary only occurred when pain was an 'indispensable stimulant to the sexual system'.[29] Among European sexologists, such a view was not controversial. Albert von Schrenck-Notzing (1862–1929) even named the phenomenon of sexual pleasure through pain: algolagnia.[30]

Spiritual ecstasies wrought by painful experiences mirror the indulgences of the flesh, or at least it is easy enough to see such a reflection if one turns back to the virtuosity of pain in religious asceticism. Was it a form of masochism? John Yamamoto-Wilson suggests that the medieval and early modern prevalence of pain and its orientation towards virtue, piety, and salvation meant that there was no need for a formal definition of something akin to masochism. Intentionalizing pain as divine love made everyone a lover of pain, in a sense. But this was phenomenologically distinct from sexual pleasure, even if the Reformation would newly mark out the sin of seeking out pain for pleasurable purposes.[31] Certainly the imagery of Catholic flagellation was employed in later iterations of sexual inversion. In *Venus im Pelz* (1870) by Leopold von Sacher-Masoch (1836–95), Severin, the central character, abandons himself through the ecstasies of martyrdom, but for all the allusions to Catholicism, his relationship with Wanda is secular and material, built on interpersonal dynamics of power and its lack. It is a misdirection to seek in masochism the pleasurable pains of the ascetic.[32]

To get at this phenomenological distinction, one can re-approach one of the most famous early modern exemplars of apparently sexually pleasurable pain. The emblem of ecstasy in pain is Teresa of Ávila (1515–82), a Carmelite nun and mystic from what is now central Spain. A devotion to the mortification of the flesh caused Teresa to become ill, and led her to numerous reflections on pain, the relation of body and soul, and to a devout wish for union with God. She recounts a vision, which she repeatedly experienced, that confounds understanding. Some scholars have tried to diagnose her in earthly terms, but it is much more important to understand her in situated terms.[33] The passage, drawn from her own account of her life, is usually reduced to a few key lines, but I reproduce it here at length so that it can be comprehensively unpacked. I use the canonical translation of E. Allison Peers, but I have altered key words according to a close reading of Teresa's Spanish, and these changes are in italics:

> It pleased the Lord that I should sometimes see the following vision. I would see beside me, on my left hand, an angel in bodily form. ... He was not tall, but short, and very beautiful, his face so aflame that he appeared to be one of the highest types of angel who seem to be all afire. ... In his hands I saw a long golden spear and at the end of the iron tip I seemed to see a point of fire. With this he seemed to pierce my heart several times so that it

penetrated to my entrails. When he drew it out, I thought he was drawing them out with it and he left me completely *scorched* [*abrasada*] with a great love for God. The pain was so *great* [*grande*] that it made me utter several moans; and so excessive was the *gentleness* [*suavidad*] caused me by this *great* [*grandisimo*] pain that one can never wish to lose it, nor will one's soul be content with anything less than God. It is not bodily pain, but spiritual, though the body has a share in it – indeed, a great share. So sweet *is the courtship* [*requiebro*] which pass[es] between the soul and God that if anyone thinks I am lying I beseech Good, in His goodness, to give him the same experience.

During the days that this continued, I went about as if in a stupor. I had no wish to see or speak with anyone, but only to *embrace my suffering* [*abrazarme con mi pena*], which caused me greater *glory* [*gloria*] than any that can come from the whole of creation. I was like this on several occasions, when the Lord was pleased to send me these raptures, and so deep were they that, even when I was with other people, I could not resist them; so, greatly to my distress, they began to be talked about … [*B*]*efore* [*antes*] this *suffering* [*pena*] of which I am now speaking begins, the Lord seems to transport the soul and to send it into an ecstasy, so that *there is no place for sorrow or for suffering* [*no hay lugar de tener pena, ni de padecer*] because it immediately begins to experience *joy* [*gozar*].[34]

The amendments to the translation seem necessary, for there is a clear transition from the first part of the account when Teresa talks of physical and spiritual pain as *dolor* to the second part of the account when she seems to talk about suffering as *pena*. To render both words as 'pain' flattens out the translation. For most purposes it may not matter, but here I think it is important. There is one other significant correction: the Spanish marks the transportation of the soul into ecstasy as *before* this suffering begins, whereas the canonical English translation has it happen *when* the suffering begins. Again, the distinction is important.

The content of the vision cannot be escaped: Teresa has her heart physically pierced and her entrails pulled out. She is burned by this. I resist the accepted translation of being 'afire' to avoid a metaphor of passion. The scorching seems more literal in this passage. Teresa frames the effect on her of the great pain – gentleness, *suavidad* – in a way that is difficult to comprehend. It is as if all potential resistance is erased by the physical/

spiritual pain, such that she is smoothed out, rendered inert, mellowed by it. It is a complete openness to the direct experience of God's love. While the standard English translation refers to the 'colloquies of love' between the soul and God in this state, Teresa more narrowly defines this as a process of wooing, an exchange of compliments perhaps, or, as I put it here, a courtship. It is the experience of the approach towards union with God.

The lexical shift from *dolor* to *pena* indicates that while there is spiritual and bodily pain, there is no *suffering*, save for the 'distress' (Teresa uses *pena* in this instance too) of these raptures being picked up in public. This is a crucial distinction, for Teresa's pathway to suffering is cut off by the transportation of her soul to a state of ecstasy *before* the pain begins.[35] She seems to look on this spiritual and bodily pain as if in the abstract, but her experience is entirely one of joy. She therefore embraces her suffering while experiencing no suffering. The context of the divine vision and her self-understanding within this vision enabled her to process pain as joy, as the experience of God's love, as ecstatic rapture.

Perhaps understandably, the popular reception of Teresa has struggled to disentangle this divine ecstasy from earthly *eros*. Famously realized by Gian Lorenzo Bernini (1598–1680) in his sculpture completed in 1652, and still standing in the church of Santa Maria della Vittoria in Rome, Teresa is captured in bodily ecstasy, compounding fleshly sensuality and spiritual abandonment, especially in the posture, tilt of the head, and facial expression. Teresa's own account of ecstasy, in which all the senses are consumed such that the body itself is frozen, would tend to negate the possibility of such a reclining swoon, for only the soul would swoon. The rapture, or trance-like state, would render her rooted in whatever position she was in. The artist, and the reader of Teresa's own words, is faced with the problem of imagining an experience and expression of the soul alone, and the effect is most easily achieved via bodily and facial metaphor. Spiritual pain and ecstasy are relocated back in the body as physical, sensual ecstasy. The visual metaphor for divine union, for this mystical combination of agony and joy, quickly became canonical. Teresa's painful ecstasy was not, despite its depiction, erotic. Nonetheless, she has long since been the model of the earth-bound orgasm.[36]

Pushing the Pain Barrier

At about the twenty-mile mark in the Berlin marathon of 2012, I looked at my feet for the first time. I had struggled with blisters throughout months of training, which had made islands of my big toes. From step one in the race, I was in pain, but I had learned to live inside it, to rely on its predictable presence with each impact to mark time, to keep pace. I was trying to abstract it, to think about it not as pain but as a curious bodily experience. For the most part, this worked as a strategy. I ran through the pain barrier. Then I looked down.

The sight of blood affects people differently depending on the context. It does not have to signify anything. When I added the sight of my own blood seeping out of the tops of both of my shoes to the pain in my feet, I was beset by a sudden and almost overwhelming sense of alarm and began to shake, to take shorter, irregular breaths, to feel burning in my eyes and a sick metallic taste in my mouth. A whole physiological and sensory process slammed into my conscious awareness and screamed a single, compelling word: stop. The blood leaking from my shoes was a visual sign that I had been consciously avoiding. Having clocked my feet, I suddenly owned them. These were *my* feet and this was *my* pain. The pain barrier through which I had been running was suddenly a far more formidable obstacle.

I did not stop. Most people don't (and people run through far worse). For the following fifty minutes or so, I tried to keep my eyes off my feet and to think only of the feeling of finishing. I was constantly aware of the wetness in my shoes and what it was, but I pushed on. In the home stretch, running towards the Brandenburg Gate, surrounded by thousands, the pain went away. I was lifted by a sudden ecstasy, a raw emotionality that I cannot name. The shaking was there, and a barely resistible urge to break down in tears, but I felt carried home. Euphoria. I felt no pain for the next few hours. The next day, I could barely walk.

There is a whole genre of sporting narratives of this type and it is not new. In 1809, Robert Barclay Allardice of Ury (Captain Barclay; 1779–1854) undertook to walk 1,000 miles in 1,000 hours at the rate of one mile per hour, making for a task of forty-two days' duration, during which time he would have little sleep or rest. A significant sum of money was on the line, and no little honour and celebrity to boot. The feat took place on a prepared course at Newmarket and generated considerable fame for the pedestrian athlete. In 1813, Walter Thom published a history of pedestrianism in which Captain Barclay's 1,000-mile challenge was documented in some detail. The word 'pain' does not appear until the twelfth night, when he 'complained of pains in the back of his neck and shoulders'. Thereafter, it appears frequently. Day 13, 'pain in the legs, particularly in the back tendons'; day 14, 'more pain in his legs'; day 15, same, but later with 'more pain than before', which ceased after about 100 yards of walking; day 16, an increase of leg pain, and so on. The pain would ebb and flow through the day, at times making it difficult to walk. Things would look better for a while and then the pain would return. By the twentieth day, the pain was 'increasing' and he was 'somewhat stiff in his motion'. The following day, he was 'much worse; pain increased; walked heavily, and not in good spirits'. The leg pain was joined by foot pain. By day 22, a doctor was called, but a warm bath and a massage with a 'small phial' of liquid did not improve matters. Still the pain ebbed and flowed, such that some miles were accomplished with great difficulty, in great agony, and others with little pain at all. On day 23, Barclay's feet and leg pains were joined by a toothache and a fever, such that he was 'very ill and fretful; complained much of his legs and feet, and walked with difficulty'.

In the early hours of day 24, Barclay was worse still, with continuing difficulty in walking, toothache, and distress 'from want of sleep'. The toothache slowly abated, but the prescribed warm bath 'had softened his feet so much, that they became unable to bear the pressure of his body'. Baths abandoned, a hot flannel was instead applied to the painful parts, which 'had the effect to cause the pains in his legs and thighs to remove from one part to another'. By the early hours of day 26, he was 'very ill and very stiff; great difficulty in walking, and complained much of pain', and by 3 a.m. was 'rather worse'. Again, the light brought some salve and on he walked, but the pattern of night-time agonies and despair continued. By day 29, he was in 'great pain; was very stiff, and had much difficulty in walking', and in the early hours of day 30 he 'was so very stiff he could scarcely rise, and when he got up could scarcely stand'. Assistance in getting up would from this point be required. By day 32, 'the back tendons of his legs shrunk up' when he rested, 'and the pain was excessive during the time of relaxing them', but there was a crucial mitigating factor. Throughout this narrative Thom documented Barclay's 'spirits' and 'appetite', but for the first time here he introduced his 'unconquerable' courage.

Still, he weakened under the weight of a great coat soaked by rain, and at the beginning of the thirty-fourth day 'the pain in his legs' was 'excessive'. He 'could not move without crying out'. At 3 a.m., he 'could scarcely move'. Same the next day, where he could not rise without being lifted: 'To have seen him at this time, one would have thought that it would be impossible for him to go on, he was so debilitated and in such agony, but he was determined to complete the match at all risques.' The next day he was still worse, 'so very ill indeed, that it became difficult to manage his time, for he … was now so slow that he had but little time for rest'. In the early morning of day 39, 'the want of rest began to affect him dreadfully; very stiff, could not stand'. So it continued until the end, save for the last day, when he was 'in better spirits than usual'. In the early afternoon, 'to appearance he was much better, and walked with less difficulty'. He completed the feat and 'the crowd gave three cheers'.[37]

Barclay's achievement remains remarkable, but the modern mass pursuit of distance running will perhaps make it seem accessible and relatable to many. Lost to most contemporary readers, however, is the context of courage and the military association of pluck in the face of adversity on the field of sport with bravery under fire. Also lost is the context of honour, which was a major factor in both sporting endeavour and sporting endurance. For the majority of the time it took to walk those 1,000 miles, Barclay complained of pain and distress, yet he continued. The pain was worth it, and by no means only in pecuniary terms.

One finds parallels in more recent times, though the affective context of going through the pain barrier has changed. Consider the account by footballer Roy Keane (b. 1971) of his later playing career at Celtic in 2006, for example, when he was 'taking painkillers before every match. An injection in the bum.' 'The cause of the pain was a labral tear of the hip,' and Keane 'understood that playing on could worsen the tear. I was taking an injection before the game and one at half-time, just to get through. And you do get through, but the consequences arrive the next day.' Why carry on like this? Because of 'the shame'. Keane was 'under contract. People had bought jerseys with my name on them. I didn't want to let anyone down.' Moreover, he lived with his own reputation as a tough guy. The memories of peak performance and peak attitude were too recent to submit to 'screaming' pain.[38] Is this kind of thing about mind over matter? To some extent, yes, but it is more the case of context over injury. The event itself, the whole context of one's goals, training, the meaning derived from the prospect of achievement, a sense of responsibility or commitment: all these things command more attention, in the moment, than the injury, which is duly relegated.

Ten years earlier, American gymnast Kerri Strug (b. 1977) was vaulting while in great pain, delivering Olympic gold to the United States in the team event by famously appearing to land on one leg after the ankle in the other one seemed to snap. She would later be diagnosed with a third-degree lateral sprain. At the time, Strug's courage was valorized in both personal and nationalist terms. The *New York Times* reported that she 'looked like a clip from one of those grainy black-and-white' war movies where 'the American platoon always had one hero who took a hit on the last patrol, but carried the flag up the hill anyway'. In the moment prior to the vault, her coach had pleaded 'we need it, we need it', with the 'we' seemingly encompassing the team and its attendants and the entire nation, with the old enemy Russia standing by waiting to snatch victory. Even then, the *Times* was aware of 'criticisms that young women's bodies are too fragile for the ever-increasing stress of training and competition', in a context of media scrutiny of 'injuries and eating disorders'. But this was antithetical to 'girl power' and the coach was unapologetic: 'All this criticism is cheap publicity. There are thousands of girls who love this sport. There are six kids [the US team] with their eyes wide open. She wants to go out there.'[39] And all of this was given an extra twist because Strug was thought to have a 'personal history of faltering under pressure', and her coach said that 'She is not a fighter like some of the others.' He contended: 'People think these girls are fragile dolls. They're not. They're courageous.'[40] Strug would reflect that 'This is what you dream about from when you're 5 years old. I wasn't going to stop.'[41] Rick Weinberg, writing for ESPN, described Strug holding 'the pose for a few seconds' when she landed, 'just long enough to please the judges, then she falls to the floor and grimaces in agonizing pain as the ovation continues'.[42] Strug went through the pain barrier in the name of nation, to a fanfare of military analogies, to chase a 'dream', under severe pressure in an asymmetrical power dynamic.

Contexts change. In the 2020 Olympics, staged a year late because of the COVID-19 pandemic, American gymnast Simone Biles (b. 1997) was almost universally praised for declining to go on when beset by mental illness. The landscape of 'bravery' and courage had entirely altered. Non-performance, saying 'no', standing up to the pressure by refusing to be pushed into its maw: all these things now amounted to courage. To say the pain was real and a barrier was a watershed moment in high-profile sport. Strug's courage in 1996 was re-appraised according to the new standard, apparently even by Strug herself. Focus was tightened on the agency of the gymnast in making decisions with her own body, with arguments that Strug had not been able to decide for herself.[43] The sport had already been blown apart by evidence of widespread abuse on many levels, such that bravely standing up and doing the right thing now meant saying 'no' and, if needs be, blowing the whistle on abusers.[44] The erasure of physical pain had been supplanted by the foregrounding of the damaging effects of emotional pain. This change had been blowing in the wind for some years.[45]

The meaning of pain on the playing field is shifting as the effect of contextual change continues to unfold. Several sports – American Football, Association Football, both Rugby codes, boxing – are coming towards a reckoning in the way they look after athletes and protect them from head injuries, in the light of damning evidence of chronic traumatic encephalopathy caused by repeated concussions.[46] The days of valorized playing through the pain may well be numbered. On an experiential level, the knowledge of what such repeated injury can do, long term, to a mind and body will change how athletes experience pain during play. In the heat of the moment, the brave decision, increasingly, will not be to play on, to run it off or shake it off, but to stop and acknowledge that the pain should be accepted as the potential sign of a serious injury. The experience of how a player feels, so long a matter to be displaced in favour of the goal, becomes paramount.

SEVEN

Embodying
Nocebo/Placebo

If you are in pain, how do you get out of it? Prescription: dig up an earthworm and place it in a wooden dish that has been split and mended with iron wire. Add water to the dish and drench the worm. Bury the worm in the ground whence it came, then drink the water from the dish. If you are suffering from a pain in the side or the loins, or sciatica, you will soon feel right as rain.

Or perhaps not. The recipe, one of dozens for sciatica, comes from *Natural Histories* by Pliny the Elder.[1] He got his information from the magicians of his time. It is one example of hundreds of his folk medicines that alleviated pain. The medicine was effective, for some. It may not work for you. How come?

Accounting for Placebo in the Past

The puzzle of placebo is increasingly understood, but it has no history to speak of. Those who have attempted to write it have repeatedly declared the history of folk cures for painful problems, especially in the era before 'scientific medicine', to be 'bizarre'. The refrain one hears most often is that the entire history of pre-modern medicine is placebo, but this is usually in order to *discount* that history. As Howard Brody noted at the end of the 1990s, to speak positively of the placebo effect, especially of the doctor's role *as* a 'walking placebo', was to 'commit an outrage against the sensibilities of many modern physicians, who view the term "placebo" as highly stigmatized and suggestive of quackery and charlatanism'.[2] Perhaps this is no longer true of most modern physicians, but the taint here described remains in the historical treatment of placebo. Instead of thus writing it off, I want to *account* for it. What happens when we take seriously the functioning of the biocultural brain in past contexts, accounting for situated beliefs, emotions, perceptions, sensations, conceptions, and knowledge? Here I aim simply to suggest

182

a framework for studying the history of the placebo effect, displacing attention from the inert medicament to the brain–body–world dynamic in which it was administered. Projecting neuroscientific and theoretical psychological work on placebo into the past, I suggest we can reach an understanding of the history of pain and pain relief, and of perceptions of feeling better, not only through analgesics and anaesthesia and active pharmaceuticals, but also through belief, ritual, and hope, and, beyond this, through the situated history of meaningful experience – of brain-bodies in temporal, cultural context.

Placebo scientists have long had an interdisciplinary instinct. In his seminal *Structural Anthropology*, Claude Lévi-Strauss (1908–2009) gives an extended critique of psychoanalysis, in the context of shamanism, that some placebo scientists have taken as a cue to understanding the cultural context of placebo rituals. Lévi-Strauss talked about psychoanalysis as a 'kind of diffuse mythology interpenetrating the consciousness of the group'. 'When this happens,' he wrote, 'the value of the system will no longer be based upon real cures from which certain individuals can benefit, but on the sense of security that the group receives from the myth underlying the cure and from the popular system upon which the group's universe is reconstructed.'[3] It is not entirely certain that Lévi-Strauss was describing something that had already happened, so much as forecasting what would happen in the future of psychoanalysis. Nonetheless, there is something in this description of the 'group's universe' that rings true for placebo research. David Grelotti, psychiatrist, and Ted Kaptchuk, professor of medicine, used these observations to introduce the notion of 'placebo by proxy': that is, when people 'other than the patient' feel better because of a placebo treatment that the patient has received, which may in turn further enhance the placebo effect on the patient.[4] Let's immediately dispense with Lévi-Strauss's distinction of the 'real' and the 'myth', since we must understand the placebo effect as 'real': an empirically measurable phenomenon. When understood as a potential series of gestures, utterances, expressions, attention, encouragement, and programmatic strategies regarding behaviour in the context of treatment, engaged in by clinicians, patients, and associates – family members, friends – of the patients, Grelotti and Kaptchuk theorize 'changes in the psychosocial context that mediate the placebo effect'.[5]

I am starting here because it usefully emphasizes that what I am calling the placebo transaction can never be siloed from the world in which it takes place. The encounter and its effects are always situated. Two things immediately strike the historian. First, contained in these few lines about placebo by proxy is a theory of situated cultural constructions that mediate how a person feels. Grelotti and Kaptchuk do not use the word 'culture', but it is clear from the way their study is orientated and directed that they refer to a highly specific context of modern American medical treatment, in which the smile is given high importance as a signal of encouragement and positivity. It is implicitly about culture. Second, they propose a theory of change over time that they think can be purposefully controlled by alterations in the psychosocial context. Change over time is the historian's *modus operandi*. This notion of a changing psychosocial context, whether controlled or uncontrolled, is appealing as a means of understanding situated historical rituals of making people feel better. The question that immediately arises is whether we can reconstruct lost psychosocial contexts and understand the experience of pain, illness, disease or dis-ease within them, including the ways in which those contexts – encompassing ritual, emotion, sensations, gesture, community, authority, setting, and so on, and including all manner of medicaments – made people feel better, or feel worse. In short, can we recover for historiography a revised account of the effectiveness of folk medicine, of pre-scientific medicine, as a story of medical effectiveness, at least to some extent?

Such is my impetus. In what follows, I'm going to sketch an outline of the most salient scientific knowledge on placebo and how that knowledge has currently been applied to the past. I want to highlight where current medical science on placebo is limited by the contemporary context of research, as well as by certain lacunae with respect to culture, ritual, and context. My hope, in building this outline, is not simply to suggest the application of contemporary scientific knowledge to the study of the past (although I think this is the most obvious way to benefit the historiography of medicine per se), but also to extend the knowledge produced by historical scholarship to see how it fits into and potentially alters contemporary medical-scientific knowledge on placebo.

The Current Outlook on Placebo

Placebo is usually followed by the word *effect*. Recent neuroscientific research on the way that placebo works disrupts its mystery. It has to do with the relationship between belief, culture, and brain chemistry, shifting the focus from the apparently magical process through which inert substances are transubstantiated into powerful pharmaceuticals. Instead, medical scientists explore how the human physiological and neurological pain management systems – the endogenous opioid, cannabinoid, and dopamine systems – work in context and, more broadly, how it is that things like placebo surgery can have similar results to real surgery.[6] Placebo is not so much an *effect* of folk cures, sugar pills, and homeopathic mystery as it is a *process* of the ordinary functioning of the biocultural brain. It is most commonly thought of as related to 'response-expectancy', perhaps in combination with conditioning: that is, the powerful belief that an intervention will work, in combination with lived experience of it having worked before, often means that it does work. Some psychological theorists have complicated this picture, pointing out that placebos work even where there is no conditioning, and even where no attitudinal position has been taken prior to the administration of placebo. There is also the problem that placebos have been shown to work even when the patient knows it is a placebo: that is, the 'magic' of human physiology is not necessarily based on deception, self-deception, or ignorance.[7]

So, the placebo process can be initiated by potentially anything that the suffering person believes will have a salving or remedying effect, including specific contextual or ritualistic practices, and in the absence of such individually held belief. Placebos can work through cultural and embodied practices that, while situated and specific, are experienced *as if* naturally. Phil Hutchison has described this in terms of 'cognition in an ethnomethodological mode', or EM-Cog, for short, encouraging placebo research via sensory ethnographies that reveal how people respond to 'meaningful loci of significance in the lifeworld', irrespective of or prior to their attitudinal position to it. Meaning, he says, is 'exhibited in their behaviour', and he furnishes the example of an emotional response to having 'a hand coming to rest on the back of your hand when you are distressed'.[8] Historians of emotion have focused on precisely this kind of thing for many years now, understanding the ways in which meaning is made through bodily practices and situated emotional and sensational experience. The example furnished by Hutchison fits readily into explainable categories of non-verbal cultural concepts that exist in dynamic relation with the bodies that experience them and give them meaning.[9]

Physical gestures, like the comforting hand, are not transhistorically meaningful but situated and specific. These things do not require, necessarily, any actor to have formed an attitude to them. They simply require that they are themselves formed within a temporal-cultural fabric. They place the emphasis on our ability to understand and reconstruct cultural context, to understand how meaning is situationally experienced. The story of placebo, therefore, is not so much about those worldly things that have been thought to have a mysterious power – from shark fins to bread pills to chicken soup – as it is about the shifting cultural contexts that frame how the brain functions and makes meaning in the world, which includes historically specific systems of belief. It is the story of bodies and biology in culture. This aligns with the limited anthropological work on placebo, such as that by Daniel Moerman, who has argued that people 'are simultaneously biological and cultural creatures. Biology and culture interact, and are equal partners in who and what we are.' To whatever extent we can look to 'biological systems of great evolutionary age', we must nonetheless accept that they are 'open' to the world in which they are situated, to 'external stimulus'. As Moerman demonstrates, one such stimulus is 'meaning, as conveyed through language, performance, ritual, art, and so on'.[10] When one adds a temporal element, it becomes a story of historical brain-bodies changing over time in a dynamic dance with their respective, always unstable, cultures. If pain is historically specific and mutable, so is its relief.

The Attitude of Placebo Scientists to the Past

Placebo scientists have addressed the history of medicine, in a limited way, but the absence of trained historians in the making of an historical narrative about placebo is telling.[11] There is one definitive text, Arthur and Elaine Shapiro's *The Powerful Placebo: From Ancient Priest to Modern Physician*, published in 1997. Both authors were clinical professors of psychiatry. Their book acknowledges something important in its opening, quoting from a 1938 article by W.R. Houston, that the doctor was always a therapeutic agent; that doctors' skill 'was a skill in dealing with the emotions of men', and that the history of medicine 'is a history of the dynamic power of the relationship between doctor and patient'.[12] So far so good. The history of medicine over the last thirty or more years has demonstrated this in countless ways. But Shapiro and Shapiro use this insight, which ought to have been the impetus for the building of a situated understanding of that dynamic power relationship, to denounce the entire history of medicine up until the twentieth century as a long procession of frauds, fads, and fabulous nonsense. Pre-modern doctors, they assert, were *fakes*. The placebo effect in their historical account is something to keep in mind as a *mistake*, remembered so as not to be repeated. Placebo effects are there to be identified, isolated, and *defeated* by real medicine. It is not surprising, therefore, that pre-modern medicines and rituals of treatment are derided as 'bizarre', irrational, emotional, 'primitive', and 'weird'.[13] The inability of the authors to attend to the situated knowledge and logic – the psychosocial context, if you will – of the past renders them unable to see any value in the power of the placebo effect in history. Most of history is simply a nonsensical multi-millennia preface to the real story of modern science. Others have followed suit.[14] For the few professional historians who have attended to placebo, this has been a source of frustration. As Nils Korsvoll has pointed out, historians of medicine, with their overwhelming focus on the Hippocratic tradition, have 'dismissed other healing options as irrational magic, while the study of magic has had little interest in the actual healing it was meant to occasion'.[15]

In the same year as the Shapiros' book came out, a collection of essays edited by the noted historian of science Anne Harrington also appeared, promising an 'interdisciplinary exploration' of the placebo effect. Perhaps inevitably, the historical chapter was written by the Shapiros, and it does in brief the same thing as their longer treatise.[16] Since then, aside from an unpublished lecture by Charles Rosenberg, which took a critical stance towards the Shapiros, there has been virtually nothing written on the topic by historians.[17] Rosenberg had closely approached the topic, years before, in a celebrated essay on the history of therapeutics, noting that the study of it 'is after all a good deal more than a series of pharmacological or surgical experiments. It involves emotions and personal relationships and incorporates all of those factors which determine belief, identity, and status,' and it focuses most importantly on the 'patterned interaction between doctor and patient, one which evolved over centuries into a conventionalized social ritual'.[18] This should have been the model for the history of placebo – it has been influential in the history of medicine more generally – but it was overlooked by the Shapiros. This absence has meant that in most introductory texts on placebo for medical researchers and students, its history is quickly dealt with by summary reference to the Shapiros. Their book became the touchstone, not merely the first word but the last word, the closed book, on the history of placebo.

As such, Fabrizio Benedetti, professor of physiology and neuroscience in Turin and one of the best-known world experts on placebo, opens his textbook account of placebo with reference to the Shapiros, and claims that pre-modern medical interventions were 'nothing but placebos', which were 'ineffective treatment for the symptoms or disorder being treated'.[19] To say that placebos were not effective for *symptoms* is an amazing stretch, but this sneering at the past is reinforced by further descriptions of pre-modern (pre-scientific, in his terms) treatments, which were, aping the Shapiros, irrational, ignorant, eccentric, and odd.[20] Despite this, Benedetti notes that 'one of the most intriguing aspects of pre-scientific medicine is not so much the existence of the myriad of bizarre and ineffective medical interventions, but rather the belief that they were effective'. He acknowledges that such 'bizarre' treatments persist today ('attributable', he says, 'to the fact that people trust, and thus use, them'), but does not capitalize on this realization, instead remarking that some of this historical weirdness is attributable to patients not actually being ill, but 'probably merely anxious, so that no real improvement actually took place'.[21] Suffice it to say that ruling out anxiety as not a real illness is suspect and that the words 'probably' and 'merely' stand in for (a) a lack of research and (b) a wilful dismissiveness of past dis-ease. Benedetti concludes his historical assessment by conceding that 'some clinical improvements might have been due to the patient's expectations of clinical benefit and to changes in their emotional state (the true psychobiological placebo effect)'.[22] Surely here is the expression of a research agenda, not the dismissal of pre-modern or pre-scientific medicine as unworthy of serious attention. In unwittingly highlighting the importance of trust and belief (with the obvious question: why did people trust and believe? Is it not because experience suggested the treatments worked for the complaint at hand?), Benedetti inadvertently points us towards an investigation of the lived experience of the administration of placebo *avant la lettre*.

In placebo research today, the structure of trust, belief, and hope usually does not encompass the doctor figure but focuses on the patient figure. In the past, such structures tended to include doctors, who were as likely as the patient to believe in the power of a ritual or a drug. What we might see as a placebo ritual was, in many cases, a medical or magical performance in which both 'doctor' – I use the term loosely – 'patient', and society were all equally invested. Grelotti and Kaptchuk imagined doctors joining in with the society of the patient in emotionally reinforcing the placebo effect, knowing that the effect was (a) real and (b) plastic. This amounts to a call for a certain amount of performance, of the making of an atmosphere of belief and hope, of tapping into the fabric of meaning to operationalize it for the patient. They are not the only ones to go down this route. In a 2013 paper in *Nature Reviews: Drug Discovery*, the efficacy of a drug or a treatment is shown to be greatly affected by the patient's 'expectations, the quality of physician–patient communication and associative learning processes'.[23] If one could 'harness' these placebo mechanisms, as the authors call them, they could be systematically used in clinical practice.[24]

From an historical point of view, how much more readily was this attained when medical personnel were convinced of the active power of the inert drugs or rituals being used? I am reminded of Rosenberg's comment that, in the nineteenth century, no 'physician doubted the efficacy of placebos (as little as he doubted that the effectiveness of a drug could depend on his manner and attitude)'.[25] Yet insofar as medical science gives rise to this question, it seems to shut it down. One impression to draw from the scientific literature on placebo is that it is not possible to study placebo without the controlled trial, since there is otherwise no way to isolate it. This puts a limit on the possibility for a history of placebo, beginning only with the second half of the twentieth century. This is unsatisfactory, born out of quantitative thinking, as opposed to the historian's qualitative approach to analysis. It behoves the historian to formulate a method.

This might be even more pressing, given recent studies that have shown that even the controlled trial is, from the point of view of placebo, not controlled enough.[26] Research has demonstrated that (a) placebos still 'work' even when patients involved in trials *know* that they are taking them and that (b) the placebo effect in controlled trials seems to be increasing over time. Both require explanation that goes beyond a focus on the human biological interior. So far, preliminary explanations have come from psychological and neuroscientific disciplines, but only an understanding of the brain as a cultural and historical artefact can fully explain the apparent tenacity and, conversely, the adaptiveness of the placebo effect. As Rosenberg presciently observed in the late 1970s, 'almost all drugs now act as placebos' because the patient's 'faith' is based on the 'physician and his imputed status' and on 'science itself'.[27] Yet the history of the controlled trial, fundamentally, is about science's attempts to defeat faith and to overcome placebo. As placebo scientists turn towards controlled trials that incorporate extra dimensions – no treatment at all, for example, to try to filter out the noise of the placebo effect altogether – and as they begin serious clinical investigations into how to harness the placebo effect (and reduce the nocebo effect – see below), they will have to reach for a deeper understanding of the contextual, symbolic, and political conditions in which placebo has taken place and might yet take place. As the science becomes yet more multidisciplinary, so its application becomes potentially less stable.

Epistles from Madeira

In practical terms, how would one set about historicizing the placebo effect? There is not much to go on, given the historiographical status of the Shapiro and Shapiro text. I can find only the beginnings of some thorough historical case studies – all recent – limited to the history of antiquity, which loosely follow the research impetus I have sketched here.[28] In a couple of studies of the Asclepius cult in ancient Greece, there is talk of the amplification of patient 'beliefs and hopes' at the healing sanctuaries of Asclepius, and of the whole culture of healing belief upon which the healing rituals were predicated.[29] Most usefully, this small investigation comes replete with testimonials: inscriptions from the fourth century BCE of the sick and the pained on their experiences of feeling better after Asclepius visited them in dreams while incubated at the sanctuary; of the prescriptions they received; and of the particular mash-up of older folk cures and early Hippocratic methods they envisioned Asclepius to prescribe or administer. We have testimony of symptoms, of procedures and encounters, and of relief. It is not, as the author of this study, Olympia Panagiotidou, points out, that such experiences were bizarre, odd, irrational, or based upon ignorance. On the contrary, they fit the description of a placebo effect in a certain psychosocial context, framed by situated knowledge, situated belief, situated practices of relief, and situated dynamics of encounter between medical authority (here embodied in the figure of a god, but reinforced by a community of medical men who practised in the god's name) and the sick, with their hopes, beliefs, and, literally, dreams. Likewise, the cocktail of earthworm and rainwater as a cure for sciatica in Pliny the Elder's *Natural Histories* might have worked, and its success can be explained. There is nothing necessarily 'bizarre' about it, any more than the rituals of bleeding and purging, from ancient China and ancient Rome down to nineteenth-century western medicine, are 'bizarre'.

I draw inspiration from this work on antiquity, using it to develop a biocultural approach that takes seriously the contextual specificity of historical constructions of experience.[30] I can employ the fundamental observation of social neuroscientists that the brain is a cultural artefact, but that means, in effect, that the only universal quality of the way the brain produces experience is its contingency.[31] This, in turn, implies a deep study of the situated context: a microhistorical focus that includes verbal and non-verbal concepts, bodily and facial expressions and gesture, the history of belief, the history of sensation (not just the canonical five senses, but the ways in which past actors have conceived of internal sensation and put their own spin on physical and sensual engagement with the world), the histories of ritual, authority, symbols, and materials. The meaning of what people say and do, through this kind of holistic and forensic approach, is revealed only through the context.

I propose a nineteenth-century example. George John Romanes (1848–94), a budding disciple of Charles Darwin, was cut off in his prime by a brain tumour, which not only killed him in his mid-forties, but also extinguished his fame and the long-standing recognition of much of his work on mental evolution. In October 1892, he corresponded with the

Prime Minister, William Ewart Gladstone (1809–98), who gave the first Romanes lecture in Oxford. Romanes laments: 'My own years have been threatened with an abrupt termination … and immediately after your lecture I have to go to Madeira for the winter. Among other things I have been left half blind, which accounts for my handwriting being even worse than it was before.'[32] To other correspondents he complained that a 'serious illness' had incapacitated him from work.[33] To Thomas Henry Huxley, Darwin's 'Bulldog', he was more explicit, noting he had 'lost the sight of one eye by effusion of serum on the retina'.[34] From other letters, I infer that Romanes was, aside from finding it difficult to see, in immense and debilitating pain, and partly paralysed.[35] He was, he says, 'ordered' by a doctor to Madeira for its inherent health benefits.[36]

There is an immense amount of scholarship on fresh air cures, water cures, altitude cures, and so on.[37] It has much to offer, but seldom does it approach anything like an appraisal of the extent to which these so-called 'cures' had a palliative effect on those who sought them, or, at least, not in a systematic way. Madeira, we know, was a resort of note for consumptives, with a reputation for dry air that somehow proved resilient against a clear lack of evidence that the climate did any good at all.[38] Vladimir Jankovic has documented the fact that the resort remained popular despite 'scientific' discredit: its 'equability was real because it was based on popular belief', pointing to 'anecdotal evidence, peripatetic culture suffused with notions of elite *Bildung* and the flight from urban civilization'.[39] Romanes' lungs were fine, but it is not so surprising, considering these terms, to find an independently wealthy gentleman of letters and science ordered to the island for his general well-being. Thus, we find Romanes, some six weeks after having told Gladstone of his illness, writing again to him from warmer climes, 'having a very pleasant winter, amid a continuous blaze of sunshine and bluest of blue skies'. The 'effects', he says, 'have certainly been beneficial. Headaches considerably diminished, and I am beginning to feel more capable of working as I used to work.'[40] Madeira, as far as Romanes was concerned, alleviated his pain. To Huxley he wrote that 'the lotus-eating life appears to be curing my headaches'.[41] He stayed on for a few more months, returning to London in the early spring. He wrote to Huxley in mid-April 1893, claiming to be 'much better, although still far from well. My eyes continue in exactly the same state, so I am afraid there is no hope of recovery in that direction.'[42] Yet he still entertained the possibility of being able to work, suggesting that the winter in Madeira had made substantial inroads into his persistent headaches.

I don't think that a culture of medical travel, a warm sun, and a blue sky are enough to explain the case. There is something else, in Romanes' correspondence itself, that speaks of historically specific epistolary practices of evoking wellness to feel wellness. His entire adult life was spent writing letters, hashing out the era's major intellectual debates through private correspondence. Despite the overwhelming intellectual content that flowed from his pen, his letters always dutifully and respectfully attended to the health of his correspondents and, notably, their wives, as well as answering those correspondents' own enquiries about his own health. Following an insight from recent placebo scientific research that the word 'placebo' can evoke a placebo response, on the basis that the concept has entered general knowledge and that patients therefore expect it to have an effect, I can trace a similar effect in the nineteenth century.[43] One can read into the practice of writing 'I am feeling better' an utterance that itself has a placebo effect: the writing of it makes it so.[44] Romanes did this often, but there is more besides. In September 1893, we find him chiding a critic who has misunderstood his work by writing 'There is none so blind as those who will not see,' all in the context of the failing health of both.[45] Romanes regularly sought solace in his work, in the life of the mind, and made light of his blindness with such quips. To physiologists he would write of his illness as if observing a physiological experiment, documenting his bodily problems as if they were not his. He told his friend Edward Sharpey Schäfer (1850–1935) that an attack of haemiplegia had left him 'utterly disabled', but described the features of this as 'curious', and 'interesting physiologically', noting that only his arm and leg were affected, with varying degrees of numbness in other parts. He asked, scientist to scientist, whether from Schäfer's 'knowledge of localisation ... anything could be made of these seemingly curious facts'.[46] Romanes was reassuring himself by distancing measures as well as seeking reassurance at a stage of remove from the personal.

There is clear evidence that his correspondents entered into epistolary stratagems designed to induce wellness. One such, having met Romanes in person in December 1893, wrote to affirm that, to him at least, Romanes' health was good: 'better than when I met you five years ago', despite a serious relapse of symptoms in the autumn of that year.[47] Romanes himself made efforts to announce that he was 'mending'.[48]

By May 1894, Romanes was dead. The whole period of his illness was thus mediated by a variety of cultural palliatives, in the absence of any medical intervention of note. We can take Romanes at his word when he said he felt better because of a change of climate, and we can infer with some assurance that he felt better through the act of writing as such. The decline of his final years is marked by a remarkable change in his handwriting, which was poor in the first place. Yet within this decline there are marked moments of improvement, of both legibility and of stamina, with long and involved letters poured out in his own hand. While the vagaries of his disease in causing such moments of attenuated pain, disability, and fatigue cannot be ruled out, the conscious engagement in a range of historically specific placebo rituals, even if they weren't called that, must be ruled in. They had a palliative effect on the worst symptoms of a painful terminal disease.

Nocebo Effects: From COVID-19 to Hysteria

The COVID-19 pandemic has raged around me throughout the process of writing this book. While many people and many politicians have made conscious rhetorical overtures in declaring the pandemic over, there remains no clear evidence of a societal placebo effect in this regard. People still sicken, still die, still face long-term recovery battles. Likewise, the various drugs promoted by non-medical social media conspiracy sites as effective COVID treatments – ivermectin, for example – do not seem to have any effect at all on those who ardently believe in their efficacy. Placebo often makes patients feel better, but seldom does it make inroads against specific pathologies. The placebo that counteracts a virus, or a cancer, or a bacterial infection would be big news indeed. Belief and expectation have their limits.

Conversely, the pandemic has drawn attention to placebo's opposite, the nocebo effect, and the potential for deleterious consequences on public health on a large scale. The nocebo effect works, essentially, in the same way as placebo, but in this case the belief, expectation, or cultural framing of certain conditions or drugs or treatments is that they will have a negative outcome: pain, sickness, even death. A range of factors have been enumerated as contributing to or causing the nocebo effect: individual mood disorders that are strongly connected to negative expectations; aspects of religious outlook or worldview in relation to the status and likelihood of suffering in the life course; self-examination in the context of particular exposure to disease (personal, or in the media, for example); diagnostic associations (such as the emotional response to finding out one has cancer); sociogenic illness (the idea of a kind of contagion that works through sociocultural networks and knowledge, rather than through specific pathogens – things like 'mass hysteria' might get filed under this heading); and invocation (the magic spell, the hex, the curse, that, despite having no intrinsic power, do have an injurious effect on their target).[49] Lack of trust in science, or in a particular medical authority, might be causative.[50]

A correspondent to the *Journal of Public Health* in August 2021 noted the high degree of probability that the pandemic could cause large-scale nocebo events, given the amount of negative information flowing through information channels over which there are no editorial or expert controls, in an environmental context that emphasizes the powerlessness of citizens in the face of a high risk of contagion, or, at the least, of the perception of such. Ultimately, it points to the importance of politics in public health, since on-target messaging, clear communication, and a kind of medical authority that exudes expertise are essential for govern-ments who hope to safeguard public health not only from a specific viral pathogen, but also from the nocebo effect that is activated through negativity, lack of clarity, inconsistent policy, and a tendency to ignore medical expertise in favour of glib ideologies or perceived political expediency.[51]

One study found that people who strongly believed themselves to be infected with COVID-19 were more likely to experience severe symptoms indicative of the virus, especially if those people had a history of anxiety.[52] It confirmed other studies that found the prevalence of negative emotions to correlate with the reporting of symptoms of illness and of treatment side-effects.[53] Meanwhile, a study in Greece on patients with autoimmune rheumatic diseases found that some 10 per cent of respondents, highly correlated with a higher level of education, experi-enced nocebo effects related to their disease, representing an increase in 'nocebo behaviour' compared with before the pandemic. The speculation here is that the pandemic's association with 'emotional distress and significant disruptions in health-care services' were causative of new nocebo effects. The atmosphere of COVID-19 is therefore presumed to generate symptoms unrelated to the virus, which points to the causative power of higher rates of health anxiety and emotional distress about the status of medicine and health provision.[54] Historians have presented us with evidence of analogous processes. Nervous conditions that have commonly been linked to modern life, and to the modern city, were in part iatrogenic illnesses, caused by anxiety *about* the potential for anxiety within the medical establishment. Once doctors provided a popular script about the myriad ways modernity, electricity, and technology might overtax the human physiological system, it was only a matter of time until overtaxed humans started presenting themselves precisely as symptomatic of neurasthenia caused by modern life.[55] Nocebo effects are real. The symptoms of illness that patients experience cannot be dismissed as phantoms or as the productions of errant minds. They are real symptoms, even if not associated directly with the diseases the patient thinks they are associated with.

Soon there will be enormous scope for nocebo studies in relation to so-called 'long-COVID' patients. Given the well-documented emotional turmoil of the pandemic, it is to be expected that some proportion of long-COVID suffering has to do with nocebo effects, correlated with this emotional atmosphere and with individual histories of emotional disorders. At time of writing, research on the matter showed that half of the patients studied who were 'seeking medical help for post-acute COVID-19 syndrome' had not had COVID, but in any case the study found that the presence of COVID-19 immunity made no difference to the symptoms of long-COVID, which were characterized by 'severe fatigue, altered quality of life and psychologic distress'. The study did find that a significant proportion of the study cohort reporting long-COVID 'had a positive screening for anxiety, depression and post-traumatic stress disorder'. Again, all temptations at dismissing these symptoms, or long-COVID itself, as social contagion of malingering, or of an elaborate hoax, must be dismissed. As the authors assert, the 'persistence of physical symptoms (related or not to COVID-19) is likely associated with the psychologic burden of the pandemic'.[56] In other words, an infection with COVID-19 is not a necessary precondition for some presentations of post-acute COVID-19 syndrome. A massive proportion of society is undergoing a nocebo effect akin to PTSD.

I find this contemporary research insightful in re-casting my eye over the history of experience of pain and disease, especially as it concerns hysteria.[57] Negative emotional conditions, even in the individual or in the social context, are a precondition for the nocebo effect, which nevertheless emerges at distinct moments, with discrete triggering causes. The problem with hysteria studies is, as with long-COVID complaints, the association of the diagnostic label with malingering, fraud, or failings in 'temperament' or 'character'. Throughout the eighteenth and nineteenth centuries in Europe, hysterical illnesses in women were attributed to their mental weakness, their sexual organs, and their emotional fragility, but in every case these were grounds to dismiss hysteria as an unreal malady, a phantasm, rather than a real illness. The gendered politics of this has been extensively studied, as have the suggestive powers of the doctor in prescribing the expectations for classical hysterical presentations.[58] There is, however, much greater room to study the experience of hysteria through the concept of nocebo: a real illness, its causes rooted in social knowledge of the disease and an atmosphere of repression that provided the necessary preconditions for emotional distress. In each theatre of its emergence, specific contextual factors would be vital for an understanding of the specific characteristics of the disease.

In the mid-1970s, François Sirois's historical survey of 'epidemic hysteria' between 1872 and 1972 found that large-scale outbreaks were common, taking place in schools, towns, and factories, and involving potentially hundreds of people at a time.[59] Sirois traces the earliest reports of mass hysteria back to 1374, with the dancing manias of Aachen, but it is easy to go further back and further afield.[60] Christopher Milnes' recent history of euphoria traced the connections between pain, hysteria, compulsive mass dancing, and St Vitus' Dance, finding an explanation of frenzied dancing souls in Aristotle, and a story of a bridge that collapsed under the weight of 200 dancers in Germany in 1278.[61] Jerri Daboo documents the extraordinary history of 'tarantism' in Italy, which dates to at least the eleventh century, but which maintained a centuries-long peak in the early modern period.[62] Nominally, the *tarantismo* was a ritual performed as 'a cure for someone bitten by the tarantula spider', whose symptoms 'can include nausea, paralysis, lethargy, spasms, headaches, irregular pulse and breathing, and fainting'. Generally, evidence of a real spider bite was wanting. The symptoms alone were sufficient to have the musicians summoned. The rhythmic approach of the musicians would gradually bring the body back into harmony and restore the health of the afflicted person, through their own dancing. While Daboo points out that there is a long historical debate about whether 'the condition of tarantism' is '"real" or not, and if the *tarantata* is "faking" rather than being genuinely ill, or even in a state of madness or hysteria', it is precisely here that a biocultural view collapses these distinctions.[63] To be in a state of madness or hysteria can be a genuine illness, the cultural and performative appearance and experience of which are specific and context-bound.

One might debate whether such cultural forms should rightfully fit within an account of hysteria, or be viewed in conjunction with contemporary problems of pandemic life. To me, they share something fundamentally in common. In Sirois's study, modern outbreaks of mass hysteria have commonly involved women, but there were marked changes over time in the ways that symptoms presented. This is in accord with numerous more recent historical accounts that have emphasized the importance of 'cultural influences' in changing the bodily form that hysteria presented, as well as the politics of its gendering.[64] Since Sirois, there have been various attempts to re-label such phenomena, in part to shift the negative connotations of the word 'hysteria' and replace it with more sensitive approaches to the lived experience of real distress and illness. Yet whether we call it mass hysteria or mass psychogenic illness or mass sociogenic illness, or even (as with COVID-19) 'reactive psychological disaster syndrome', we are nonetheless faced with similar phenomena and the same puzzle.[65] And while 'hysteria' is most commonly deployed in contemporary parlance pejoratively, with an air of dismissal or an accusation of malingering, the reality is that hysteria-like phenomena are all around us and receive serious treatment from scholars and the medical community alike, for their psychological and bodily effects are no less real to those who experience them for having no apparent material pathological cause.[66] Similarly to hysteria, the words 'nocebo' and 'placebo' tend still to be received negatively, as if they refer to the faulty imagination of the patient, rather than to something that can be properly described and explained. A series of historical reflections on the past experiences of pain and illness with no apparent physical cause might help to contextualize and authenticate those people who are suffering today under similar terms. While many will reject the notion that long-COVID has nothing necessarily to do with the COVID-19 virus itself but is rather based in the atmosphere of fear, anxiety, and stress, it is likely that palliation, for some, will follow a more widespread entertainment of the idea.

Voodoo? Nocebo and the Enduring Puzzle of the Hex

In 1942, the famous Harvard physiologist Walter B. Cannon published a treatise on '"voodoo" death'. It was a serious experimental investigation into the possibility that apparently innocuous activity – a curse or hex or magic spell – could cause death. He asked: could 'an ominous and persistent state of fear … end the life of a man'?[67] This took place in a context where scientists and clinicians had for years struggled to understand the phenomenon of shock: the sudden and irreversible disintegration of human regulatory functions, such that a sight, sound, or otherwise innocuous injury might cause some people to die. The mystery unfolded during the First World War and has been forensically documented by Stefanos Geroulanos and Todd Meyers.[68] What is most striking is the astonishing constellation of disciplinary expertise. Psychiatrists, physiologists, and anthropologists all thought that their discipline had the necessary tools to crack the puzzle of catastrophic shock, but it is in their interweaving that we find the most surprising results.

Cannon was inspired by the anthropologists and, in turn, the anthropologists were inspired by his work. Voodoo death was a means of accessing the contextual and individual vagaries of shock. It showed the power of magic and provided an explanatory framework for why not all human systems always behaved the same way, despite their obvious functional similarities. It opened the door to the imprint of culture and society upon the body, upon the balance between life and death, and it paved the way for nocebo studies.[69] For the medical scientists, it pointed the way to an understanding of the brain-body's capacity to produce pain and to cause death as if from nowhere. Cannon set about the experiment by using animals, trying to find the physiological phenomena that might lead to the otherwise inexplicable demise of a living being, but he had made the connection between stories of voodoo death collected from anthropological readings and those who died from shock in those recent wars among 'civilized' nations with breath-taking ease. As a 'consequence of sorcery', a person may die 'from a true state of shock, in the surgical sense – a shock induced by prolonged and tense emotion'.[70] On the battlefield, 'a shocking experience' could have 'persistent effects', such that anxiety, coupled with insufficient food and water and rapid pulse, was sufficient to kill. It 'would fit well with the conditions reported from primitive tribes'. '"[V]oodoo death" may be real, and … it may be explained as due to shocking emotional distress – to obvious or repressed terror.'[71]

Since Cannon's explosive article, many have adopted its thesis, and many have critiqued it. But most scientists of placebo and nocebo agree that words and ritual practices do have the power to cause pain and even to give rise to dangerous emotions that can kill, in certain circumstances and contexts where the emotional/physiological response to them is predicated on the reality of their power (this can include feelings of helplessness or hopelessness).[72] In a revised form, voodoo death is still a reference point in contemporary medical science.[73] According to Otniel Dror, 'postwar biomedicine "discovered" that voodoo-like phenomena were ubiquitous in modern Western experience'.[74] Dror specifies Cannon's reluctance to entertain that voodoo death and Christian healing practices were connected, insisting that they functioned according to different 'logic'.[75] The incorporation of Cannon's experimental work into the broader understanding of nocebo and placebo is an insight only afforded by later research, but Dror notes that the 'formulation of a theory of placebo' was part of a series of 'mechanisms that explained alternative knowledge claims' – mesmerism, spiritualism, psychical research, and so on – 'in terms of orthodox theory' as part of the consolidation and institutionalization of power and authority of 'orthodox physicians', against the prevailing nineteenth-century influence of 'alternative approaches and cosmologies'. Placebo and nocebo seemed to work, as it were, outside the framework of a formalized scientific system of knowledge production, but nonetheless within situated cultural processes of knowledge production and belief. While there is an attempt in Cannon's work to emphasize the distance between civilized America and the kind of voodoo practices carried on by those subjected to the anthropological gaze, there is an inescapable appropriation of a form of knowledge in this work. As Dror points out, Cannon's work was part of a process of contesting 'what constituted scientific knowledge' and policing 'who could make knowledge claims' and 'how to maintain authority' over such claims.[76] If Cannon's examination of voodoo was rhetorically at arm's length, his attempt to experiment on it in his laboratory brought it into the affective, practical, and disciplinary logic of western medical experimentation. The legacy, and value, of this remains with us.

Martin Samuels, for example, Founding Chair of Neurology at the Brigham and Women's Hospital, Harvard Medical School, revisited Cannon's '"Voodoo" death' in a 2007 article in the *Cleveland Clinic Journal of Medicine*, demonstrating through the autonomic nervous system the 'connection between neuropsychiatric illness and the visceral organs', which could explain all manner of sudden unexpected deaths. He connected a number of forms of sudden death, including sudden death in middle-aged men, sudden infant death syndrome, voodoo death (or being scared to death), sudden death during a natural catastrophe, sudden death caused by grief or a major loss, sudden death in a panic attack or from mental stress, and sudden death during war.[77] It is of profound importance, to medical science, to historians, and to society at large, that there is a wealth of experimental evidence that 'stress alone can result in the production' of cardiac lesions that lead to death. To avoid any confusion, the definition of stress here is broad: 'restraint, surgery, bacteremia, vagotomy, toxins and others'.[78] The 'neurologic catastrophe' is caused by the 'overactivity of the sympathetic limb of the autonomic nervous system', causing 'major cardiac and pulmonary pathologies'.[79] The heart literally breaks, in certain conditions. Fear, it seems, is sufficient to break it. Belief in the power of a curse might result in the most extreme nocebo effects: severe pain, even death.

For the anthropologists, voodoo death gave them a situated understanding of the potential *reality* of magical beliefs and practices, which justified a tight focus on cultural symbols, rituals, and practices as having biological power. Bronisław Malinowski (1884–1942) had approached this as early as 1925 in *Magic, Science and Religion*, but the thesis was delivered with greater verve by Marcel Mauss (1872–1950) in 1926, in an essay entitled (in translation) 'The physical effect on the individual of the idea of death suggested by the collectivity'.[80] Claude Lévi-Strauss later enfolded the physiological insight, building directly on 'the pioneering work of Cannon'.[81] We can see all of this echoing through contemporary work on the subject.[82] And, as a coda to this intellectual history of the entanglement of physiological, psychological, and anthropological research on the reality of nocebo, the idea of it has given some historians the scope to entertain the historical reality of witchcraft in the past, even if such cases were in the minority at the high (or rather low) points of the witch-hunting crazes in Europe and elsewhere.[83]

Routes Forward

How does all of this potentially play out with respect to the production of knowledge about placebo and nocebo? If applied to medical-scientific research on the placebo effect, what does an historiographical contribution potentially do? Placebo research is already an interdisciplinary endeavour, but it is dominated by psychological and neuroscientific approaches, with a clear focus on the brain. I propose to radicalize the interdisciplinarity, not by removing the focus on the brain, but by following to their full extent the logical implications of assertions that the brain is a biocultural organ. The brain must be put in the world.

History has the potential to balance the focus of placebo researchers, who overwhelmingly tend to look to the brain-body interior, by compelling them to pay greater attention to the exterior, to cultural context. An influential article published in *Nature Reviews: Neuroscience* promised to connect 'context, learning and health' via a neuroscientific approach to placebo effects, declaring that placebo effects 'are attributable to the brain-mind responses to the context in which a treatment is delivered'. Yet the overwhelming focus of the piece is the specific actions of that response, leaving the question of context to the side, despite a conclusion that 'a substantial part of the therapeutic benefit patients experience when undergoing medical treatment is caused by their brain's response to the treatment context'. What specifically comprises that context? If it is desirable to (a) control for placebo in trials and (b) make the best use of placebo as therapy, understanding this is surely of vital importance, equal to the importance of what happens in the brain. Yet the medical-scientific impetus is generally to try to get at 'the brain mechanisms underlying these effects', at the expense of seeing the context as one such underlying mechanism, which will never show up on an fMRI scanner. The authors attest that 'the creation of robust placebo effects across disorders and outcomes seems to require appropriate conceptual beliefs ... that are supported by experience-dependent learning', but they say that those conceptual beliefs are 'maintained in prefrontal cortical networks' and that the experience-dependent learning takes place in 'striatal and brainstem circuits'.[84] I say both are maintained and take place in the cultural context as well as in the brain, that the two are irrevocably entangled, and that it is fruitless to examine one without the other.

Similarly, in a recent prominent article in the *New England Journal of Medicine*, there is due and careful attention to context, expectations, and sociocultural 'framing', but there are said to be 'molecular events and neural network changes underlying placebo and nocebo effects', which are 'mediated by expectancies'.[85] It seems unlikely that placebo will be fully controlled or harnessed if this casual priority for biological processes is maintained, as if they are not *always* dynamically involved with mediating external conditions. The conditions for *knowing* or *believing* a thing to be helpful or harmful exist outside the brain as well as inside it. Moreover, this biocultural dynamic is unstable. Change in both concepts and experience has occurred and does occur, but this change cannot be accounted for by only examining one side of the equation. There is something to be gained by incorporating historical and humanities-based methods into laboratory-based research. It necessarily changes the questions being asked and it changes the status of the knowledge being produced. To furnish a terminal example, a ground-breaking study on the increase of placebo responses over time in US clinical trials of neuropathic pain found that the increased placebo effect might have to do, in part, with distinctive American recruitment methods, which rely principally upon advertising, and which result in 'differing patient characteristics in US studies'.[86] The observation is pregnant with research possibilities that are centred precisely upon the question of the physiological effect of cultural and contextual specificity. At present, I cannot see such studies taking place, but one might dare to hope that work on placebo in the humanities might inspire it.

Conclusion
The Mutable Patient

A patient is, literally, a sufferer. *Patior*: I suffer or endure. Also, I submit. It is to this experiential category, rather than to the modern subject of medical treatment, that I refer by the phrase 'the mutable patient'. There is no one way to suffer, or to interpret meaningfully what it is to experience pain, or to experience feeling relief from pain. While in some respects every reader will know pain, the only thing that can be generalized from this knowledge is that pain is plastic: it is personal, it is social; it is subjective but formed and alleviated through intersubjective and collective dynamics; it is cultural, insofar as the experience of pain must be learned according to the conceptual framing of the culture in which a person is formed; it is therefore unstable, even in a single individual over the course of life, perhaps even from one moment to the next. Pain is universal only in the meaningless sense that (almost) everybody has experienced something 'painful' at some point, but it is in fact conceptually plural. I can talk about 'pain' in this general sense, but to do justice to the myriad ways of encountering, enduring, or even celebrating pain, one must examine the conceptual and cultural specificities of different contexts of suffering; one must come to know the signs, symbols, and expressions of situated pains, of 'patients' in their own worlds. This rubric applies to historians researching the history of pain knowledge and pain experience. More importantly, perhaps, it should apply to contemporary physicians and nurses, and to insightful public health policy makers everywhere. The temptation to discount the overwhelming evidence of the mutability and contingency of the experience of pain, the incorporation of this fact into the most authoritative definition of pain notwithstanding, remains almost overwhelming. It must be resisted.

I conclude by gathering the threads of the narrative together to finally disrupt any notion of pain as a great universal. The argument has shown that the experience of pain is *always* situated and mediated in many ways. It calls for a greater focus on these forms of mediation and suggests that the broad collective of academic disciplines that form 'pain studies' should take them more seriously in their desire both to say what pain is and what should be done about it. Moreover, it highlights the fact that for most of human history most pain has gone unalleviated, untreated, unmedicated. To live was to suffer, but to live was to submit to this suffering and to find situated ways to account for, evaluate, and manage it. Patience has, literally, been a virtue in many cultures, and for a variety of reasons. Is patience still a virtue, or can it be? I leave off with a reflection on the meaninglessness of pain in contemporary civilizations, on the tide of chronic pain and the lack of options either for treating it or for making sense of it: the apparent futility, in this case, of knowing our own pain.

For the most part, I have tried in this book to focus tightly on the relation of pain knowledge and pain experience, but relief (actual or the pursuit thereof) has, perhaps always, been a part of this dynamic, as seen in the final chapter. Worlding pain is often inherently intertwined with the quest for alleviation. To some extent, the capacity to make one's pain known to the world, or the ability to place one's pain into an applicable context, has served as an intrinsic salve. The human endogenous pain-killing systems function in part through this capacity not merely to put pain into the world, but also to have it received in an appropriate manner. What of more explicitly targeted instrumental attempts to kill pain? What about drugs? The experience of pain is often about the practices employed to endure or alleviate it, and to that extent the painkiller must make its entry. But one can only divert so much attention to analgesics without disrupting a matter-of-fact understanding of what they are for and what they do. Analgesic use is itself part of the experiential history of pain. Since the beginning of the era of controlled pharmaceutical trials, the problem of the objective collection of pain data from test subjects has not been cracked. The realization of the bearing of 'personality', or of emotionality, as well as attention, fear, or inhibition, on the experience of pain and the extent to which patients feel comfortable reporting it to a medical authority means that there could be little statistical gain from asking a patient how a drug made them feel.[1]

The modern desire to 'kill pain', paired with and fuelled by an indus-trial-capitalist desire to supply painkillers, pertains to a specific context in which the experience of pain is narrowly channelled through negativity and aversion: a paucity of meaning. Modern western pain might be defined by 'our' eagerness to get out of it. This book largely eschews a focus on attempts to relieve pain (although I have had to address pain-killing drugs, pharmaceutical trials, and anaesthesia in certain historical contexts) in favour of instances of being in and remaining in pain. The turn, at the end, to placebo and relief only further highlights the extent to which the phenomenon of pain is contextually experienced. But however powerful placebo or other painkillers may be, pain abides. This speaks to the fact that 'our' hopes about living in an anaesthetic age, or about the prospect for a pain-free future, have been dashed against the rocks of suffering *despite* and indeed *through* painkillers. The personal and social pains of opioid addiction, which skyrocketed after the intro-duction of OxyContin in 1995, have shown the risk-free relation of the use of painkillers for pain – a common enough refrain by pain specialists since the 1980s – to be altogether too sanguine. If anything, 'we' live in an age of pain and the painkiller occupies an ambiguous but complex part of the culture, politics, and economic logic of the presence of pain, not its elimination.[2] So-called 'diseases of despair' have opioids at their heart, as both cause and symptom: not just the drugs, but the companies that make them and the institutions of medicine that supply them.[3]

The medicalized and biologized understandings of pain that are now predominant in the way that people think about and perceive their own pains raise a major problem for sufferers when they understand that those pains are either insufficiently important or insufficiently under-stood to permit medical attention. While it is common for biologists to pronounce that chronic pain serves no adaptive purpose, that is, it is useless, they present it as a problem for science to solve. Such an appraisal overlooks the centuries of suffering in which pains long endured were fitted into cosmologies that not only made sense of them but also put a positive value on them. How much more endurable were chronic pains when one understood them to be necessary experiences on the road to salvation in the hereafter? But the 'useless' appraisal filters down into lay understandings of chronic pain, such that the millions who endure unending pain often now do so in the knowledge that it is a biological anomaly. In worlds drained of moral and religious frameworks of expla-nation about the value of pain, suffering without recourse to relief seems meaningless and unrelenting. While to some extent such sufferers might find ways to commiserate or share their pain narratives, the result of chronic pain in western civilization commonly leads to despair. It is highly related to self-harm and to suicidality. Moreover, in cultures that emphasize meaningful existence through work, capital, and sociality, chronic pain's tendency towards unfitness for work, impoverishment, and isolation only enhances the sense of hopelessness and futility that comes bundled with the pain syndrome. These entanglements are, in fact, definitive of the kinds of pain experience that are undergone.

The outlook is bleak. Once the experiential repertoire that made positive meanings out of suffering – that made such suffering bearable – is gone, it cannot be easily reinstituted. Dwindling numbers in the West find any solace or meaning for their suffering in spiritual practices or theological interpretations. Rather than looking for solutions from the patient outwards – from the cosmology, emotionology, and sensorium of the individual – the solution now seems to be from the social inwards: to relieve loneliness in substantial ways; to campaign for relief, both financial and social, from the capitalist or neoliberal logic of self-help through work; to provide access to and education in contemporary artforms that might provide an outlet for blocked channels of expression; to connect, in person or online, communities of suffering in the spirit of shared understanding. If the moral economy of religion that was at the core of western cultures has dwindled, it is to be replaced – for the sufferer – with an infrastructure of social connections, social support, and a new canon of social-artistic means of communication.

Where such things have been organized and implemented (and it should be said that these kinds of initiative have reached only the smallest fraction of chronic pain sufferers), there has been a clear sign that the worst experiences of suffering can be alleviated. The provision of an outlet of expression has provided, in the realization of an objective sign of a person's pain in a painting, a photograph, a poem, or whatever it may be, a reified instance of meaning for that pain, realized outside of the body. In turn, it allows a person to know their pain in a new way and to live it through a new medium.

The surface has barely been scratched. The logics of the economy, of the politics of disability and of the responsibility of government to provide relief, and of the institutions of medicine and medical education, mean that new practices of providing both meaning and relief must overcome an enormous obstacle of social inertia. To be a 'patient', in western societies, is limited only to those captured by the medical system and its practices of diagnosis and therapeutics. To medicine, the sufferer submits. There is little scope, outside of this framework, to suffer meaningfully or to seek remedy. The sufferer without recourse to medical salvation also submits, but with fatalism. It is submission to a system that cannot, according to its own processes, provide a cure.

For most, resignation becomes part and parcel of what they know of their pain. For others, resistance to submission – refusal to be *patient* – defines what their pain drives them to do. Thus, we have seen in recent years major campaigns for recognition for sufferers of endometriosis, fibromyalgia, chronic fatigue syndrome, long-COVID, and so on, which are defined by their demand to have the lived experiences of pain that typifies each of these categories acknowledged as *real*, and their concomitant demand for medical validation – through research and through treatment – of these conditions as true diagnoses. Such demands require others to look, to bear witness, to accede to the truthfulness of pain claims and pain knowledge acquired through painful experience. They are borne on the hopes of relief that can only come through widespread acceptance (and significant research funding) within orthodox medicine. They are fuelled by hope, determination, and anger, which in turn are part of the colour of the painful experience. By what measure might that experience change if such campaigns prevail?

The takeaway, for me, is the emphasis on the narrow bandwidth in which pain syndromes can make sense, and the extent to which the authority to validate a sufferer as a 'patient' is limited to medical personnel. If the hope is for a cure, or rather a set of cures, perhaps this is just as well. If the hope is for a shift in meaning within the pain experience – for the transformation of the experience of pain from futility and despair to something else, something bearable, instrumental, if not positive, then at least useful – then medical recognition alone seems likely to come up short. Where people have found each other – remotely, online – the specific salvation seems to reside in the quality of the community or the collective: to share in a common framework of understanding is itself an act of reification, meaning-making, bearing witness, validation. For those in pain, especially those in pain that endures or never seems to end, modernity's stress on the individual, on self-reliance or individual responsibility, on subjectivity over notions of society, collective experience, or community, comes at a great cost. It is not only that these structural qualities of modernity underwrite the modern disease of loneliness, it is that they also seem to thwart inter-subjective and relational solutions to pain syndromes. As pain takes hold and forces withdrawal, an apparent lack of sociality logically superadds isolation to the pain syndrome, worsening its experience. The sufferer becomes invisible. It is not a submission. This is not a willing patient. It is a quality of society that care in the community, where it exists, unfortunately cannot rebuild or replace the community that should be at the heart of care. Thus, the mutable patient exists online, in the twenty-first-century equivalent of an epistolary network, not so much a world of letters as it is a world of emojis, sharing of information and misinformation, campaigning, fund-raising, and, in whatever limited way, consolation. The shared experience of suffering – the pain collective – is disembodied and removed from personal or face-to-face interaction.

Yet on another level, the history of modern civilization is the history of collective suffering to which no name is ascribed, save a promise to remember that often seems to lack a subject. The nation, an ineffable collective, provided a sense of identity, a sense of purpose, a sense of motivation for action, whether it was for or against the very idea. The twentieth century's history of wars, slaughter, and genocide was, in every theatre, carried out in the name of a nation, of the ways in which people could be identified as belonging or not belonging, whether because of creed or colour or confession. The bodies of the maimed and the bodies of the dead, meaningfully innumerable, are the cipher for the pain of those identified with the nation and identified as outside the nation. In war, the collective suffers together, sharing an experience often through a resistance to sharing: by not talking about it. The private torments of survivors, their mute suffering, in loneliness, without overt complaint, nonetheless scream in a chorus of silence.

Perhaps this much is obvious. But the nation is the canvas upon which other mute sufferings are painted in obscurity. Poverty and loneliness, often conjoined, are the price of modern capitalist and neoliberal politics, couched within a framework of national ideologies. Can one suffer loneliness collectively? Yes. It is, by all accounts, an epidemic. In their isolation, cut painfully from community, the lonely can hear and read of the commonality of their plight. There is something ironic and deeply distasteful about this kind of collective experience. It is a form of knowledge about the common suffering of people, who, given the chance, might identify with each other in such a way as to palliate the suffering they endure. Yet while the means of shared knowledge remain open and seem to grow, so the prospects afforded to people to find community in the collective, to share in an experience and therefore break that experience, seem only to diminish. Paul McCartney wistfully asked where all the lonely people belong. There is no real doubt any more about where this distinctly modern group, in alarming numbers, have come from. They are the product of capitalism, of war, of underfunding, of austerity, of secularism, anti-society politics, the degradation of traditional industries, community hubs, guilds, training, education, and on and on. When everything must turn a profit to survive, what does not turn a profit produces suffering. The biggest cause of pain in modern societies is capitalism, especially in its strident individualist strain. Under it, most of us patiently submit.

We all know *our own* pain. But how much of pain does anyone know? For pain is not, as I hope this book has shown, a great universal that afflicts all humans alike. It is far more political than that. What a person is, where they are, when they are, and in what circumstances – these make pain, or rather the person in pain, what it is. Pain is plastic. Pain is plural. Pain is sometimes from somewhere: neck pain, back pain; pain is sometimes from somewhere else: referred pain; phantom pain; pain is the wound of an imaginary weapon that stabs, shoots, and pierces; pain is somatic, psychosomatic, emotional, ranging from trauma to 'trauma'; pain is loss: grief, anguish, a broken heart; pain is a heart attack; pain is chronic *or* acute, chronic *and* acute; pain is an ache, a headache, a tension headache, a splitting headache; pain is migraine; pain is *there*, visible; pain is inside, *invisible*, invalid: endometriosis, fibromyalgia, nervous, not recognized; pain is nerve pain, burning pain, pounding pain, boring pain, suicidal pain; pain is trigeminal neuralgia; pain is labour; pain is pleasure; pain is pressure; pain is weight: depression, despair, anxiety, angst, loneliness; pain is anything but unnameable: pain is *álgos, lúpē, odúnē, pashein, pathos, poena, pati, dolor, douleur, dolore, duḥkh, dard, 'alam, wajʿ, bol, Schmerz, tuska, tóng, kurushimi,* hurt, suffering. Pain is pain. And on, and on.

Epilogue

It is 2007. I am visiting the Hamburger Bahnhof art gallery in Berlin with a student, precocious, arrogant, fascinating, disturbing. He has told me that, as a younger teenager, he once stoned a seagull to see if *he* would feel anything. He did not. Now we stand examining an exhibition devoted to *Schmerz*, the perceptions and allure thereof, in science, in medicine, in everyday experience. Nietzsche's death mask does not move us, though we wonder about the black dog that stalked him. What does stimulate is a 'game' – a piece of immersive art based on an arcade video game – called *PainStation* (2001, but frequently updated), designed by Tilman Reiff and Volker Morawe (under the auspices of their company, //////////fur//// art entertainment interfaces). The cuboid terminal has a place on opposing sides so that one player can face off against another in a game reminiscent of Pong. Two information signs flank the machine. On one side, 'Instructions' to play the game. The left hand must be kept in contact with the 'sensorfield' to stay in the game. This 'sensorfield' delivers all the game's punishments and maltreatments. The right hand controls the action. On the other side, 'Warning': the game 'causes real pain', including 'third-degree burns', 'paralysis of the left body', caused by electric shocks, and 'haematoma and open wounds' on the left hand, caused by repeated whipping.

The setting adds a wrinkle of extra tension, for in a gallery space where nothing must be touched, an object that may be touched has added allure. We stand and look on. The game immediately invokes the Milgram experiments on the authoritarian personality, in which subjects willingly caused pain to another (or thought they did), simply because the authority figure instructed them to do so.[1] But here there is no authority, but a warning sign and the compelling semiotics of play. So we watch as couple after couple line up to compete to inflict pain on one another. The pain, at first, is not severe, but to win one must endure. As the game designers put it, 'no pain, no game'. Those punished wince, start, invariably remove their left hands, and then *laugh*. What wager are these people taking in coming forward to play? And what about us, the witnesses, who watch it play out again and again? It troubles me.

It has troubled me ever since. The 'game' is now part of the permanent exhibition at the Computerspielemuseum in Berlin. It matters, I think, if you go there specifically to play the game, just as it matters if you encounter it at a BDSM party, to which events the *PainStation* has toured. At that event in 2007, most people would have had no idea that they would encounter such a thing. Context is everything. It was a curio, in which people willingly engaged. Standing by, doing nothing, the players to me became part of the exhibition, their pain part of the art, part of the *display*. Vaunt empathy as a human universal if you will, but here was a clear example of how easily such things are disrupted, disengaged, or displaced, for I did not wonder about their pain, but about their humanity, and mine. The spectacle of pain, and others' willingness to make a game of it, seemed to me to be the point, and it would be trite if it were not that this somehow chimes with everyday experience of the world of pain. For every day, to some degree, you and I casually watch the spectacle of others in pain and do nothing, *feel* nothing, most of the time.[2] While in 2007 I did nothing but stare in a kind of stupefaction at the cosmic *PainStation*, concerning the pain that we encounter every day do we even look, or allow ourselves to see? Do we trust our eyes, our senses? What do I feel confronted by a never-ending screed of pain testimony, pain imagery, and pain sounds, of war, suffering, death, and grief? What do you feel? The answer, for me, is that at times I am overwhelmed by bewilderment, grief, despair, and rage. But being overwhelmed is not a sustainable state. Most of the time, I feel nothing. It is not nothingness as compassion fatigue. It is not nothingness as a failure of empathy. I am not inhuman. It is nothingness by necessity, nothingness by force of distraction, so that life – my life – and joy may go on. I am forcing this terminal reflection because it is one that most of us resist, most of the time. To own it is a necessary discomfort and, perhaps, a reminder to not let most of the time fall into all of the time; a reminder to continue to know pain.

Notes

Prologue

1 Alex Scott-Samuel et al., 'The impact of Thatcherism on health and well-being in Britain', *International Journal of Health Services*, 44 (2014): 53–71; Iain Crinson, 'Putting patients first: the continuity of the consumerist discourse in health policy, from the radical right to New Labour', *Critical Social Policy*, 55 (1998): 227–39.

Introduction: Disrupting a Definition

1 Rob Boddice and Bettina Hitzer, 'Emotion and experience in the history of medicine: elaborating a theory and seeking a method', in *Feeling Dis-ease in Modern History: Experiencing Medicine and Illness*, eds Rob Boddice and Bettina Hitzer (London: Bloomsbury, 2022), 3–19.

2 Excellent recent examples of the history of pain include: Joanna Bourke, *The Story of Pain: From Prayer to Painkillers* (Oxford: Oxford University Press, 2014); Javier Moscoso, *Pain: A Cultural History* (Houndmills: Palgrave, 2012); and Rachel Ablow, *Victorian Pain* (Princeton: Princeton University Press, 2017).

3 John Bonica, 'The need of a taxonomy', and H. Merskey et al., 'Pain terms: a list with definitions and notes on usage', *Pain*, 6 (1979): 247–52, at 250.

4 Srinivasa N. Raja et al., 'The revised International Association for the Study of Pain definition of pain: concepts, challenges, and compromises', *Pain*, 161 (2020): 1976–82, at 1977.

5 Rob Boddice, 'Hurt feelings', in *Pain and Emotion in Modern History*, ed. Rob Boddice (Houndmills: Palgrave, 2014), 1–15.

6 Ronald Melzack and Patrick Wall, *The Challenge of Pain* (London: Penguin, 1996), 15–18; Patrick Wall, 'Introduction to the fourth edition of *Textbook of Pain*', *Topical Issues in Pain*, 4 (2013): 7.

7 Serge Marchand, 'The physiology of pain mechanisms: from the periphery to the brain', *Rheumatic Disease Clinics of North America*, 34 (2008): 285–309.

8 N.I. Eisenberger, M.D. Lieberman, and K.D. Williams, 'Does rejection hurt? An fMRI study of social exclusion', *Science*, 302 (2003): 209–92; Lucas B. Mazur, 'The importance of cultural psychological perspectives in pain research:

towards the palliation of Cartesian anxiety', *Theory & Psychology*, 32 (2022): 183–201.

9   Nikola Grahek, *Feeling Pain and Being in Pain*, 2nd edition (Cambridge, MA: MIT Press, 2007).

10 Jan Plamper, *The History of Emotions: An Introduction* (Oxford: Oxford University Press, 2015); Rob Boddice, *The History of Emotions* (Manchester: Manchester University Press, 2018).

11 Deborah Padfield and Joanna M. Zakrzewska, eds, *Encountering Pain: Hearing, Seeing, Speaking* (London: UCL Press, 2021).

Chapter 1 *Scripting*: The Politics of Knowledge

1   John B. de C.M. Saunders and Charles Donald O'Malley, *Andreas Vesalius Bruxellensis: The Bloodletting Letter of 1539* (New York: Schuman, 1947), 11.

2   Galen, 'De locis affectis', in *Claudii Galeni opera omni*, ed. Karl Gottlob Kühn (Leipzig, 1826), vol. 8, 1–452.

3   Daniel King, *Experiencing Pain in Imperial Greek Culture* (Oxford: Oxford University Press, 2018), esp. 67–102.

4   Courtney Roby, 'Galen on the patient's role in pain diagnosis: sensation, consensus, and metaphor', in *Homo Patiens: Approaches to the Patient in the Ancient World*, eds Georgia Petridou and Chiara Thumiger (Leiden: Brill, 2016), 304–22, at 319.

5   Galen, *De locis affectis* (K.8.118). Roselyne Rey, *The History of Pain* (Cambridge, MA: Harvard University Press, 1998), 33. The translations here are all Roby's, but between works the translation choices change. Given that the purpose is to refer to common experiences, the subtleties of change are important. Roby, 'Galen on the patient's role', 318; Courtney Roby, 'Galen on Pain', MA Thesis, University of Colorado, 2005, 44; Nicole Wilson, 'The semantics of pain in Greco-Roman antiquity', *Journal of the History of Neurosciences*, 22 (2013): 129–43.

6   Adil S. Gamal, *Medieval Islamic Medicine*, trans. Michael W. Dols (Berkeley: University of California Press, 1984), 6–8.

7   Roby, 'Galen on Pain', 39–40.

8   Rey, *History of Pain*, 33; Roby, 'Galen on Pain', 45.

9   Ibn Sina, *al-Qānūn fī al-Ṭibb* (lithograph of 1867, McGill University Library).

10 I have cross-read the Arabic against a modern translation in Farsi because it is likely that Ibn Sina's categories had a vernacular possibility in Farsi and because of the likelihood of helpful conceptual continuity between co-extensive languages. I am also reading against Latin translations and attempts to put the work into English, especially O. Cameron Gruner, trans. and ed., *The Canon of*

Medicine of Avicenna (New York: AMS Press, 1973), 246–51; Osama A. Tashani and Mark I. Johnson, 'Avicenna's concept of pain', *Libyan Journal of Medicine*, 5 (2010).

11 There are reasons to view chronic itch and chronic pain through the same lens, but that is not the sense here. Tong Liu and Ru-Rong Ji, 'New insights into the mechanism of itch: are pain and itch controlled by distinct mechanisms?', *Pflügers Archiv – European Journal of Physiology*, 465 (2013): 1671–85.

12 Avicenna, *Canon medicinae*, trans. Gerardus Cremonensis, Spain, late thirteenth century, 1:2: xix–xx (105–7); Avicenna, *Canon medicinae*, trans. Gerardus Cremonensis (Gerardus Sablonetanus) (Venice: Bertochus, 1489/90), book 1, section 2, cap. xix–xx (63–4); Avicenna, *Clarissimi Abuali ibn Tsina canon medicinae*, ed. Edmund Castell, trans. Vopiscus Fortunatus Plemp (1658), book 1, section 2, ch. 19–20 (110–12).

13 Tashani and Johnson, 'Avicenna's concept of pain'; Sadia Nikhat, Yasmeen Shamsi, and Mohd. Fazil, 'Overcoming pain: an exploration of analgesia in Ibn Sina's *Al-Qanoon Fil Tibb*', *Journal of Drug Delivery and Therapeutics*, 9 (2019): 571–4, at 572; Mojtaba Heydari et al., 'The origin of the concept of neuropathic pain in early medieval Persia (9th–12th century CE)', *Acta medico-historica Adriatica*, 13 (2015): 9–22; Saeidimehr Mohammad, 'Avicenna on the causes of pain', *Avicinian Philosophy Journal*, 20 (2016–17): 5–16.

14 See the previous note and Murat Çetkin et al., 'The pain in the *Canon of Medicine*: types, causes and treatment', *European Journal of Therapeutics*, 25 (2019): 164–9.

15 Petri Brissoti [Pierre Brissot], *Apologetica disceptatio* (Basel: Thomae VVolffii, 1529).

16 Saunders and O'Malley, *Andreas Vesalius Bruxellensis*, 40–1.

17 That Vesalius operated in good knowledge of the Arabic school of medicine is well documented. Abdul Haq Compier, 'Rhazes in the Renaissance of Andreas Vesalius', *Medical History*, 56 (2012): 3–25.

18 Saunders and O'Malley, *Andreas Vesalius Bruxellensis*, 19.

19 Judy F. Pugh, 'The semantics of pain in Indian culture and medicine', *Culture, Medicine and Psychiatry*, 15 (1991): 19–43, at 19.

20 Sarah M. Whitman, 'Pain and suffering as viewed by the Hindu religion', *The Journal of Pain*, 8 (2007): 607–13, at 609.

21 Pugh, 'Semantics of Pain', 21, 33.

22 Pugh, 'Semantics of Pain', 26.

23 Pugh, 'Semantics of Pain', 36.

24 Pugh, 'Semantics of Pain', 38.

25 Paolo Santangelo, 'The perception of pain in late-imperial China', in *Pain*

and Emotion, ed. Boddice, 36–52; Angelika C. Messner, 'Towards a history of the corporeal dimensions of emotions: the case of pain', *Asiatische Studien*, 66 (2012): 943–72.

26 Paul U. Unschuld and Hermann Tessenow, trans., *Huang Di nei jing su wen* (Berkeley: University of California Press, 2011), vol. 1, 102.

27 Paul U. Unschuld, *Huang Di nei jung su wen: Nature, Knowledge, Imagery in an Ancient Chinese Medical Text* (Berkeley: University of California Press, 2003), 131.

28 Unschuld, *Huang Di*, 132.

29 Unschuld and Tessenow, *Huang Di*, vol. 1, 584–92.

30 Unschuld and Tessenow, *Huang Di*, vol. 1, 592–3.

31 Unschuld and Tessenow, *Huang Di*, vol. 1, 594–7.

32 Keith Wailoo, *Pain: A Political History* (Baltimore: Johns Hopkins University Press, 2014), 33–5, 39, 76–95, 87–93.

33 Mark D. Sullivan, 'Finding pain between minds and bodies', *The Clinical Journal of Pain*, 17 (2001): 246–56, at 247–8.

34 Edward R. Perl, 'Ideas about pain, a historical view', *Nature Reviews Neuroscience*, 8 (2007): 71–80, at 73.

35 Ronald Melzack and Patrick Wall, 'Pain mechanisms: a new theory', *Science*, n.s. 150 (1965): 971–9.

36 Henry K. Beecher, 'Pain in men wounded in battle', *Annals of Surgery*, 123 (1946): 96–105; Henry K. Beecher, 'Relationship of significance of wound to pain experienced', *Journal of the American Medical Association*, 161 (1956): 1609–13.

37 Howard L. Fields, 'Setting the stage for pain: allegorical tales from neuro-science', in *Pain and Its Transformations: The Interface of Biology and Culture*, eds Sarah Coakley and Kay Kaufman Shelemay (Cambridge, MA: Harvard University Press, 2007), 36–61, at 46.

38 Joanna Bourke, 'Phantom suffering: amputees, stump pain and phantom sensations in modern Britain', in *Pain and Emotion*, ed. Boddice, 66–89; Wilfried Witte, 'The emergence of chronic pain: phantom limbs, subjective experience and pain management in post-war West Germany', in *Pain and Emotion*, ed. Boddice, 90–110; Alastair Minnis, *Phantom Pains and Prosthetic Narratives* (Cambridge: Cambridge University Press, 2021).

39 Ambroise Paré, *La manière de traicter les playes faictes tant par hacquebutes …* (Paris: Arnoul l'Angelié, 1552), 59

40 Tommy L. Lott, 'Descartes on phantom limbs', *Mind & Language*, 1 (1986): 243–71.

41 S.W. Mitchell, 'Phantom limbs', *Lippincott's Magazine of Popular Literature and*

Science, 8 (1871): 563–9; Aura Satz, '"The conviction of its existence": Silas Weir Mitchell, phantom limbs and phantom bodies in neurology and spiritualism', in *Neurology and Modernity: A Cultural History of Nervous Systems, 1800–1950*, eds Laura Salisbury and Andrew Shail (London: Palgrave, 2010), 113–29.

42 Ronald Melzack, 'Phantom limbs', *Regional Anesthesia*, 14 (1989): 208–11; Ronald Melzack, 'Phantom limbs and the concept of a neuromatrix', *Trends in Neuroscience*, 13 (1990): 88–92; Ronald Melzack, 'From the gate to the neuro-matrix', *Pain*, 82 (1999): S121–6; Ronald Melzack, 'Pain and the neuromatrix in the brain', *Journal of Dental Education*, 65 (2001): 1378–82; Ronald Melzack, 'Evolution of the neuromatrix theory of pain', *Pain Practice*, 5 (2005): 85–94; Ronald Melzack and Joel Katz, 'Pain in the 21st century: the neuromatrix and beyond', in *Psychological Knowledge in Court: PTSD, Pain, and TBI*, eds Gerald Young, Keith Nicholson, and Andrew W. Kane (New York: Springer, 2006), 129–48.

43 Apostol Vaso et al., 'Peripheral nervous system origin of phantom limb pain', *Pain*, 155 (2014): 1384–91.

44 Kirsty Bannister and Anthony H. Dickenson, 'What is the pain experience and how can we control it? Perspectives from neuroscience', in *Encountering Pain*, eds Padfield and Zakrzewska, 355–69, at 355, 363, 368.

45 George L. Engel, 'The need for a new medical model: a challenge for biomedicine', *Science*, 196 (1977): 129–36, at 133, 135

46 Robert J. Gatchel et al., 'The biopsychosocial approach to chronic pain: scientific advances and future direction', *Psychological Bulletin*, 133 (2007): 581–624; Kelley Bevers et al., 'The biopsychosocial model of the assessment, prevention, and treatment of chronic pain', *US Neurology*, 12 (2016): 98–104.

47 David Borsook, Simona Sava, and Lino Becerra, 'The pain imaging revolution: advancing pain into the 21st century', *The Neuroscientist*, 16 (2010): 171–85; Debbie L. Morton, Javin S. Sandhu, and Anthony K.P. Jones, 'Brain imaging of pain: state of the art', *Journal of Pain Research*, 9 (2016): 613–24.

48 Ewen Callaway, 'Can brain scans reveal behaviour? Bombshell study says not yet', *Nature*, 17 March 2022.

Chapter 2 *Experiencing*: Objectivity versus Subjectivity

1 This concept was developed by Erin Sullivan, *Beyond Melancholy: Sadness and Selfhood in Renaissance England* (Oxford: Oxford University Press, 2016).

2 Otniel E. Dror, 'Visceral pleasures and pains', in *Knowledge and Pain*, eds Esther Cohen et al. (Leiden: Brill, 2012), 147–68.

3 Mark Paterson, 'On pain as a distinct sensation: mapping intensity, affects, and difference in "interior states"', *Body & Society*, 25 (2019): 100–35.

4 Moscoso, *Pain*, 106–7.

5 Noémi Tousignant, 'A quantity of suffering: measuring pain as emotion in the mid-twentieth-century USA', in *Pain and Emotion*, ed. Boddice, 111–29, at 112.

6 David Hord, *The Criminal Body: Lombroso and the Anatomy of Deviance* (New York: Routledge, 2015); Mark Paterson, 'The biopolitics of sensation, techniques of quantification, and the production of a "new" sensorium', *Resilience: A Journal of the Environmental Humanities*, 5 (2018): 67–95; Andy Williams, *Forensic Criminology* (New York: Routledge, 2014), 93–4.

7 Cesare Lombroso, *Criminal Man* (New York and London: G.P. Putnam's Sons, 1911), 25–6, 246–7.

8 Lombroso, *Criminal Man*, 39.

9 Dolores Martín Moruno's translation of Mantegazza's words in *Fisiologia del dolore* (Florence, 1880), 'Pain as practice in Paolo Mantegazza's science of emotions', *Osiris* 31 (2016): 137–62, at 141.

10 Moruno, 'Pain as practice', 142.

11 Tousignant, 'Quantity of suffering', 113.

12 Tousignant, 'Quantity of suffering', 114; Joanna Bourke, 'Pain sensitivity: an unnatural history from 1800 to 1965', *Journal of the Medical Humanities*, 35 (2014): 310–19; Jessica Pykett and Mark Paterson, 'Stressing the "body electric": history and psychology of the techno-ecologies of work stress', *History of the Human Sciences* (2022).

13 Xine Yao, *Disaffected: The Cultural Politics of Unfeeling in Nineteenth-Century America* (Durham, NC: Duke University Press, 2021), 18. Jefferson is quoted on the same page.

14 Quoted in Yao, *Disaffected*, 19.

15 Dror, 'Visceral pleasures and pains', 147.

16 Tousignant, 'Quantity of suffering', 116; Noémi Tousignant, 'The rise and fall of the dolorimeter: pain, analgesics, and the management of subjectivity in mid-twentieth-century United States', *Journal of the History of Medicine and Allied Sciences*, 66 (2011): 145–79.

17 Tousignant, 'Quantity of suffering', 118.

18 R. Melzack and W.S. Torgerson, 'On the language of pain', *Anesthesiology*, 34 (1971): 50–9, at 50.

19 Kenneth Woodrow et al., 'Pain tolerance: differences according to age, sex and race', *Psychosomatic Medicine*, 34 (1972): 548–56; D.F. Zatzick and J.E. Dimsdale, 'Cultural variations in response to painful stimuli', *Psychosomatic Medicine*, 52 (1990): 544–57.

20 Peggy Eastman, 'Genetic and ethnic differences reported in pain perception', *Neurology Today*, 9 (2009): 20–2.

21 Mary Gibson, 'On the insensitivity of women: science and the woman question in liberal Italy, 1890–1910', *Journal of Women's History*, 2 (1990): 11–41.

22 Angie L.F. Soetanto, Joanne W.Y. Chung, and Thomas K.S. Wong, 'Are there gender differences in pain perception?', *Journal of Neuroscience Nursing*, 38 (2006): 172–6. There are countless other examples.

23 Marie-Pierre Cyr et al., 'Reliability and convergent validity of the algometer for vestibular pain assessment in women with provoked vestibulodynia', *Pain Medicine*, 17 (2016): 1220–8.

24 Sander L. Gilman, *Illness and Image: Case Studies in the Medical Humanities* (New Brunswick, NJ: Transaction Publishers, 2015), ch. 5; Danny Rees, 'Down in the mouth: faces of pain', in *Pain and Emotion*, ed. Boddice, 164–86.

25 Esther Cohen, 'The animated pain of the body', *American Historical Review*, 105 (2000): 36–68, at 37.

26 Sarah R. Cohen, 'Searching the animal psyche with Charles Le Brun', *Annals of Science*, 67 (2010): 353–82. I am grateful to Benedict Robinson for pointing out the link to John of Damascus and scholastic passions (see his *Passion's Fictions from Shakespeare to Richardson: Literature and the Sciences of Soul and Mind* [Oxford: Oxford University Press, 2021], 127).

27 Chloé Hogg, 'Subject of passions: Charles Le Brun and the emotions of absolutism', *Philological Quarterly*, 93 (2014): 65–94; Zhang Ying, 'Descartes's theory of passion and Le Brun's theory of expression: a study of details regarding the French classicist aesthetics during the 17th century', *Theoretical Studies in Literature and Art*, 38 (2018): 49–60; Paola Giacomoni, 'The light of emotions: passions and emotions in seventeenth-century French culture', *Nuncius: annali di storia della scienza*, 33 (2018): 56–87; Caecilie Weissert, 'Charles Le Bruns *Expression des passions* und die *Têtes d'expression* im Kontext physiologischer Betrachtungen', in *Ars – Visus – Affectus: Visual Cultures of the Affective in the Early Modern Era*, eds Anna Pawlak, Lars Zieke, and Isabella Augart (Berlin: De Gruyter, 2016), 251–72.

28 Charles Le Brun, *Méthode pour apprendre à dessiner les passions* (Amsterdam: François van der Plaats, 1702), 15.

29 Lynda Nead, 'Response: the art of making faces', *Textual Practice*, 22 (2008): 133–43, at 135.

30 Linda Walsh, 'The expressive face', in *Early Modern Emotions: An Introduction*, ed. Susan Broomhall (London: Routledge, 2016), 81–6; Jennifer Montagu, *The Expression of the Passions: The Origin and Influence of Charles Le Brun's Conférence sur l'expression générale et particulière* (New Haven: Yale University Press, 1994).

31 Charles Bell, *Essays on the Anatomy and Philosophy of Expression* (London: John Murray, 1824), 61–2.

32 Charles Bell, *Essays on the Anatomy of Expression in Painting* (London: Longman, Hurst, Rees, and Orme, 1806), 117.

33 Bell, *Essays* (1824), 92, 95, 96.

34 Bell, *Essays* (1806), 112; Nead, 'Response', 135.

35 Alexander Bain, *Emotions and the Will* (London: John W. Parker, 1859); Herbert Spencer, *The Principles of Psychology* (London: Longman, Brown, Green, and Longmans, 1855); Wilhelm Wundt, *Beiträge zur Theorie der Sinneswahrnehmung* (Leipzig: Winter, 1862).

36 G.-B. Duchenne (de Boulogne), *Mécanisme de la physionomie humaine* (Paris: Jules Renouard, 1862) 2, 35–8.

37 Duchenne, *Mécanisme*, 74, 79.

38 Charles Darwin, *The Expression of the Emotions in Man and Animals* (London: John Murray, 1872), 74

39 Darwin, *Expression*, 177

40 Darwin, *Expression*, 342.

41 Cf. Paolo Mategazza, *Atlante della espressione del dolore: fotografie prese dal vero e da molte opere d'arte, che illustrano gli studi sperimentali sull'espressione del dolore* (Florence, 1876); Moruno, 'Pain as practice', 150–9.

42 Paul Ekman and Wallace V. Friesen, 'Constants across cultures in the face and emotion', *Journal of Personality and Social Psychology*, 17 (1971): 124–9; Charles Darwin, *The Expression of the Emotions in Man and Animals*, Introduction, Afterword, and Commentaries by Paul Ekman, 4th edition (Oxford: Oxford University Press, 2009).

43 Ruth V.E. Grunau and Kenneth D. Craig, 'Pain expression in neonates: facial action and cry', *Pain*, 28 (1987): 395–410; for criticism, see Manon Ranger, C. Céleste Johnston, and K.J.S. Anand, 'Current controversies regarding pain assessment in neonates', *Seminars in Perinatology*, 31 (2007): 283–8.

44 Paul A. Flecknell, 'Do mice have a pain face?', *Nature Methods*, 7 (2010): 437–8.

45 Niek Andresen et al., 'Towards a fully automated surveillance of well-being status in laboratory mice using deep learning: starting with facial expression analysis', *PLoS ONE*, 15 (2020); Larry Carbone, 'Do "prey species" hide their pain? Implications for ethical care and use of laboratory animals', *Journal of Applied Animal Ethics Research*, 2 (2020): 216–36.

46 Kenneth M. Prkachin, 'The consistency of facial expressions of pain: a comparison across modalities', *Pain*, 51 (1992): 297–306. Ekman's support is directly acknowledged.

47 Prkachin, 'Consistency', 305.

48 Michel-Pierre Coll et al., 'Repeated exposure to vicarious pain alters

electrocortical processing of pain expressions', *Experimental Brain Research*, 234 (2016): 2677–86.

49 Prkachin, 'Consistency', 304, 305.

50 Kenneth D. Craig, Kenneth M. Prkachin, and Ruth Eckstein Grunau, 'The facial expression of pain', in *Handbook of Pain Assessment*, eds Dennis C. Turk and Ronald Melzack, 2nd edition (New York: Guilford Press, 2001), 153–69, at 160.

51 Kenneth M. Prkachin, 'Facial pain expression', *Pain Management*, 1 (2011): 367–76, at 369–70. Meanwhile, in the third edition of the *Handbook of Pain Assessment* (New York: Guilford Press, 2011), the reference to much-needed cross-cultural studies was simply deleted.

52 Donna Lee Wong and Connie Morain Baker, 'Pain in children: comparison of assessment scales', *Pediatric Nursing*, 14 (1988): 9–17, at 11.

53 Wong and Baker, 'Pain in children', 16.

54 C.T. Chambers and K.D. Craig, 'An intrusive impact of anchors in children's face pain scales', *Pain*, 78 (1998): 27–37.

55 IASP, 'Faces Pain Scale – Revised', https://www.iasp-pain.org/resources/faces-pain-scale-revised/; C.L. Hicks et al., 'The Faces Pain Scale – Revised: toward a common metric in pediatric pain measurement', *Pain*, 93 (2001): 173–83.

56 Miriam Kunz, Kenneth Prkachin, and Stefan Lautenbacher, 'Smiling in pain: explorations of its social motives', *Pain Research and Treatment* (2013): 1–8, at 1, 7.

57 Kenneth M. Prkachin, 'Inferring pain from avatars', *Scandinavian Journal of Pain*, 21 (2020): 5–7, an editorial comment on Eleonora Meister et al., 'Decoding of facial expressions of pain in avatars: does sex matter?', *Scandinavian Journal of Pain*, 21 (2020): 174–82.

58 Prkachin, Inferring pain', 6.

59 Meister et al., 'Decoding of facial expressions', 175, 181.

60 Lisa Feldman Barrett, *How Emotions Are Made: The Secret Life of the Brain* (Boston: Houghton Mifflin Harcourt, 2017); Daniel M. Gross and Stephanie D. Preston, 'Darwin and the situation of emotion research', *Emotion Review*, 12 (2020): 179–90.

61 Robert Burton, *The Anatomy of Melancholy* (1621; Philadelphia: E. Claxton, 1883), 18.

62 Burton, *Anatomy*, 163.

63 Burton, *Anatomy*, 162.

64 Burton, *Anatomy*, 164.

65 Burton, *Anatomy*, 164–5.

66 Burton, *Anatomy*, 166.

67 Burton, *Anatomy*, 167.

68 Burton, *Anatomy*, 170.

69 Burton, *Anatomy*, 209.

70 Sullivan, *Beyond Melancholy*; Moscoso, *Pain*.

71 Mark Savage, 'Lady Gaga had a "psychotic break" after sexual assault left her pregnant', BBC News, 21 May 2021.

72 Bourke, *Story of Pain*, 53ff.

73 Rob Boddice, 'Hysteria or tetanus? Ambivalent embodiments and the authenticity of pain', in *Emotional Bodies: The Historical Performativity of Emotions*, eds Dolores Martín-Moruno and Beatriz Pichel (Urbana-Champaign: University of Illinois Press, 2019), 19–35; Daniel Goldberg, 'Pain without lesion: debate among American neurologists, 1850–1900', *19: Interdisciplinary Studies in the Long Nineteenth Century*, 15 (2012).

74 Jonathan Shay, *Achilles in Vietnam: Combat Trauma and the Undoing of Character* (New York: Scribner, 1994); Ronald Pies, 'The anatomy of sorrow: a spiritual, phenomenological, and neurological perspective', *Philosophy, Ethics, and Humanities in Medicine*, 3 (2008): art. 17.

75 Joanna Bourke, 'Forensic sense: sexual violence, medical professionals and the senses', in *Feeling Dis-ease*, eds Boddice and Hitzer, 157–74.

76 Jaipreet Virdi, 'A tale of three hospitals', *Synapsis*, 3 April 2022.

77 William Reddy, 'The unavoidable intentionality of affect: the history of emotions and the neurosciences of the present day', *Emotion Review*, 12 (2020): 168–78, at 172.

78 Stephanos Geroulanos and Todd Meyers, *The Human Body in the Age of Catastrophe: Brittleness, Integration, Science, and the Great War* (Chicago: University of Chicago Press, 2018); Manos Tsakiris and Helena De Preester, eds, *The Interoceptive Mind: From Homeostasis to Awareness* (Oxford: Oxford University Press, 2019).

79 Rob Boddice, 'Pain', in *Routledge History of Emotions in the Modern World*, eds Katie Barclay and Peter Stearns (New York: Routledge, 2022), 77–89.

80 Allan Young, *The Harmony of Illusions: Inventing Post-Traumatic Stress Disorder* (Princeton: Princeton University Press, 1995).

81 Ville Kivimäki, 'Experiencing trauma before trauma: posttraumatic memories, nightmares and flashbacks among Finnish soldiers', in *Trauma, Experience and Narrative in Europe during and after World War II*, eds Ville Kivimäki and Peter Leese (London: Palgrave Macmillan, 2022), 89–117; Ville Kivimäki, 'Languages of the wound: Finnish soldiers' bodies as sites of shock in the Second World War', in *Languages of Trauma: History, Memory, and Media*, eds Peter Leese, Julia Barbara Köhne, and Jason Crouthamel (Toronto: University of Toronto Press, 2021), 70–96.

82 Geoff MacDonald and Lauri Jensen-Campbell, eds, *Social Pain: Neuropsychological and Health Implications of Loss and Exclusion* (Washington, DC: American Psychological Association, 2011).

83 N.I. Eisenberger, M.D. Lieberman, and K.D. Williams, 'Does rejection hurt? An fMRI study of social exclusion', *Science*, 302 (2003): 209–92.

84 Grahek, *Feeling Pain*.

85 Daniel Randles, Steven J. Heine, and Nathan Santos, 'The common pain of surrealism and death: acetaminophen reduces compensatory affirmation following meaning threats', *Psychological Science*, 24 (2013): 966–73; C. Nathan DeWall et al., 'Acetaminophen reduces social pain: behavioral and neural evidence', *Psychological Science*, 21 (2010): 931–7.

86 Makoto Harris Takao, 'Beyond nostalgia and the prison of English: positioning Japan in a global history of emotions', *Zeithistorische Forschungen*, 18 (2021): 21–43; Susan J. Matt, *Homesickness: An American History* (New York: Oxford University Press, 2014); Juliane Brauer, 'Nostalgie unde Heimweh: Zum politischen Gehalt von Heimatgefühlen', *Zeithistorische Forschungen*, 18 (2021): 151–65.

87 Rob Boddice, *A History of Feelings* (London: Reaktion, 2019), 21–9.

88 Achilles' name is a compound of grief/pain and 'host of fighting men'. Gregory Nagy, 'The name of Achilles: questions of etymology and "folk-etymology"', *Illinois Classical Studies*, 19 (1994): 3–9.

89 Emily Austin, 'Grief as πoθή: understanding the anger of Achilles', *New England Classical Journal*, 42 (2015): 147–63; Emily Austin, 'Achilles' desire for lament: variations on a theme', *Classical World*, 114 (2020): 1–23.

90 David Konstan, 'Understanding grief in Greece and Rome', *Classical World*, 110 (2016): 3–30; Christos Tsagalis, *Epic Grief: Personal Laments in Homer's Iliad* (Berlin: De Gruyter, 2004).

91 D.L. Cairns, 'Weeping and veiling: grief, display and concealment in ancient Greek culture', in *Tears in the Graeco-Roman World*, ed. Thorsten Fögen (Berlin: De Gruyter, 2009), 37–58, at 41.

92 Cairns, 'Weeping', 44.

93 Cairns, 'Weeping', 48.

94 Kyriaki Mystakidou et al., 'Death and grief in the Greek culture', *Omega*, 50 (2004–5): 23–34, at 26.

95 Cf. Svend Brinkmann, 'The body in grief', *Mortality*, 24 (2019): 290–303.

Chapter 3 *Worlding*: Expressing and Managing

1 Elaine Scarry, *The Body in Pain: The Making and Unmaking of the World* (New York: Oxford University Press, 1985).

2 Wolfgang Wagner, 'Cancer and the arts: La Madonna dei Tumori, Ravenna, Italy', *European Society for Medical Oncology Open*, 1 (2016); Michele A. Riva and Giancarlo Cesana, 'Our Lady of Tumours', *Cancer and Society*, 18 (2017): 180.

3 Taken from the prayer, printed and available in the Basilica: http://www .sanvitaleravenna./madonna-dei-tumori/.

4 Boddice, *History of Feelings*, 84–6.

5 Thanks to Karen McCluskey for discussing this painting with me.

6 Ariel Glucklich, *Sacred Pain: Hurting the Body for the Sake of the Soul* (Oxford: Oxford University Press, 2003). For more historically minded research on pain as virtue, see Moscoso, *Pain*, esp. chs 1 and 2; Bourke, *Story of Pain*, 88–130; Esther Cohen, *The Modulated Scream: Pain in Late Medieval Culture* (Chicago: University of Chicago Press, 2009), 168–97; L. Stephanie Cobb, *Divine Deliverance: Pain and Painlessness in Early Christian Martyr Texts* (Berkeley: University of California Press, 2017).

7 Judith Perkins, *The Suffering Self: Pain and Narrative Representation in the Early Christian Era* (London: Routledge, 1995).

8 Marla Carlson, *Performing Bodies in Pain: Medieval and Post-Modern Martyrs, Mystics, and Artists* (Houndmills: Palgrave, 2010).

9 Cohen, *Modulated Scream*.

10 Karen McCluskey, Louise St Guillaume, and Daniela Da Silva, 'Ability and disability in the pictorial *vitae* of *Beata* Fina in fifteenth-century San Gimignano', in *Routledge Companion to Art and Disability*, eds Keri Watson and Timothy W. Hiles (New York: Routledge, 2022), 94–114; Sari Katajala-Peltomaa, Jenni Kuuliala, and Iona McCleery, eds, *A Companion to Medieval Miracle Collections* (Leiden: Brill, 2021).

11 Louise Marshall, 'Manipulating the sacred: image and plague in Renaissance Italy', *Renaissance Quarterly*, 47 (1994): 485–532.

12 Gavin Flood, *The Ascetic Self: Subjectivity, Memory and Tradition* (Cambridge: Cambridge University Press, 2004); Lih-Mih Chen et al., 'Concepts within the Chinese culture that influence the cancer pain experience', *Cancer Nursing*, 31 (2008): 103–8.

13 C.S. Lewis, *The Problem of Pain* (1940; New York: HarperCollins, 2001), 91; Angela Platt, 'Pain as spiritual barometer of health: a sign of divine love, 1780–1850', *Studies in Church History*, 58 (2022): 1–21.

14 Herbert Spencer, 'Consciousness under chloroform', *Popular Science Monthly*, 13 October 1878: 694–8, at 694–6.

15 For context on the association of medicine and the Gothic, see William Hughes, 'Victorian medicine and the Gothic', *Victorian Gothic: An Edinburgh*

Companion, eds Andrew Smith and William Hughes (Edinburgh: Edinburgh University Press, 2014), 186–201; Louise Benson James, 'Hysterical bodies and Gothic spaces: Lucas Malet's "moral dissecting-room"', in *Lucas Malet, Dissident Pilgrim: Critical Essays*, eds Jane Ford and Alexandra Gray (London: Routledge, 2019).

16 Spencer, 'Consciousness under chloroform', 696–8.

17 George H. Savage, 'Insanity following the use of anaesthetics in operations', *British Medical Journal*, 3 December 1887: 1199–200.

18 Boddice, *History of Feelings*, 144–63; Liz Gray, 'Body, mind and madness: pain in animals in nineteenth-century comparative psychology', *Pain and Emotion*, ed. Boddice, 148–63.

19 Rob Boddice, 'Species of compassion: aesthetics, anaesthetics, and pain in the physiological laboratory', *19: Interdisciplinary Studies in the Long Nineteenth Century*, 15 (2012); Rob Boddice, *The Science of Sympathy: Morality, Evolution, and Victorian Civilization* (Urbana-Champaign: University of Illinois Press, 2016), esp. ch. 4; Tarquin Holmes and Carrie Friese, 'Making the anaesthetised animal into a boundary object: an analysis of the 1875 Royal Commission on Vivisection', *History and Philosophy of the Life Sciences*, 42 (2020): art. 50.

20 Kate Cole-Adams, '"I could hear things, and I could feel terrible pain": when anaesthesia fails', *Guardian*, 9 February 2018.

21 Cole-Adams, '"I could hear things"'; Michael Wang, 'Inadequate anaesthesia as a cause of psychopathology', *Bulletin of the Royal College of Anaesthetists*, 40 (1998): 20–2.

22 J.J. Pandit et al., 'A national survey of anaesthetists (NAP5 Baseline) to estimate an annual incidence of accidental awareness during general anaesthesia in the UK', *British Journal of Anaesthesia*, 110 (2013): 501–9, at 501, 508; J. Bruhn et al., 'Depth of anaesthesia monitoring: what's available, what's validated and what's next?', *British Journal of Anaesthesia*, 97 (2006): 85–94, at 86–7.

23 Darwin to Gray, 22 May 1860, Darwin Correspondence Project, 'Letter no. 2814', https://www.darwinproject.ac.uk/letter/?docId=letters/DCP-LETT-2814 .xml.

24 Charles Darwin, *On the Origin of Species by Means of Natural Selection* (London: John Murray, 1859), 200–1, 472.

25 John Bowring, ed., *The Works of Jeremy Bentham* (Edinburgh: William Tait, 1843), vol. 11, 81.

26 John Stuart Mill, *Utilitarianism*, 2nd edition (London: Longman, Green, Longman, Roberts and Green, 1864), 13.

27 Cathy Gere, *Pain, Pleasure, and the Greater Good: From the Panopticon to the Skinner Box and Beyond* (Chicago: University of Chicago Press, 2017); Rob

Boddice, *Humane Professions: The Defence of Experimental Medicine, 1876–1914* (Cambridge: Cambridge University Press, 2021), 13–15.

28 Boddice, *Science of Sympathy*; Daniel M. Gross, 'Defending the humanities with Charles Darwin's *The Expression of the Emotions in Man and Animals* (1872)', *Critical Inquiry*, 37 (2010): 34–59; Ablow, *Victorian Pain*, 94.

29 Darwin to Romanes, 5 February 1880, Darwin Correspondence Project, 'Letter no. 12461', https://www.darwinproject.ac.uk/letter/?docId=letters/DCP-LETT -12461.xml.

30 Ablow, *Victorian Pain*, ch. 4.

31 Patrick Wall, *Pain: The Science of Suffering* (New York: Columbia University Press, 2002), 49.

32 Wall, *Pain*, 19.

33 Gere, *Pain*, 165ff.

34 Martin Schiavenato et al., 'Neonatal pain facial expression: evaluating the primal face of pain', *Pain*, 138 (2008): 460–71.

35 Bourke, *Story of Pain*, 214–22.

36 Rousseau, quoted in Larry Wolff, 'When I imagine a child: the idea of childhood and the philosophy of memory in the Enlightenment', *Eighteenth-Century Studies*, 31 (1998): 377–401, at 395.

37 Rachel E. Horton, 'Mothers' facial expressions of pain and fear and infants' pain response during immunization', *Infant Mental Health Journal*, 31 (2010): 397–411.

38 Bourke, *Story of Pain*, 292–3.

39 Irene Ridgers, Katherine McCombe, and Andrew McCombe, 'A tongue-tie clinic and service', *British Journal of Midwifery*, 17 (2009): 230–3, at 231–2.

40 Helen Wallace and Susan Clarke, 'Tongue tie division in infants with breast feeding difficulties', *International Journal of Pediatric Otorhinolaryngology*, 70 (2006): 1257–61.

41 Prim Auychai, Andreas Neff, and Poramate Pitak-Arnnop, 'Tongue-tie children with a severe Hazelbaker score or difficult breastfeeding benefit greatly from frenotomy or frenuloplasty with/without anaesthesia – first do or do no harm?', *Journal of Stomatology, Oral and Maxillofacial Surgery* (2021).

42 B.R. Paix, 'Circumcision of neonates and children without appropriate anaesthesia is unacceptable practice', *Anaesthesia and Intensive Care*, 40 (2012): 511–16.

43 R. Goldman, 'The psychological impact of circumcision', *BJU International*, 83 (1999): 93–102; Hanoch Ben-Yami, 'Circumcision: what should be done?', *Journal of Medical Ethics*, 39 (2013): 459–62.

44 Benjamin T. Many et al., 'A contemporary snapshot of circumcision in US children's hospitals', *Journal of Pediatric Surgery*, 55 (2020): 1134–8; D.B.

Andropoulos, 'Effect of anaesthesia on the developing brain: infant and fetus', *Fetal Diagnosis and Therapy*, 43 (2018): 1–11; C. Ing et al., 'Long-term differences in language and cognitive function after childhood exposure to anesthesia', *Pediatrics*, 130 (2012): e476–85.

45 Gayle Giboney Page, 'Are there long-term consequences of pain in newborn or very young infants?', *Journal of Perinatal Education*, 13 (2004): 10–17.

46 Donald Canton, *What a Blessing She Had Chloroform: The Medical and Social Response to the Pain of Childbirth from 1800 to the Present* (New Haven: Yale University Press, 1999).

47 Isabel M. Córdova, *Pushing in Silence: Modernizing Puerto Rico and the Medicalization of Childbirth* (Austin: University of Texas Press, 2018); Whitney Wood, *Birth Pangs: Maternity, Medicine, and Feminine Delicacy in English Canada, 1867–1940* (Montreal: McGill-Queens University Press, forthcoming); Richard W. Wertz and Dorothy C. Wertz, *Lying-In: A History of Childbirth in America*, new edition (New Haven: Yale University Press, 1989); Barbara M. Cooper, *Countless Blessings: A History of Childbirth and Reproduction in the Sahel* (Bloomington: Indiana University Press, 2019); Nancy Rose Hunt, *A Colonial Lexicon: of Birth Ritual, Medicalization, and Mobility in the Congo* (Durham, NC: Duke University Press, 1999); Chiaki Shirai, 'Historical dynamism of childbirth in Japan: medicalization and its normative politics, 1868–2017', *Technology and Culture*, 61 (2020): 559–80; Jennifer Evans and Ciara Meehan, eds, *Perceptions of Pregnancy from the Seventeenth to the Twentieth Century* (London: Palgrave, 2016); Moscoso, *Pain*, 96–104.

48 Maria Cizmic, *Performing Pain: Music and Trauma in Eastern Europe* (Oxford: Oxford University Press, 2011); Maria Pia Di Bella and James Elkins, eds, *Representations of Pain in Art and Visual Culture* (London: Routledge, 2013); Maj Hasager, 'Memory and trauma: two contemporary art projects', in *Languages of Trauma*, eds Leese, Köhne, and Crouthamel, 197–210; Dyah Pitaloka and Hans Pols, 'Performing songs and staging theatre performances: working through the trauma of the 1965/66 Indonesian mass killings', in *Languages of Trauma*, eds Leese, Köhne, and Crouthamel, 141–59; Carol A. Courtney, Michael A. O'Hearn, and Carla C. Franck, 'Frida Kahlo: portrait of chronic pain', *Physical Therapy*, 97 (2017): 90–6; Siobhan M. Conaty, 'Frida Kahlo's body: confronting trauma in art', *Journal of Humanities in Rehabilitation* (2015); Nigel Spivey, *Enduring Creation: Art, Pain, and Fortitude* (Berkeley: University of California Press, 2001).

49 There are two paintings with this title in English, the first is qualified by *Sick Mood at Sunset*. The second is from 1894. In Norwegian, they are both *Fortvilelse*.

50 Thor Arvid Dyrerud, '"Nordic Angst": Søren Kierkegaard and *The Concept of Anxiety* in Norway', *Kierkegaard Studies Yearbook* (2001): 364–77, at 365–6.

51 Quotes from Sue Prideaux, *Edvard Munch: Behind the Scream* (New Haven: Yale University Press, 2005), 2.

52 The Norwegian is taken from the Munch Museum website, https://munch .emuseum.com/no/objects/6213/fortvilelse?ctx=b2d416f5-e9de-429a-bd12 -70888da3cd24&idx=2. The English is partly based on the translation on this site, but I have adapted it here to be (a) more literal and (b) more faithful to the original.

53 Quoted in J. Gill Holland, ed., *Edvard Munch: We Are Flames which Pour Out of the Earth* (Madison: University of Wisconsin Press, 2005), 64–5.

54 Mladen Stilinović, 'Dictionary – pain', in *Preoccupations* (Lyon: Galerie l'Ollave, 1994), quoted on https://mladenstilinovic.com/works/625-2/.

55 For analysis, James R. Hamilton, 'Handke's *Kaspar*, Wittgenstein's *Tractatus*, and the successful representation of alienation', *Journal of Dramatic Theory and Criticism* (1995): 3–26.

56 Ludwig Wittgenstein, *Philosophical Investigations*, trans. G.E.M. Anscombe, P.M.S. Hacker, and Joachim Schulte (1953; Oxford: Wiley Blackwell, 2010), part 1§293.

57 Stilinović, 'Dictionary – pain'.

58 Eugen Blume et al., eds, *Schmerz: Kunst und Wissenschaft* (Cologne: DuMont, 2007).

59 Louise Bourgeois, *I Want to be Accurate, Not Shocking: In Conversation with Christiane Meyer-Thoss* (Berlin: Mikrotext, 2020), n.p.

60 Christiane Meyer-Thoss, *Designing for Free Fall* (Amman: Zurich, 1992), 189.

61 Boddice, 'Hysteria or tetanus?'

62 Sander L. Gilman, 'The image of the hysteric', in *Hysteria beyond Freud*, ed. Sander L. Gilman et al. (Berkeley: University of California Press, 1993), 345–452; Mark Micale, *Approaching Hysteria: Disease and Its Interpretations* (Princeton: Princeton University Press, 1995); Mark Micale, *Hysterical Men: The Hidden History of Male Nervous Illness* (Cambridge, MA: Harvard University Press, 2008); Andrew Scull, *Hysteria: The Biography* (Oxford: Oxford University Press, 1993).

63 Boddice, 'Hysteria or tetanus?'

64 Maria Nadotti, 'La distruzione del padre: an interview with Louise Bourgeois', *Salmagundi*, 202–3 (2019). The interview is from 1993: Ulf Küster, *Louise Bourgeois* (Ostfilden: Hatje Cantz, 2012).

65 Meyer-Thoss, *Designing for Free Fall*, 200.

66 Marta Equi Pierazzini, '"The subject of pain is the business I am in": Louise

Bourgeois and the iconography of hysteria: reclaiming the visibility of pain', *Ikon*, 12 (2019): 203–12.

67 Meyer-Thoss, *Designing for Free Fall*, 177

68 Meyer-Thoss, *Designing for Free Fall*, 200.

69 Nadotti, 'La distruzione del padre'.

Chapter 4 *Suffering*: Chronicity and Pain Syndromes

1 Andrew Hodgkiss, *From Lesion to Metaphor: Chronic Pain in British, French and German Medical Writings, 1800–1914* (Amsterdam: Rodopi, 2000).

2 Clifford J. Woolf and Michael W. Salter, 'Neuronal plasticity: increasing the gain in pain', *Science*, 288 (2000): 1765–8.

3 Eva Kosek et al., 'Do we need a third mechanistic descriptor for chronic pain states?', *Pain*, 157 (2016): 1382–6; quote from Jo Nijs et al., 'Central sensitization in chronic pain conditions: latest discoveries and their potential for precision medicine', *Lancet Rheumatology*, 3 (2021): e383–92, at e383.

4 Kosek et al., 'Do we need a third mechanistic descriptor', e383–4.

5 Kosek et al., 'Do we need a third mechanistic descriptor', e387.

6 Lars-Petter Granan, 'We do not need a third mechanistic descriptor for chronic pain states! Not yet', *Pain*, 158 (2017): 179.

7 Amy Lewandowski Holley, Anna C. Wilson, and Tonya M. Palermo, 'Predictors of the transition from acute to persistent musculoskeletal pain in children and adolescents: a prospective study', *Pain*, 158 (2017): 794–801, at 799.

8 Michael Von Korff and Gregory Simon, 'The relationship between pain and depression', *British Journal of Psychiatry Supplement*, 30 (1996): 101–8; Marion Tegethoff et al., 'Comorbidity of mental disorders and chronic pain: chronology of onset in adolescents of a national representative cohort', *Journal of Pain*, 16 (2015): 1054–64.

9 Maaike Leeuw et al., 'The fear-avoidance model of musculoskeletal pain: current state of scientific evidence', *Journal of Behavioral Medicine*, 30 (2007): 77–94; Peter J. Norton and Gordon J.G. Asmundson, 'Anxiety sensitivity, fear, and avoidance behavior in headache pain', *Pain*, 111 (2004): 218–23; Anna C. Wilson, Amy S. Lewandowski, and Tonya M. Palermo, 'Fear-avoidance beliefs and parental response to pain in adolescents with chronic pain', *Pain Research and Management*, 16 (2011): 178–82.

10 Judy Foreman, *A Nation in Pain: Healing Our Biggest Health Problem* (New York: Oxford University Press, 2014), 3.

11 Rob Boddice, *Pain: A Very Short Introduction* (Oxford: Oxford University Press, 2017), 95.

12 R.M. Leadley et al., 'Chronic diseases in the European Union: the prevalence

and health cost implications of chronic pain', *Journal of Pain & Palliative Care Pharmacopathy*, 26 (2012): 310–25; Ceri J. Phillips, 'The cost and burden of chronic pain', *Reviews in Pain*, 3 (2009): 2–5; Miriam N. Raftery et al., 'The economic cost of chronic noncancer pain in Ireland: results from the PRIME Study, Part 2', *Journal of Pain*, 13 (2012): 139–45; Marina T. van Leeuwen et al., 'Chronic pain and reduced work effectiveness: the hidden cost to Australian employers', *European Journal of Pain*, 10 (2006): 161–6.

13 Rafia S. Rasu et al., 'Cost of pain medication to treat adult patients with nonmalignant chronic pain in the United States', *Journal of Managed Care + Specialty Pharmacy*, 20 (2014): 921–8.

14 Steven F. Brena, *Chronic Pain: America's Hidden Epidemic* (New York: Atheneum, 1978), 3–11.

15 John J. Bonica, 'Preface', in *New Approaches to Treatment of Chronic Pain: A Review of Multidisciplinary Pain Clinics and Pain Centers*, ed. Lorenz K.Y. Ng (Washington, DC: Government Printing Office, 1981), vii–x, at vii.

16 Fay Bound Alberti, *A Biography of Loneliness* (Oxford: Oxford University Press, 2019); Boddice, *History of Feelings*, ch. 6; Edgar Cabanas and Eva Illouz, *Manufacturing Happy Citizens: How the Science and Industry of Happiness Control our Lives* (Cambridge: Polity, 2019); William Davies, *The Happiness Industry: How the Government and Big Business Sold Us Well-Being* (London: Verso, 2015).

17 Ma Carmen Castillejos et al., 'Prevalence of suicidality in the European general population: a systematic review and meta-analysis', *Archives of Suicide Research*, 25 (2021): 810–28.

18 Jordana L. Sommer, Caitlin Blaney, and Renée El-Gabalawy, 'A population-based examination of suicidality in comorbid generalized anxiety disorder and chronic pain', *Journal of Affective Disorders*, 257 (2019): 562–7.

19 Melzack and Torgerson, 'On the language of pain', 50.

20 Melzack and Torgerson, 'On the language of pain', 53.

21 Melzack and Torgerson, 'On the language of pain', 53–8.

22 Ronald Melzack, 'The McGill Pain Questionnaire: major properties and scoring methods', *Pain*, 1 (1975): 277–99, at 283.

23 Melzack, 'McGill Pain Questionnaire', 288.

24 Melzack, 'McGill Pain Questionnaire', 294.

25 Melzack, 'McGill Pain Questionnaire', 296.

26 Mamoru Hasegawa et al., 'The McGill Pain Questionnaire, Japanese version, reconsidered: confirming the reliability and validity', *Pain Research and Management*, 1 (1996): 233–7, at 236.

27 Ann Harrison, 'Arabic pain words', *Pain*, 32 (1988): 239–50, at 240, 248.

28 Heikki Ketovuori and P.J. Pöntinen, 'A pain vocabulary in Finnish – the Finnish Pain Questionnaire', *Pain*, 11 (1981): 247–53.

29 Ivan Kiss, Harald Müller, and Manfred Abel, 'The McGill Pain Questionnaire – German version. A study on cancer pain', *Pain*, 29 (1987): 195–207, at 205, 207.

30 Giuseppina Maiani and Ezio Sanavio, 'Semantics of pain in Italy: the Italian version of the McGill Pain Questionnaire', *Pain*, 22 (1985): 399–405, at 401, 404.

31 Luciola sa Cunha Menezes Costa et al., 'Systematic review of cross-cultural adaptations of McGill Pain Questionnaire reveals a paucity of clinimetric testing', *Journal of Clinical Epidemiology*, 62 (2009): 934–43.

32 Harriet Martineau, *Life in the Sick-Room* (Boston: William Crosby, 1845), 19.

33 Martineau, *Life in the Sick-Room*, 24.

34 Hanna Kienzler, 'SymptomSpeak: women's struggle for history and health in Kosovo', *Culture, Medicine, and Psychiatry*, 46 (2022): 739–60, at 756, 755.

35 Kivimäki, 'Experiencing trauma before trauma', 100.

36 Deborah Padfield, *Perceptions of Pain* (Stockport: Dewi Lewis, 2003), 19.

37 Padfield, *Perceptions of Pain*, 41–3.

38 Kesherie Gurung, 'Bodywork: self-harm, trauma, and embodied expressions of pain', *Arts and Humanities in Higher Education*, 17 (2018): 32–47, at 32; Anna Motz, 'Self-harm as a sign of hope', *Psychoanalytic Psychotherapy*, 24 (2010): 81–92; Outi Horne and Emese Csipke, 'From feeling too little and too much, to feeling more and less? A nonparadoxical theory of the functions of self-harm', *Qualitative Health Research*, 19 (2009): 655–67.

39 Ana Finel Honigman, 'Enabling art: self-expression/self-harm in the work and reception of L.A. Raven', *Third Text*, 28 (2014): 177–89.

40 Padfield and Zakrzewska, eds, *Encountering Pain*, esp. 147–252, the section on 'seeing'; Tara Parker-Pope, 'Pain as an art form', *New York Times*, 22 April 2008.

41 Katherine Foxhall, *Migraine: A History* (Baltimore: Johns Hopkins University Press, 2019), 184–210.

42 Lisa Olstein, *Pain Studies* (New York: Bellevue Press, 2020), 142–3.

43 Arthur Kleinman et al., 'Pain as human experience: an introduction', in *Pain as Human Experience: An Anthropological Perspective*, eds Mary-Jo DelVechhio Good et al. (Berkeley: University of California Press, 1992), 1–28, at 5.

44 Daniel Goldberg, *The Bioethics of Pain Management: Beyond Opioids* (New York: Routledge, 2017), 27.

45 Marja-Liisa Honkasalo, 'What is chronic is ambiguity: encountering biomedicine with long-lasting pain', *Journal of the Finnish Anthropological Society*, 24 (1999): 75–92, at 79.

46 Travis Chi Wing Lau, 'The crip poetics of pain', *Amodern*, 10 (2020).

47 Marcus Aurelius, *Marcus Aurelius [Meditations]*, trans. C.R. Haines (Cambridge, MA: Harvard University Press, 1916), VII, 16.

48 *Meditations*, VII, 33.

49 *Meditations*, VII, 16.

50 Troels Engberg-Pedersen, 'Marcus Aurelius on emotions', in *The Emotions in Hellenistic Philosophy*, eds Juha Sihvola and Troels Engberg-Pedersen (Dordrecht: Springer Science+Business Media, 1998), 305–38.

51 *Meditations*, VII, 35.

52 Jo-Marie Claassen, 'Cornelius Fronto: a "Libyan nomad" at Rome', *Acta Classica: Proceedings of the Classical Association of South Africa*, 52 (2009): 47–71; J.E.G. Whitehorne, 'Was Marcus Aurelius a hypochondriac?', *Latomus*, 36 (1977): 413–21.

53 Edward Champlin, *Fronto and Antonine Rome* (Cambridge, MA: Harvard University Press, 1980), esp. ch. 4 and appendix A; Michael P.J. van den Hout, *A Commentary on the Letters of M. Cornelius Fronto* (Leiden: Brill, 1999); Amy Richlin, 'Parallel lives: Domitia Lucilla Cratia, Fronto and Marcus', *EuGeStA*, 1 (2011): 163–203; Amy Richlin, *Marcus Aurelius in Love* (Chicago: University of Chicago Press, 2007); cf. Christian Laes, 'What could Marcus Aurelius feel for Fronto?' *Studia Humaniora Tartuensia*, 10 (2009).

54 The various extracts from the correspondence are from *The Correspondence of Marcus Cornelius Fronto*, trans. C.R. Haines (London: Heinemann, 1919), vol. 1, 185–253, from c.144 CE–c.156 CE. Marcus's philosophical language was Greek; the vernacular in the letters is Latin.

55 Whitehorne, 'Was Marcus Aurelius a hypochondriac?', 415, n. 16.

56 Andrea Marculescu, 'Narrating pain and healing in Andrieu de la Vigne, *Mystère de saint Martin* (1496)', in *Lived Religion and Everyday Life in Early Modern Hagiographic Material*, eds Jenni Kuuliala, Rose-Marie Peake, and Päivi Räisänen-Schröder (London: Palgrave, 2019), 215–33, at 222; Amelia Kennedy, 'Crip time in the medieval monastery: Cistercian writers on the time-scapes of infirmity, c. 1150–1250', *Journal of Medieval Monastic Studies*, 10 (2021): 67–87.

57 Emma Sheppard, 'Performing normal but becoming crip: living with chronic pain', *Scandinavian Journal of Disability Research*, 22 (2020): 39–47.

58 McCluskey, St Guillaume, and Da Silva, 'Ability and disability', 109–10.

59 Clementine Morrigan, 'Trauma time: the queer temporalities of the traumatized mind', *Somatechnics*, 7 (2017): 50–8.

60 Ellen Samuels, 'Six ways of looking at crip time', *Disability Studies Quarterly*, 37 (2017).

Chapter 5 *Commiserating*: Sensing, Feeling, and Witnessing the Other in Pain

1 Susan Sontag, *Regarding the Pain of Others* (New York: Picador, 2003).
2 Goldberg, *Bioethics of Pain Management*, 26; Mark D. Sullivan, 'Finding pain between minds and bodies', *The Clinical Journal of Pain*, 17 (2001): 146–56; Konrad Ehlich, 'The language of pain', *Theoretical Medicine*, 6 (1985): 177–87, at 180.
3 Rod Preece, *Brute Souls, Happy Beasts and Evolution: The Historical Status of Animals* (Vancouver: UBC Press, 2005).
4 This was not actually what the early Utilitarians argued for. Rob Boddice, 'The moral status of animals and the historical human cachet', *JAC*, 30 (2010): 457–89.
5 Boddice, *Science of Sympathy*; Boddice, *Humane Professions*.
6 Anon., 'Comparative psychology', *New Monthly Magazine*, 14 (1820): 297; Gray, 'Body, mind and madness'.
7 Philanthropos [Gerald Yeo], *Physiological Cruelty; or, Fact v. Fancy: An Inquiry into the Vivisection Question* (London: Tinsley, 1883), 4.
8 Shira Shmuely, 'From mules to cephalopods: animal sentience and the law', *Europe Now*, 45 (2021).
9 Boddice, *History of Feelings*, 145–6.
10 *The Times*, 4 August 1875.
11 Cf. Bernard Rollin, *The Unheeded Cry: Animal Consciousness, Animal Pain and Science* (Oxford: Oxford University Press, 1990); Lorraine Daston and Gregg Mitman, eds, *Thinking with Animals: New Perspectives on Anthropomorphism* (New York: Columbia University Press, 2005).
12 Mark Bekoff, *The Emotional Lives of Animals: A Leading Scientist Explores Animal Joy, Sorrow, and Empathy – and Why They Matter* (Novato: New World Library, 2007); Frans de Waal, *Mama's Last Hug: Animal Emotions and What They Tell Us about Ourselves* (New York: W.W. Norton, 2019).
13 Lisa Feldman Barrett, 'The theory of constructed emotion: an active inference account of interoception and categorization', *Social Cognitive and Affective Neuroscience*, 12 (2017): 1–23, at 13.
14 Rob Boddice and Mark Smith, *Emotion, Sense, Experience* (Cambridge: Cambridge University Press, 2020), 54.
15 Barrett, 'Theory of constructed emotion', 14.
16 Thomas Nagel, 'What is it like to be a bat?', *Philosophical Review* (1974): 435–50.
17 Rob Boddice, 'The end of anthropocentrism', in *Anthropocentrism: Humans, Animals, Environments*, ed. Rob Boddice (Leiden: Brill, 2011), 1–11.
18 Boddice, *History of Feelings*, 38–43.

19 Boddice, *Science of Sympathy*.

20 David Konstan, *Pity Transformed* (London: Duckworth, 2001), 15.

21 Adam Smith, *The Theory of Moral Sentiments* (1759; Los Angeles: Logos, 2018), 10.

22 Jeremy Bentham, *An Introduction to the Principles of Morals and Legislation* (London: T. Payne and Son, 1789), XVII, 5n; Boddice, 'Moral status of animals'.

23 Mill, *Utilitarianism*, 14.

24 For more on Mill's vision of pain, an imagined 'distance between self and experience that suggests one learns ... "pain behavior" in the process of becoming a recognizable member of a community', see Ablow, *Victorian Pain*, 24–47, quotation at 26.

25 Edmund Gurney, 'A chapter in the ethics of pain', *Fortnightly Review*, 36 (1881): 778–96, at 784.

26 Boddice, *Science of Sympathy*, 116–36.

27 Yao, *Disaffected*.

28 Thomas Haskell, 'Capitalism and the Origins of the Humanitarian Sensibility', part 1, *American Historical Review*, 90 (1985): 339-61.

29 Brenda Lynn Edgar, Valérie Gorin, and Dolores Martín Moruno, eds, *Making Humanitarian Crises: Emotions and Images in History* (London: Palgrave, 2022).

30 Ablow, *Victorian Pain*, 48–71.

31 Martineau, *Life in the Sick-Room*, 25

32 Martineau, *Life in the Sick-Room*, 26

33 Martineau, *Life in the Sick-Room*, 26–7.

34 Martineau, *Life in the Sick-Room*, 38.

35 Martineau, *Life in the Sick-Room*, 29.

36 Martineau, *Life in the Sick-Room*, 30.

37 Martineau, *Life in the Sick-Room*, 37.

38 Martineau, *Life in the Sick-Room*, 40–1.

39 Alberti, *Biography of Loneliness*.

40 Martineau, *Life in the Sick-Room*, 41.

41 Martineau, *Life in the Sick-Room*, 41–2.

42 See Anka Ryall, 'Medical body and lived experience: the case of Harriet Martineau', *Mosaic: An Interdisciplinary Critical Journal*, 33 (2000): 35–53; T. Spencer Wells, 'Remarks on the case of Miss Martineau', *British Medical Journal*, 5 May 1877: 543.

43 Franziska Gygax, 'Feeling (and falling) ill: finding a language of illness', in *Feeling Dis-ease*, eds Boddice and Hitzer, 125–39.

44 Giovanni Mazzotti et al., 'The diagnosis of the cause of the death of Venerina', *Journal of Anatomy*, 216 (2010): 271–4.

45 Jessica R. Adkins, 'The Disgust of Anatomy', unpublished PhD thesis, Saint Louis University, 2020, 41.

46 C. Wagner, 'Replicating Venus: art, anatomy, wax models and automata', *19: Interdisciplinary Studies in the Long Nineteenth Century*, 20 (2017); Cristiana Bastos, 'Displayed wounds, encrypted messages: hyper-realism and imagination in medical moulages', *Medical Anthropology*, 36 (2017): 533–50.

47 Rob Boddice, *A History of Attitudes and Behaviours toward Animals in Eighteenth- and Nineteenth-Century Britain: Anthropocentrism and the Emergence of Animals* (Lewiston, NY: Edwin Mellen Press, 2009).

48 Herbert Spencer, *Principles of Psychology*, 3rd edition (1899; Osnabrück: Otto Zeller, 1966), vol. 2, §§ 689–91.

49 Spencer, *Principles*, 3rd edition, §§ 253, 583.

50 *Oxford English Dictionary*, third edition, 2014.

51 E.B. Titchener, *Lectures on the Experimental Psychology of Thought-Processes* (New York: Macmillan, 1909).

52 Susan Lanzoni, *Empathy: A History* (New Haven: Yale University Press, 2018), 29.

53 Vernon Lee, *Beauty and Ugliness* (London: John Lane, 1912); *The Beautiful* (Cambridge: Cambridge University Press, 1913); Lanzoni, *Empathy*, ch. 1; Carolyn Burdett, 'Is empathy the end of sentimentality?', *Journal of Victorian Culture*, 16 (2011): 259–74; Carolyn Burdett, '"The subjective inside us can turn into the objective outside": Vernon Lee's psychological aesthetics', *19: Interdisciplinary Studies in the Long Nineteenth Century*, 12 (2011).

54 Sara Ahmed, 'Affective economies', *Social Text*, 22 (2004): 117–39; Sara Ahmed, *The Cultural Politics of Emotion*, 2nd edition (London: Routledge, 2014), ch. 1.

55 Ahmed, 'Affective economies', 125.

56 Monique Scheer, 'Are emotions a kind of practice (and is that what makes them have a history)? A Bourdieuian approach to understanding emotion', *History and Theory*, 51 (2012): 193–220, at 202.

57 Jean Decetey and Philip L. Jackson, 'The functional architecture of human empathy', *Behavioural and Cognitive Neuroscience Reviews*, 3 (2004): 71–100; L.S. McGrath, 'Historiography, affect, and the neurosciences', *History of Psychology*, 20 (2017): 129–47; B.M. Hood, *The Self Illusion: How the Social Brain Creates Identity* (Oxford: Oxford University Press, 2012), 63–70; Allan Young, 'Mirror neurons and the rationality problem', in *Rational Animals, Irrational Humans*, eds Shigeru Watanabe et al. (Tokyo: Science University Press, 2009), 55–69.

58 Ruth Leys, *The Ascent of Affect: A Genealogy* (Chicago: University of Chicago Press, 2017).

Chapter 6 *Contextualizing*: Pleasure and Punishment

1 Scarry, *Body in Pain*, 27.
2 Scarry, *Body in Pain*, 34.
3 Scarry, *Body in Pain*, 161.
4 Jeannine Bell, '"Behind this mortal bone": the (in)effectiveness of torture', *Indiana Law Journal*, 83 (2008): 339–61; Christopher Michael Sullivan, 'The (in)effectiveness of torture for combating insurgency', *Journal of Peace Research*, 51 (2014): 388–404; Jeannine Bell, 'One thousand shades of gray: the effectiveness of torture', *IU Law-Bloomington*, Research Paper No. 37 (2005); Ronnie Janoff-Bulman, 'Erroneous assumptions: popular belief in the effectiveness of torture interrogation', *Peace and Conflict: Journal of Peace Psychology*, 13 (2007): 429–35.
5 Mark A. Costanzo, 'The effects and effectiveness of using torture as an interrogation device: using research to inform the policy debate', *Social Issues and Policy Review*, 3 (2009): 179–210.
6 Lisa Silverman, *Tortured Subjects: Pain, Truth, and the Body in Early Modern France* (Chicago: University of Chicago Press, 2001).
7 Nancy Park, 'Imperial Chinese justice and the law of torture', *Late Imperial China*, 29 (2008): 37–67.
8 Mitchell B. Merback, *The Thief, the Cross and the Wheel: Pain and the Spectacle of Punishment in Medieval and Renaissance Europe* (Chicago: University of Chicago Press, 1999); Robert Mills, ed., *Suspended Animation: Pain, Pleasure and Punishment in Medieval Culture* (London: Reaktion, 2006); Cohen, *Modulated Scream*, 52–86.
9 Cohen, *Modulated Scream*, 54.
10 Rebecca Evans, 'The ethics of torture: definitions, history, and institutions', *Oxford Research Encyclopedia of International Studies*, https://oxfordre.com/internationalstudies/view/10.1093/acrefore/9780190846626.001.0001/acrefore-9780190846626-e-326; Cohen, *Modulated Scream*, 52.
11 Merback, *The Thief*.
12 Margaret Abruzzo, *Polemical Pain: Slavery, Cruelty, and the Rise of Humanitarianism* (Baltimore: Johns Hopkins University Press, 2011); Sara M. Butler, *Pain, Penance, and Protest: Peine Forte et Dure in Medieval England* (Cambridge: Cambridge University Press, 2022); Ian Gibson, *The English Vice: Beating, Sex and Shame in Victorian England and After* (London: Duckworth, 1978).
13 Ralph Gardiner, *Englands grievance discovered in relation to the coal-trade*

(London, 1655), 110–11. Daniel Defoe documented the same bridle (Newcastle under Lyme, Staffs) in 1753, explicitly mentioning it as a shaming practice: *A tour thro' the whole island of Great Britain* (London: S. Birt, etc., 1752), vol. 2, 384.

14 Lynda E. Boose, 'Scolding Brides and bridling scolds: taming the woman's unruly member', *Shakespeare Quarterly*, 42 (1991): 179–213, at 197; John G. Harrison, 'Women and the Branks in Stirling, c.1600 to c.1730', *Scottish Economic & Social History*, 18 (1998): 114–31.

15 Quoted in Kate Aughterson, ed., *Renaissance Women: A Sourcebook: Constructions of Femininity in England* (London: Taylor & Francis, 1995), 242–3.

16 Quoted in Aughterson, ed., *Renaissance Women*, 243. For context, Althea Stewart, 'Good Quaker Women, tearful sentimental spectators, readers, and auditors: four early-modern Quaker narratives of martyrdom and witness', *Prose Studies*, 29 (2007): 73–85.

17 B.H. Cunnington, 'The "brank" or scold's bridle', *The English Illustrated Magazine*, 26 (1905): 116–20; 'Muzzles for ladies', *Strand Magazine*, 8 (1894): 485–9. Cunnington (116) states that there is a record of a mayor imposing the bridle on Anne Runcorn, complete with public parade, in Congleton in 1824.

18 Robin Blackburn, *The Making of New World Slavery: From the Baroque to the Modern, 1492–1800* (London: Verso: 1998), 324.

19 Joan Durrant, 'More than a symbol: Canada's legal justification of corporal punishment of children', in *A Question of Commitment: The Status of Children in Canada*, ed. Thomas Waldock (Waterloo: Wilfrid Laurier Press, 2020), 179–204.

20 Irwin A. Hyman, Wendy Zelikoff, and Jacqueline Clarke, 'Psychological and physical abuse in the schools: a paradigm for understanding post-traumatic stress disorder in children and youth', *Journal of Traumatic Studies*, 1 (1988): 243–67; Jonathan Benthall, 'Invisible wounds: corporal punishment in British schools as a form of ritual', *Child Abuse & Neglect*, 15 (1991): 377–88.

21 Rosemary Barnes and Nina Josefowitz, 'Indian residential schools in Canada: persistent impacts on Aboriginal students' psychological development and functioning', *Canadian Psychology/Psychologie canadienne*, 60 (2019): 65–76; Amy Bombay, Kimberly Matheson, and Hymie Anisman, 'The intergenerational effects of Indian Residential Schools: implications for the concept of historical trauma', *Transcultural Psychiatry*, 51 (2014): 320-38; Amy Bombay, Kim Matheson, and Hymie Anisman, 'Intergenerational trauma: convergence of multiple processes among First Nations peoples in Canada', *International Journal of Indigenous Health*, 5 (2009): 6–47.

22 Valerie E. Michaelson and Joan E. Durrant, eds, *Decolonizing Discipline:*

Children, Corporal Punishment, Christian Theologies, and Reconciliation (Winnipeg: University of Manitoba Press, 2020).

23 Gibson, *English Vice*.

24 I am indebted to Lesley Hall's 2004 article 'Pain and the erotic' for guiding me to and through many of the relevant sources in this subsection. It has been removed from its original location but can be found through the internet archive: https://web.archive.org/web/20121105162207/https://wellcome.ac.uk/en/pain/microsite/culture1.html.

25 Richard Burton, trans., *The Kama Sutra of Vatsyayana* (London: Kama Shastra Society, 1883), 46.

26 John Cleland, *Fanny Hill: Memoirs of a Woman of Pleasure* (London: G. Fenton, 1749).

27 Johann Heinrich Meibom, *A Treatise of the Use of Flogging in Venereal Affairs* (London, 1761).

28 Havelock Ellis, *Studies in the Psychology of Sex* (Philadelphia: F.A. Davis, 1906), vol. 3 [*Love and Pain*], 57. For context, Ivan Crozier, 'Philosophy in the English boudoir: Havelock Ellis, *Love and Pain*, and sexological discourses on algophilia', *Journal of the History of Sexuality*, 13 (2004): 275–305; Richard von Krafft-Ebing, *Psychopathia Sexualis. Eine Klinisch-Forensische Studie* (Stuttgart: Ferdinand Enke, 1886); Albert Moll, *Die konträre Sexualempfindung*, 2nd edition (Berlin: Fischer's Medicinische Buchhandlung, 1893).

29 Ellis, *Studies*, vol. 3, 138, 151.

30 A. von Schrenck-Notzing, *Therapeutic Suggestion in Psychopathia Sexualis* (Philadelphia: F.A. Davis, 1895).

31 John Yamamoto-Wilson, *Pain, Pleasure and Perversity* (Farnham: Ashgate, 2013), 61–88.

32 Leopold von Sacher-Masoch, 'Venus im Pelz', in *Das Vermächtniß Kains. Erster Theil. Die Lieber. Zweiter Band* (Stuttgart: Cotta, 1870), 121–368.

33 Marcella Biro Barton, 'Saint Teresa of Ávila: did she have epilepsy?', *The Catholic Historical Review*, 68 (1982): 581–98.

34 E. Allison Peers, trans. and ed., *The Complete Works of Saint Teresa of Jesus* (New York: Sheed & Ward, 1946), vol. 1, 192–3. For the Spanish original, *Obras de Sta. Teresa de Jesus*, ed. P. Sliverio de Santa Teresa (Burgos: El Monte Carmelo, 1915), vol. 1, 234–5.

35 Cf. Susanne Warma, 'Ecstasy and vision: two concepts connected with Bernini's *Teresa*', *The Art Bulletin*, 66 (1984): 508–11.

36 Jacques Lacan, Seminar XX, *Encore*, 1972–3, quoted in Juliet Mitchell and Jacqueline Rose, eds, *Feminine Sexuality: Jacques Lacan and the École Freudienne* (New York: Norton, 1985), 147; Dany Nobus, 'The sculptural iconography of

feminine jouissance: Lacan's reading of Bernini's *Saint Teresa in Ecstasy*, *The Comparatist*, 39 (2015): 22–46; Alana Louise Bowden, 'The saint behind the sculpture: (re)interpreting Saint Teresa's ecstasy through a feminist analysis of Bernini's *The Ecstasy of Saint Teresa*', *Literature & Aesthetics*, 31 (2021): 132–47; Annamarie Jagose, *Orgasmology* (Durham, NC: Duke University Press, 2012), 135f.; Maria Berbara, '"Esta pena tan sabrosa": Teresa of Ávila and the figurative arts', in *The Sense of Suffering: Constructions of Physical Pain in Early Modern Culture*, eds Jan Frans van Dijkhuizen and Karl A.E. Enenkel (Leiden: Brill, 2009), 267–97.

37 Walther Thom, *Pedestrianism; or, an account of the performances of celebrated pedestrians during the last and present century; with a full narrative of Captain Barclay's public and private matches; and an essay on training* (Aberdeen: D. Chalmers, 183), 129–54. See also Peter Radford, *The Celebrated Captain Barclay: Sport, Money and Fame in Regency Britain* (London: Headline, 2001).

38 Roy Keane with Roddy Doyle, *The Second Half* (London: Weidenfeld & Nicolson, 2014), 98–9, 102.

39 George Vecsey, 'A hurting Kerri Strug wasn't ready to stop yet', *New York Times*, 24 July 1996.

40 Rick Weinberg, 'The ESPN Take, 51: Kerri Strug fights off pain, helps US win gold', ESPN.com, 29 June 2008, https://web.archive.org/web/20080629004458 /http://sports.espn.go.com/espn/espn25/story?page=moments%2F51.

41 Vecsey, 'A hurting Kerri Strug'.

42 Weinberg, 'The ESPN Take, 51'.

43 Rebecca Schuman, 'Kerri Strug shouldn't have been forced to do that vault', *Slate*, 31 July 2021, https://slate.com/culture/2021/07/kerri-strug-simone-biles -vault-atlanta-legacy-injuries.html.

44 Mitch Weiss and Holbrook Mohr, 'US gymnasts say sport rife with verbal and emotional abuse', *NBC Los Angeles*, 23 February 2018, https://www .nbclosangeles.com/news/national-international/us-gymnasts-say-sport-rife -with-verbal-and-emotional-abuse/2051941/; Rachel Denhollander, *What Is a Girl Worth? My Story of Breaking the Silence and Exposing the Truth about Larry Nassar and USA Gymnastics* (New York: Tyndale Momentum, 2019).

45 Robert Weinberg, Daniel Vernau, and Thelma S. Horn, 'Playing through pain and injury: psychosocial considerations', *Journal of Clinical Sport Psychology*, 7 (2013): 41–59; Samantha O'Connell and Theo C. Manschreck, 'Playing through the pain: psychiatric risks among athletes', *Current Psychiatry* (July 2012): 16–20.

46 Stephen T. Casper, 'The anecdotal patient: brain injury and the magnitude of harm', *Notes and Records of the Royal Society Journal of the History of Science*,

76 (2022): 663–82; Stephen T. Casper, 'Punch-drunk slugnuts: violence and the .vernacular history of disease', *Isis*, 113 (2022); Stephen T. Casper et al., 'Toward complete, candid, and unbiased international consensus statements on concussion in sport', *Journal of Law, Medicine, and Ethics*, 49 (2021): 372–7.

Chapter 7 *Embodying*: Nocebo/Placebo

1 Book 30:15.
2 Howard Brody, 'The doctor as therapeutic agent: a placebo effect research agenda', in *The Placebo Effect: An Interdisciplinary Exploration*, ed. Anne Harrington (Cambridge, MA: Harvard University Press, 1999), 77–92.
3 Claude Lévi-Strauss, *Structural Anthropology* (New York: Basic Books, 1963), 184.
4 David J. Grelotti and Ted J. Kaptchuk, 'Placebo by proxy', *BMJ*, 343 (2011): 343d4345.
5 Grelotti and Kaptchuk, 'Placebo by proxy'.
6 Jacqui Wise, 'Heart stents for stable angina show no benefit over placebo, study finds', *BMJ*, 359 (2017): j5076.
7 Phil Hutchison, 'The "placebo" paradox and the emotion paradox: challenges to psychological explanation', *Theory & Psychology*, 30 (2020): 617–37.
8 Hutchison, 'The "placebo" paradox', 632.
9 Imke Rajamani and Margrit Pernau, 'Emotional translations: conceptual history beyond language', *History and Theory*, 55 (2016): 46–65.
10 Daniel Moerman, *Meaning, Medicine and the 'Placebo Effect'* (Cambridge: Cambridge University Press, 2002), 154. See also David B. Morris, 'Placebo, pain, and belief: a biocultural model', in *The Placebo Effect*, ed. Harrington, 187–207.
11 Jacqueline E. Raicek, Bradley H. Stone, and Ted J. Kaptchuk, 'Placebos in 19th century medicine: a quantitative analysis of the *BMJ*', *BMJ*, 345 (2012): e8326.
12 Shapiro and Shapiro, *Powerful Placebo*, 2.
13 Shapiro and Shapiro, *Powerful Placebo*, 13, 23.
14 Stewart Justman, 'Imagination's trickery: the discovery of the placebo effect', *The Journal of the Historical Society*, 10 (2010): 57–73, at 72–3.
15 Nils H. Korsvoll, 'Introduction: using placebo research to explore belief and healing in late antiquity', *Trends in Classics*, 13 (2021): 1–20, at 2.
16 Arthur K. Shapiro and Elaine Shapiro, 'The placebo: is it much ado about nothing?', in *The Placebo Effect*, ed. Harrington, 12–36.
17 The nearest theoretical approach to my argument here is that by Morris, 'Placebo, pain, and belief'.
18 Charles Rosenberg, 'The therapeutic revolution: medicine, meaning and social

change, in nineteenth-century America', *Perspectives in Biology and Medicine*, 20 (1977): 485–506, at 485–6.

19 Fabrizio Benedetti, *Placebo Effects: Understanding the Mechanisms in Health and Disease* (Oxford: Oxford University Press, 2008), 2.

20 Benedetti, *Placebo Effects*, 2–3.

21 Benedetti, *Placebo Effects*, 5, 3.

22 Benedetti, *Placebo Effects*, 3.

23 Paul Enck et al., 'The placebo response in medicine: minimize, maximize or personalize?', *Nature Reviews: Drug Discovery*, 12 (2013): 191–204, at 202.

24 Brody, 'Doctor as therapeutic agent'.

25 Rosenberg, 'Therapeutic revolution', 499.

26 Kathryn T. Hall, Joseph Loscalzo, and Ted J. Kaptchuk, 'Genetics and the placebo effect: the placebome', *Trends in Molecular Medicine*, 21 (2015): 285–94, at 285–6, 289–90.

27 Rosenberg, 'Therapeutic Revolution', 504.

28 Nils H. Korsvoll, ed. 'Special Issue: Healing, Belief, and Placebo: Medical and Religious Plurality in Late Antiquity', *Trends in Classics*, 13 (2021).

29 Olympia Panagiotidou, 'Religious healing and the Asclepius cult: a case of placebo effects', *Open Theology*, 2 (2016): 79–91.

30 Christian Büchel et al., 'Placebo analgesia: a predictive coding perspective', *Neuron*, 81 (2014): 1223–39.

31 Cf. Maria Gendron, Batja Mesquita, and Lisa Feldman Barrett, 'The brain as cultural artifact', in *Culture, Mind, and Brain: Emerging Concepts, Models, and Applications*, eds Laurence J. Kirmayer et al. (Cambridge: Cambridge University Press, 2020), 188–222; Rob Boddice, 'The cultural brain as historical artifact', in *Culture, Mind, and Brain*, eds Kirmayer et al., 367–74.

32 George John Romanes to William Ewart Gladstone, 20 October 1892. British Library, London, Add. 44516ff., 196–7.

33 George John Romanes to John T. Gulick, 27 October 1892, Linnean Society, London, MS396, 191.

34 George John Romanes to Thomas H. Huxley, 18 June 1892, Imperial College, London, Huxley Papers, 25.238–9.

35 George John Romanes to Edward Albert Sharpey-Schäfer, 12 September 1893, Wellcome Library, London, PP/ESS/B.16/8.

36 Romanes to Gulick, 27 October 1892, Linnean Society, London, MS396, 191.

37 George Weisz, 'Historical reflections on medical travel', *Anthropology and Medicine*, 18 (2011): 137–44.

38 Vladimir Jankovic, *Confronting the Climate: British Airs and the Making of Environmental Medicine* (Houndmills: Palgrave, 2010), 140–50.

39 Jankovic, *Confronting the Climate*, 146, 150.

40 Romanes to Gladstone, 2 December 1892, British Library, London, Add. 44516ff., 293–4.

41 Romanes to Huxley, 1 December 1892, Imperial College, London, Huxley Papers, 25.246–7.

42 Romanes to Huxley, 18 April 1893, Imperial College London, Huxley Papers, 25.248–9.

43 Gary J. Bennett, 'Does the word "placebo" evoke a placebo response?', *Pain*, 159 (2018): 1928–31.

44 An insight inspired by Arlie Russel Hochschild, 'Emotion Work, feeling rules, and social structure', *The American Journal of Sociology*, 85 (1979): 551–75 and William M. Reddy, 'Against constructionism: the historical ethnography of emotions', *Current Anthropology*, 38 (1997): 327–51.

45 George John Romanes to William Turner Thiselton-Dyer, 15 September 1893, Linnean Society, London, MS395, 17.

46 Romanes to Schäfer, 12 September 1893, Wellcome Library, London, PP/ESS/B.16/8.

47 Gulick to Romanes, 6 December 1893, Linnean Society, London, MS396, 195.

48 Romanes to Gulick, 9 October 1893, Linnean Society, London, MS396, 194.

49 Robert A. Hahn, 'The nocebo phenomenon: scope and foundations', in *The Placebo Effect*, ed. Harrington, 56–76, at 59–67.

50 Anita Slomski, '"Important conversations" are needed to explain the nocebo effect', *Journal of the American Medical Association*, 325 (2021): 707–9.

51 Andrew A. Siguan, 'Conspiracies and the nocebo effect during the COVID-19 pandemic', *Journal of Public Health*, 23 August 2021.

52 Hojjat Daniali and Magne Arve Flaten, 'Experiencing COVID-19 symptoms without the disease: the role of nocebo in reporting symptoms', *Scandinavian Journal of Public Health*, 50 (2022): 61–9. See also by the same authors, 'What psychological factors make individuals believe they are infected by coronavirus 2019?', *Frontiers in Psychology*, 12 (2021): 667722, where the authors demonstrate that belief of infection was correlated with higher levels of conscientiousness and health anxiety.

53 Kate Faasse and Keith J. Petrie, 'The nocebo effect: patient expectations and medication side effects', *Postgraduate Medical Journal*, 89 (2013): 540–6; Luana Colloca and Fabrizio Benedetti, 'Nocebo hyperalgesia: how anxiety is turned into pain', *Current Opinions in Anesthesiology*, 20 (2007): 435–9.

54 George E. Fragoulis et al., 'Nocebo-prone behaviour in patients with autoimmune rheumatic diseases during the COVID-19 pandemic', *Mediterranean Journal of Rheumatology*, 31 (2020): 288–94.

55 Amelia Bonea et al., *Anxious Times: Medicine and Modernity in Nineteenth-Century Britain* (Pittsburgh: University of Pittsburgh Press, 2019), esp. the introduction; Andreas Killen, *Berlin Electropolis: Shock, Nerves, and German Modernity* (Berkeley: University of California Press, 2005).

56 Marc Scherlinger et al., 'Refining "long-COVID" by a prospective multimodal evaluation of patients with long-term symptoms attributed to SARS-CoV-2 infection', *Infectious Diseases and Therapy*, 10 (2021): 1747–63.

57 See Boddice, 'Hysteria or tetanus?'

58 Gilman, 'The image of the hysteric'; Micale, *Approaching Hysteria*; Micale, *Hysterical Men*; Scull, *Hysteria*.

59 François Sirois, 'Epidemic hysteria', *Acta Psychiatrica Scandinavica*, 50: s252 (1974): 7–44.

60 Kélina Gotman, *Choreomania: Dance and Disorder* (Oxford: Oxford University Press, 2018).

61 Christopher Milnes, *A History of Euphoria: The Perception and Misperception of Health and Well-Being* (New York: Routledge, 2019), 107–8.

62 Jerri Daboo, *Ritual, Rapture and Remorse: A Study of Tarantism and Pizzica in Salento* (Bern: Peter Lang, 2010); Jean Fogo Russell, 'Tarantism', *Medical History*, 23 (1979): 404–25; Pilar León Sanz, 'Medical theories of tarantism in eighteenth-century Spain', in *Music as Medicine: The History of Music Therapy since Antiquity*, ed. Peregrine Horden (London: Routledge, 2000), 273–92; David Gentilcore, 'Ritualized illness and music therapy: views of tarantism in the Kingdom of Naples', in *Music as Medicine*, ed. Horden, 255–72.

63 Daboo, *Ritual*, 4.

64 Edward Shorter, 'Paralysis: the rise and fall of a "hysterical symptom', *Journal of Social History*, 19 (1986): 549–82, at 549; Gilbert H. Glaser, 'Epilepsy, hysteria and "possession": a historical essay', *Journal of Nervous and Mental Disease*, 166 (1978): 268–74.

65 Leslie P. Boss, 'Epidemic hysteria: a review of the published literature', *Epidemiologic Reviews*, 19 (1997): 233–43.

66 Marc Schuilenburg, *Hysteria: Crime, Media, and Politics* (Oxford: Routledge, 2021); Johanna Braun, ed., *Performing Hysteria: Images and Imaginations of Hysteria* (Leuven: Leuven University Press, 2020).

67 Walter B. Cannon, '"Voodoo" death', *American Anthropologist*, 44 (1942): 169–81, at 176.

68 Geroulanos and Meyers, *The Human Body*.

69 Geroulanos and Meyers, *The Human Body*, 267–91.

70 Cannon, '"Voodoo" death', 179.

71 Cannon, '"Voodoo" death', 180.

72 David Lester, 'Voodoo death', *Omega*, 59 (2009): 1–18.
73 Fabrizio Benedetti et al., 'Nocebo and the contribution of psychosocial factors to the generation of pain', *Journal of Neural Transmission*, 127 (2020): 687–96, at 689.
74 Otniel Dror, '"Voodoo death": fantasy, excitement, and the untenable boundaries of biomedical science', in *The Politics of Healing: Histories of Alternative Medicine in Twentieth-Century North America*, ed. Robert D. Johnston (New York: Routledge, 2004), 71–81, at 72.
75 Dror, '"Voodoo death"', 76.
76 Dror, '"Voodoo death"', 77.
77 Martin A. Samuels, '"Voodoo" death revisited: the modern lessons of neurocardiology', *Cleveland Clinic Journal of Medicine*, 74 (2007): S8–16, at S11–12.
78 Samuels, '"Voodoo" death revisited', S13.
79 Samuels, '"Voodoo" death revisited', S16.
80 Bronisław Malinowski, *Magic, Science and Religion* (1925; Boston: Beacon Press, 1948); Marcel Mauss, 'The physical effect on the individual of the idea of death suggested by the collectivity' (1926), in *Sociology and Psychology*, trans. B. Brewster (London: Routledge & Kegan Paul, 1979), 35–56.
81 Lévi-Strauss, *Structural Anthropology*, ch. 9.
82 Simon Dein, 'Psychogenic death: individual effects of sorcery and taboo violation', *Mental Health, Religion & Culture*, 6 (2003): 195–202; Jana Králová, 'What is social death?', *Contemporary Social Science*, 10 (2015): 235–48; Robert A. Hahn, 'Expectations of sickness: concept and evidence of the nocebo phenomenon', in *How Expectancies Shape Experience*, ed. Irving Kirsch (Washington, DC: American Psychological Association, 1999), 333–56.
83 Robin Briggs, 'Emotion and affect in Lorrain witchcraft trials', in *Emotions in the History of Witchcraft*, ed. Laura Kounine (Houndmills: Palgrave, 2016), 137–53, at 146; Edward Bever, *The Realities of Witchcraft and Popular Magic in Early Modern Europe: Culture, Cognition, and Everyday Life* (Houndmills: Palgrave, 2008); Edward Bever, 'Bullying, the neurobiology of emotional aggression, and the experience of witchcraft', in *Emotions in the History of Witchcraft*, ed. Kounine, 193–212.
84 Tor D. Wager and Lauren Y. Atlas, 'The neuroscience of placebo effects: connecting context, learning and health', *Nature Reviews: Neuroscience*, 16 (2015): 403–18, at 415.
85 Luana Colloca and Arthur J. Barsky, 'Placebo and nocebo effects', *New England Journal of Medicine*, 382 (2020): 554–61, at 555.
86 Alexander H. Tuttle et al., 'Increasing placebo responses over time in US clinical trials of neuropathic pain', *Pain*, 156 (2015): 2616–26, at 2624.

Conclusion: The Mutable Patient

1 Bourke, *Story of Pain*, 298–9; Wailoo, *Pain*, 64–7.

2 Wailoo, *Pain*, 168–201.

3 Anne Case and Angus Deaton, *Deaths of Despair and the Future of Capitalism* (Princeton: Princeton University Press, 2020).

Epilogue

1 Stanley Milgram, 'Behaviour study of obedience', *Journal of Abnormal and Social Psychology*, 67 (1963): 371–8.

2 Sontag, *Regarding the Pain of Others*.

Bibliography

I limit my bibliography to only the most essential selected secondary works. Primary and secondary sources are fully referenced in the notes corresponding to the text.

Ablow, Rachel, *Victorian Pain* (Princeton: Princeton University Press, 2017)

Bankoff, George, *The Conquest of Pain: The Story of Anaesthesia* (London: Macdonald & Co., 1940)

Baszanger, Isabelle, *Inventing Pain Medicine: From the Laboratory to the Clinic* (New Brunswick, NJ: Rutgers University Press, 1998)

Bending, Lucy, *The Representation of Bodily Pain in Nineteenth-Century English Culture* (Oxford: Oxford University Press, 2000)

Berry, Michael, *A History of Pain: Trauma in Modern Chinese Literature and Film* (New York: Columbia University Press, 2008)

Biro, David, *The Language of Pain: Finding Words, Compassion, and Relief* (New York: Norton, 2000)

Boddice, Rob, ed., *Pain and Emotion in Modern History* (Houndmills: Palgrave, 2014)

Bourke, Joanna, *The Story of Pain: From Prayer to Painkillers* (Oxford: Oxford University Press, 2014)

Butler, Sara M., *Pain, Penance, and Protest: Peine Forte et Dure in Medieval England* (Cambridge: Cambridge University Press, 2022)

Canton, Donald, *What a Blessing She Had Chloroform: The Medical and Social Response to the Pain of Childbirth from 1800 to the Present* (New Haven: Yale University Press, 1999)

Cizmic, Maria, *Performing Pain: Music and Trauma in Eastern Europe* (Oxford: Oxford University Press, 2011)

Cohen, Esther, *The Modulated Scream: Pain in Late Medieval Culture* (Chicago: University of Chicago Press, 2010)

Cohen, Esther, et al., eds, *Knowledge and Pain* (Leiden: Brill, 2012)

Daudet, Alphonse, *In the Land of Pain*, trans. Julian Barnes (London: Jonathan Cape, 2002)

Davies, Jeremy, *Bodily Pain in Romantic Literature* (New York and London: Routledge, 2014)

Di Bella, Maria Pia, and James Elkins, eds, *Representations of Pain in Art and Visual Culture* (New York and London: Routledge, 2013)

Dijkhuizen, Jan Frans van, *Pain and Compassion in Early Modern English Literature and Culture* (Cambridge: D.S. Brewer, 2012)

Dijkhuizen, Jan Frans van and Karl A.E. Enenkel, eds, *The Sense of Suffering: Constructions of Physical Pain in Early Modern Culture* (Leiden and Boston: Brill, 2009)

Dormandy, Thomas, *The Worst of Evils: The Fight against Pain* (New Haven: Yale University Press, 2006)

Ellis, E.S., *Ancient Anodynes: Primitive Anaesthesia and Allied Conditions* (London: Heinemann, 1946)

Flood, Gavin, *The Ascetic Self: Subjectivity, Memory and Tradition* (Cambridge: Cambridge University Press, 2004)

Folkmarson Käll, Lisa, *Dimensions of Pain: Humanities and Social Science Perspectives* (London and New York: Routledge, 2013)

Foreman, Judy, *A Nation in Pain: Healing Our Biggest Health Problem* (New York: Oxford University Press, 2014)

Foxhall, Katherine, *Migraine: A History* (Baltimore: Johns Hopkins University Press, 2019)

Fülöp-Miller, René, *Triumph over Pain* (Indianapolis: Bobbs-Merrill, 1938)

Gere, Cathy, *Pain, Pleasure, and the Greater Good: From the Panopticon to the Skinner Box and Beyond* (Chicago: University of Chicago Press, 2017)

Glucklich, Ariel, *Sacred Pain: Hurting the Body for the Sake of the Soul* (Oxford: Oxford University Press, 2003)

Goldberg, Daniel, *The Bioethics of Pain Management: Beyond Opioids* (New York: Routledge, 2014)

Grahek, Nikola, *Feeling Pain and Being in Pain*, 2nd edition (Cambridge, MA: MIT Press, 2007)

Hodgkiss, Andrew, *From Lesion to Metaphor: Chronic Pain in British, French and German Medical Writings, 1800–1914* (Amsterdam: Rodopi, 2000)

King, Daniel, *Experiencing Pain in Imperial Greek Culture* (Oxford: Oxford University Press, 2018)

Lalkhen, Abdul-Ghaaliq, *An Anatomy of Pain: How the Body and the Mind Experience and Endure Physical Suffering* (New York: Scribner, 2021)

Livingston, William K., *Pain and Suffering* (Seattle: IASP Press, 1998)

MacDonald, Geoff and Lauri A. Jensen-Campbell, eds, *Social Pain: Neuropsychological and Health Implications of Loss and Exclusion* (Washington, DC: American Psychological Association, 2011).

Mann, Ronald D., *The History of the Management of Pain: From Early Principles to Present Practice* (Carnforth: Parthenon Publishing, 1988)

McTavish, Jan R., *Pain and Profits: The History of the Headache and Its Remedies in America* (New Brunswick, NJ: Rutgers University Press, 2004)

Melzack, Ronald and Patrick D. Wall, *The Challenge of Pain* (London: Penguin, 1996)

Merback, Mitchell B., *The Thief, the Cross and the Wheel: Pain and the Spectacle of Punishment in Medieval and Renaissance Europe* (Chicago: University of Chicago Press, 1999)

Mills, Robert, ed., *Suspended Animation: Pain, Pleasure and Punishment in Medieval Culture* (London: Reaktion, 2006)

Minnis, Alastair, *Phantom Pains and Prosthetic Narratives: From George Dedlow to Dante* (Cambridge: Cambridge University Press, 2021)

Mintz, Susannah B., *Hurt and Pain: Literature and the Suffering Body* (London: Bloomsbury, 2013)

Morris, David B., *The Culture of Pain* (Berkeley and Los Angeles: University of California Press, 1991)

Moscoso, Javier, *Pain: A Cultural History* (Houndmills: Palgrave, 2012)

Norridge, Zoe, *Perceiving Pain in African Literature* (Houndmills: Palgrave, 2013)

Padfield, Deborah, *Perceptions of Pain* (Stockport: Dewi Lewis, 2003)

Padfield, Deborah and Joanna Zakrzewska, eds, *Encountering Pain: Hearing, Seeing, Speaking* (London: UCL Press, 2021)

Pascual, Nieves, ed., *Witness to Pain: Essays on the Translation of Pain into Art* (Bern: Peter Lang, 2005)

Perkins, Judith, *The Suffering Self: Pain and Narrative Representation in the Early Christian Era* (London: Routledge, 1995)

Pernick, Martin S., *A Calculus of Suffering: Pain, Professionalism, and Anesthesia in Nineteenth-Century America* (New York: Columbia University Press, 1985)

Pöll, Johan Sebastian, *The Anaesthetist, 1890–1960: A Historical Comparative Study between Britain and Germany* (Rotterdam: Erasmus, 2011)

Rey, Roselyne, *The History of Pain* (Cambridge, MA: Harvard University Press, 1998)

Scarry, Elaine, *The Body in Pain: The Making and Unmaking of the World* (Oxford: Oxford University Press, 1985)

Silverman, L., *Tortured Subjects: Pain, Truth, and the Body in Early Modern France* (Chicago: University of Chicago Press, 2001)

Sontag, Susan, *Regarding the Pain of Others* (New York: Picador, 2003)

Spivey, Nigel, *Enduring Creation: Art, Pain, and Fortitude* (Berkeley and Los Angeles: University of California Press, 2001)

Wailoo, Keith, *Pain: A Political History* (Baltimore: Johns Hopkins University Press, 2014)

Wall, Patrick, *Pain: The Science of Suffering* (New York: Columbia University Press, 2002)

Yamamoto-Wilson, John R., *Pain, Pleasure and Perversity: Discourses of Suffering in Seventeenth-Century England* (Farnham: Ashgate, 2013)

Index

Achilles 37, 70–3, 75, 153
acupuncture 27–8
Aδ fibres 29
Agatha, St 77–9
Agnes, St 77
Ahmed, Sara 158–9
AI 55
algolagnia 173
anaesthesia 27, 83–9, 96–7, 140–1, 155, 183, 206
analgesics (painkillers) ix, 27, 69, 83, 96, 120, 183, 205–6
anatomical Venus (*Venerina*)154–6, 159–60
Anatomy of Melancholy, see Burton, Robert
anger 7, 70–1, 112, 173, 208
Angst 7, 98–102, 127, 210
anguish 17, 22, 49, 65, 80, 100–3, 127, 138, 157, 159, 210
Anstruther-Thomson, Kit 156
anxiety 7, 34, 65, 69, 96–8, 102, 112, 114, 116, 131, 163–4, 188, 195–6, 199–200
Archigenes 14
arthritis 118, 121, 131
asceticism 81–2, 171, 174
Asclepius 190–1
Association for the Advancement of Medicine by Research 140
attention 42, 120, 134, 144, 160, 163, 183, 205
authenticity 65
automaticity 6, 29–30, 32, 36, 94
Avicenna, *see* Ibn Sina (Avicenna)

Barclay, Robert (Captain) 177–9
Barrett, Lisa Feldman 61, 143–4
Basilica Santa Maria Maggiore 76–7, 79, 82
Sancta Maria a tumoribus 76–8
Beecher, Henry 29–30
Bell, Charles 46, 49–53
Benedetti, Fabrizio 188–9
Bentham, Jeremy 91, 147
Bernini, Gian Lorenzo 154, 176
Bible 80
Biles, Simone 181
biocultural approach 2, 63, 137, 182, 185, 191, 198, 202–3
biopsychosocial approach 33, 37
Blackburn, Robin 171
bleeding (bloodletting) 11–13, 19–21, 191
blisters 177
Bonica, John 27
Bourgeois, Louise 105–9
brain plasticity 2, 8, 31, 69, 112, 142
Brena, Steven 116
Brissot, Pierre 20
British Migraine Association 128
broken heart 23, 70, 210
burns 4, 28, 31, 120, 163, 165, 171, 210
Burton, Robert 63–6

C-fibres 29
Cairns, Douglas 72
cancer 76–9, 121, 123, 194–5
Cannon, Walter B. 199–202
capitalism 34, 112, 115, 136, 205, 207, 209–10
catastrophizing 114